M000004947

The Best of

Slate

FORTHCOMING SLATE TITLES FROM ATLAS BOOKS

The Wall Street Self-Defense Manual
by Henry Blodget

**Backstabbers, Crazed
Geniuses, and Animals We Hate:
Slate Writers Tell It Like It Is**
edited by David Plotz

THE BEST OF

Slate

A 10TH ANNIVERSARY ANTHOLOGY

Edited by **DAVID PLOTZ**

Introduction by **JACOB WEISBERG**

Foreword by **MICHAEL KINSLEY**

 ATLAS BOOKS

New York

The Best of Slate: *A 10th Anniversary Anthology*
Copyright © 2006 by *Slate*

"Not Dead at All: Why Congress was right to stick up for Terri Schiavo," by Harriet McBryde Johnson. Copyright 2005 by Harriet McBryde Johnson.

All rights reserved.

Printed in the United States of America
No portion of this publication may be reproduced or transmitted in any form or by any means, electronic or mechanical, including photocopy, recording, scanning, or any information or storage retrieval system, without permission in writing from the publisher.
Atlas Books are available at special discounts for bulk purchases in the U.S. by corporations, institutions, and other organizations. For more information, please contact the Special Markets Department at the Perseus Books Group, 11 Cambridge Center, Cambridge, MA 02142, call (617) 252–5298, or email special.markets@perseusbooks.com.

Atlas Books, LLC
10 E. 53rd St., 35th Fl.
New York NY 10022
www.atlasbooks.net

DESIGNED BY JEFF WILLIAMS

Library of Congress Cataloging-in-Publication Data
The best of Slate : a 10th anniversary anthology / edited by David Plotz ; introduction by Jacob Weisberg ; foreword by Michael Kinsley.
p. cm.
ISBN 0-9777433-0-6
1. United States—Politics and government—1993-2001. 2. United States—Politics and government—2001- 3. United States—Social conditions—1980- 4. Popular culture—United States.
I. Plotz, David. II. Slate (Redmond, Wash.)

E885.B48 2006

973.929—dc22

First Edition
1 2 3 4 5 6 7 8 9 10

Contents

Contents

Contents

2005

Foreword

BY MICHAEL KINSLEY

IN AUGUST 1995, I made a secret trip to Seattle to talk with Microsoft about starting an online magazine (whatever that might be). On the plane back home to Washington, D.C., I found myself sitting next to Christopher Buckley, the comic novelist. Like an idiot, I immediately asked him, "Why were you in Seattle?" He said he had been giving a speech, and, like a gentleman, naturally asked me the same question. To which I was forced to reply, like a parody of the Washington self-importance in Chris' novels, "I can't tell you. It's a secret." When the secret came out a few weeks later, Chris sent me a note: "I figured it wasn't Boeing."

It wasn't Boeing. But Microsoft's suburban corporate campus was still an odd place to be practicing journalism. My interest in the project and Microsoft's interest were very different, but a good fit. Like many magazine editors, and journalists generally, I dreamed of starting a magazine of my own. And I had discovered that the magic words "on" and "line" were a way to interest others in this solipsistic proposition. Microsoft, meanwhile, had no particular interest in starting a magazine. But, like many companies in those early days, it was flinging anything it could find at the Internet to see what might stick. After two decades in Washington, I moved to Seattle on Christmas Day, 1995. (I'm still here, and married to one of the Microsoft executives I met that day in August. But that's another story.) I had an office cube in a long hall (otherwise populated by software developers), a computer, and a memo I had written about what this online magazine might be like. Almost everything in the memo was completely wrong. Fortunately, I soon had colleagues who took pleasure in telling me so.

Slate began publishing in June 1996 with a small staff based primarily on the Microsoft campus in Redmond, Wash., plus even smaller offices in Washington and New York. In Washington, we sublet space from the American Enterprise Institute. The rent included feeding privileges in the conservative think tank's almost-lavish dining room, where young *Slate*sters could chow down with eminences of the right like Robert Bork, Jeane Kirkpatrick, and Irving Kristol. On the other hand, those of us in Redmond enjoyed the splendors of the Microsoft cafeteria, with its legendary free soft drinks.

Soon, though, we were truly publishing in cyberspace. A typical staff meeting might include three or four people in Redmond, two or three each in Washington and New York, foreign affairs columnist Anne Applebaum on the phone from Warsaw, the late Scott Shuger (original author of *Slate*'s "Today's Papers") from Los Angeles or one year (when his wife had a fellowship there) from Berlin, copy editor Sian Gibby from Cincinnati, me (late as usual) from the Microsoft parking garage, and so on. These various locations weren't just branches of the Redmond HQ. It was a single operation in which geography was irrelevant. Of the four original top editors, Jodie Allen was in Washington, Judith Shulevitz was in New York, and Jack Shafer and I were in Redmond, but it made no difference since 99 percent of our communication was via e-mail. When Jack moved back to Washington, it was hardly noticeable. This all seemed more remarkable at the time than it does now.

But one measure of *Slate's* success is that being online is no longer central to its definition. *Slate* is now part of the journalistic establishment. When quoted or referred to in the media, it is no longer "*Slate*, the experiment in online journalism that Bill Gates is bankrolling for Mike Kinsley, who used to be somebody on television," or "*Slate*, the online magazine published by Microsoft," or even "*Slate*, the online magazine." It's just *Slate*. Like *Time* or *Newsweek*. In 2002, Jacob Weisberg took over from me as the editor. In 2005, Microsoft sold *Slate* to the Washington Post Co., and it now operates out of more traditional journalistic surroundings in Washington and New York.

Please forgive a short victory lap. *Slate* was one of several on- and off-line publications launched with a lot of hype and a lot of money in the past decade. Most of the others (*Talk*, *Brill's Content*) are dead. Where is the analyst at a firm called Forrester Research who used to be quoted everywhere calling us, witlessly, "the Slatanic"? Haven't heard much from him lately. And while it's certainly true that Microsoft was a generous, tolerant, patient, and hands-off backer during *Slate's* early years, it is not true that "Bill Gates' deep pockets" are the only reason *Slate* is still around while these others are not. If we had spent money the way some other publications did during the late '90s Internet bubble, Microsoft would have shut us down long ago. If these projects had guarded their pennies the way we did, they might still be publishing.

From the beginning, our test of success was financial: We wanted to break even. And there have been quarters during the past two or three years when *Slate* has indeed broken even or nosed slightly into the black, though to be honest, this is not yet a regular habit. But why is breaking even so important? Obviously *Slate* was a flyspeck on Microsoft's balance sheet and looms only slightly larger on the Washington Post Co.'s. What difference does a few million dollars of profit or loss matter while billions course around us? It makes a big difference. For a publication, like an individual, financial independence brings intellectual independence. The technical term for this, I believe, is "fuckyouability" (FUA). If you're self-supporting, you can say "fuck you" to anyone, which is one important function of a magazine on almost any subject and in any medium.

The theory that *Slate* set out to prove was that the Internet made FUA more widely available. From the beginning, the economics of publishing on the Internet—no paper, no printing, no postage—were more important to us than the hyperlinks and the multimedia. In a way, though, we got this point wrong. *Slate* is sleek compared with equivalent paper magazines, but we are a galumphing contraption compared with blogs and wikis and instant messaging and other Internet innovations. Individuals with no corporate backing have done more than *Slate* has done to upturn A.J. Liebling's famous dictum, "Freedom of the press is guaranteed only to those who own one." On the other hand, *Slate* has gone far beyond anything I contemplated at the beginning in creative use of the new medium (what I tended, foolishly, to dismiss as "bells and whistles"). My original idea, believe it or not, was a publication that you would download and print out once a week. It would have been an inferior version of a print magazine—a bunch of pages stapled together (if you had a stapler nearby).

By the time *Slate* was launched, we had already moved beyond that primitive once-a-week notion. I remember, with some embarrassment, the eureka moment when it dawned on me that an online magazine didn't have to publish an entire issue at once. Pretty soon, I even figured out that you didn't need to have "issues" at all. Nevertheless, when we launched, *Slate*—probably at my insistence—had page numbers, so that people could flip through it page-by-page or use a traditional table of contents. In my defense, even 10 years later there is no consensus about the best way to guide a reader through a Web site. Print has conventions—like page numbers—so ingrained that we don't even think about them. The Web doesn't.

Of the many things I got wrong at the beginning, the most notoriously wrong was my insistence that readers should have to pay for the privilege. I thought that was a test of seriousness, as well as an economic necessity. We launched as a free site, but down the road there was a period of about a year when we demanded $19.95 for an annual subscription. It wasn't a dismal failure: At the end of the year, we had more than 20,000 paid subscribers—a third of what the *New Republic* (my former employer) had after 75 years. But meanwhile our "front porch" (the free part) was attracting 400,000 different visitors a month. (Now that figure is more like 8 million.)

And subscribers don't really pay for print magazines: Even very successful glossy magazines often don't get enough from subscribers to cover the cost of finding them (through junk mail) and signing them up. The reason they bother to extract money from people is to persuade advertisers that these people really want the magazine and therefore are likely to actually read it. On the Web, you don't have to do that indirectly: You know exactly how many people have clicked their way onto a page. That makes the whole system of soliciting and charging subscribers unnecessary. There will probably be a small role for subscriber-paid journalism on the Web, but *Slate's* feeling is been there, done that.

The magazine I dreamed of starting was a newsmagazine. On paper, on the Web, painted on the walls of caves—I didn't care. My theory was that *Time* and *Newsweek* had basically abandoned their mission. They responded to every crisis of identity for the past half-century in exactly the wrong way. From television to the Internet, the newsmags always assumed that new developments were making their central function of intelligently summarizing the news obsolete. So, for half a century or more they have been in retreat from that true function into features, consumerism, photographs, investigative reporting, health, sex—anything but telling and trying to explain what is going on in the world at the moment.

In fact (or so I theorize), the explosion of information, analysis, and opinion between 1950 and today makes a smart summarizing function more necessary, not less so. And that is what I thought *Slate* could provide, occupying the ground abandoned by its betters. Happily, the Web is made for this kind of thing. With links backward to the original story, or forward to a report due out next Tuesday, easy-to-use charts and graphs and photos, etc., the Web could perform "intelligent synthesis" on the world and the news a lot better than the traditional newsmagazines could. Or that was my theory. For 10 years, *Slate* has tried to do that and—especially under the current editor, Jacob—a lot more.

Has *Slate* succeeded? Recently I was out of town and out of touch for about a week. Coming home, I read *Time* and *Newsweek* on the plane, then spent about 45 minutes with *Slate* when I got to a computer. So, which would I pick if I had to choose just one to bring me up to speed? Although I've had nothing to do with *Slate's* management now for almost half its existence, I suppose my objectivity may still be suspect. I say only that the answer made me very, very happy.

Introduction

BY JACOB WEISBERG

IN THE LAST DECADE, *Slate* has gone from fairly well-kept secret to near-household name, with a monthly audience that has risen from the thousands to the millions. Yet our readers persist in regarding us as a great little restaurant that hasn't yet been discovered.

That's fine by us. The ability to remain at least partially invisible promotes the pleasant sense that *Slate* is a kind of club. I'm not thinking here of a country club, or the Rotary, or a book club (though we have one of those). What I mean is that *Slate* has from the start fostered a loose and cozy sense of belonging for both its writers and its readers, creating a kind of no-admission, dues-free society akin to Grateful Deadheads, bird-watchers, or amateur chefs. It's a secondary affiliation, but a strong one.

The magazine's feeling of clubbiness can be further explained by the intimate tone of Web journalism in general and of *Slate* in particular. This was one of our earliest discoveries after we started publishing in 1996. Recessive writers like myself, who in print used to avoid the first person at all costs, soon found our copy sprouting a stubble of *I*'s and *me*'s as we stretched to speak to readers in the more personal and direct way that seemed natural to the medium. We soon came to recognize that writing for a magazine on the Web called for a cross between the more formal diction of the expository essay and the to-the-point, in-your-face tone of e-mail.

Many of Slate's most familiar early rubrics, including our "Dialogues" (see Dahlia Lithwick and Emily Bazelon discussing miscarriage, p. 144), the "Diary" (see New York bartender Toby Cecchini describing some irksome customers, p. 86), and "The Breakfast Table" (see Timothy Noah and Marjorie Williams arguing about Jennifer Lopez's butt, p. 39), were essentially journalistic adaptations of this emerging form of mass communication. "Pretend you're writing me a letter," an old editor of mine used to say when I was struggling to get started on a piece. At Slate, we really do write you the letter.

Some of these popular epistolary features have faded as the novelty of e-mail has worn off (and as print publications trying to sound hipper have copied its tone). But we are experimenters by inclination, and Web-inspired forms have continued to incubate on Slate in the years since our founding. Perhaps the most notable is blogging, whose now familiar and oft-parodied voice (see "Rappers and Bloggers," p. 244) I first encountered in Mickey Kaus' "Chatterbox" column in January 1998—six years before the term "blog" became ubiquitous. The stepchild of this feature, Mickey's "Kausfiles" (see "Fifty-Fifty Forever," p. 136), is recognizably an exercise in political journalism but in 'tude is more like the messages in the editor's inbox than it is like a David Broder column. The newest forms of Internet journalism, which unfortunately cannot be captured in a printed book like this one, combine audio, video, photographs, and text in various and novel ways. Among them are slide shows, interactive photo essays, and podcast audio tours, all emerging and flourishing on Slate.com.

The members of our club, those who enjoy Slate's distinctive style of writing and penchant for journalistic experimentation, are not, for the most part, passive readers. They are by nature correspondents, interlocutors, and complainers, who break off frequently from their gargantuan media diets to fire off a critique to an author, post a comment on our reader discussion board, propose a correction when they think they've caught us in an error, or blog their own views and quips.

If many of our readers function as unpaid writers, our contributors retain a sense of jolly amateurism that marks another distinction from old media. Though we do demarcate turf here and there, our correspondents don't walk the standard newspaper beats or cover them in anything like the traditional manner. We pride ourselves on having thrown away the rule book of our profession. *Slate* has little use for such journalistic crutches as sources, quotations, fact-checking, neutrality, objectivity, balance, the Chinese walling-off of fact from opinion, and the semicolon (which our founder, Michael Kinsley, deems "pretentious"). It's not that we reject all such conventions in principle—we are often the first to complain when newspapers depart from them. Rather, we substitute a set of imperatives that seem more suitable to an interpretative, analytical, and intangible magazine: Be accurate, be intellectually honest, and above all don't waste any of the reader's precious time.

The call to purposeful and ruthless efficiency becomes a special challenge when we write about ourselves, which is what we are doing through much of this anthology. A good deal of what is in *Slate* takes the form of the first-person account, but it tends to be written in a different vein from the kind of personal revelations and extrapolation one finds in other publications. *Slate*sters tend to examine their problems and passions mercilessly and methodically. When Jeffrey Steingarten sets out to conquer his culinary aversions ("Learning To Eat Everything," p. 7), or Seth Stevenson attempts to overcome his shyness with the help of Paxil ("Extroverted Like Me," p. 90), or Masha Gessen asks a Harvard economist to help her decide whether to have a preventive mastectomy ("A Medical Quest," p. 199), they are using themselves as the natural subjects of unconventional investigations. *Slate*'s most regular voices, including Dahlia Lithwick, David Plotz, Daniel Gross, Fred Kaplan, Emily Yoffe, William Saletan, Bryan Curtis, Seth Stevenson, and Jack Shafer, are hardly exhibitionists. But if you've been reading them over the years, you've gotten to know them in a way it's hard to ever know anyone who writes a column for the *New York Times*.

What these very different writers have in common is a quality that around the office we call *Slate*-iness. We have struggled to define this term over the years and failed miserably, mostly falling back on the cop-out that we know it when we see it, or perhaps more precisely, we know when we're not seeing it. Something is *Slatey* when it does something useful—summarizes the five national newspapers every day or tells you how to pronounce "Qatar," understand Bush, or enjoy Faulkner—without feeling like an obligation or a task. To be a *Slatey* writer, you must cut through the media welter, not by speaking more loudly or crudely than others, but by engagingly clarifying and sorting something out for your fellow club members.

This can be done in a number of ways. One mode of *Slate*-iness is simply to finish off a subject once and for all in the minimum necessary number of words. See, for instance, Michael Kinsley on Bill O'Reilly (p. 97), Christopher Hitchens on *Fahrenheit 9/11* (p. 206), or Amanda Fortini on low-rise pants ("Hello, Moon," p. 157). Another is to make the contrarian case that all the common assumptions about a subject are simply and hopelessly wrong. See David Plotz's dismissal of Lewis and Clark (p. 120), June Thomas' defense of Prince Charles (p. 252), or Harriet McBryde Johnson's argument that Congress was right to stick up for Terri Schiavo (p. 247). Another way to write *Slate*-ily is to answer a clever question, perhaps that the rest of us were too embarrassed to ask. See Bryan Curtis on why men have trouble peeing at ballparks (p. 108), or Atul Gawande on why more accidents seem to happen on Friday the 13th (p. 35), or Daniel Engber on how to reattach a severed limb (p. 242). Yet another definition of *Slate*-iness is something that manages to make you think while making you laugh. See "Shag the Dog" by William Saletan (p. 100).

It was not painfully funny, but merely painful, to make the selection for this volume, and apologies to all the deserving pieces that didn't make it. Our tech guy estimates that *Slate* has, in just under 10 years, published some 32,000 articles under 2,000 different bylines. David Plotz, *Slate*'s deputy editor and a *Slate*ster from the very beginning, culled these 50, relying heavily on his own favorites and recommendations from his colleagues.

Whatever else they are, these are some of the *Slate*-iest pieces we've published. If you are not already a member, they will initiate you into the club.

1996

IT WAS ORIGINALLY GOING TO BE called *Boot*, in tribute to the protagonist of Evelyn Waugh's novel *Scoop*. Then someone informed Michael Kinsley that "boot" was slang for "vomit." So Kinsley picked *Slate* instead. In our inaugural issue, June 25, 1996, he wrote that the name "means nothing, or practically nothing. We chose it as an empty vessel into which we can pour meaning. We hope *Slate* will come to mean good original journalism in this new medium. Beyond that, who knows?"

The magazine, as we all insisted on calling it, was a fortunate product of Kinsley's curiosity, Microsoft's money, and the emerging infatuation with the Internet. Tired of playing the liberal on *Crossfire* and of working for unprofitable journals beholden to whimsical benefactors, Kinsley approached college acquaintance Steve Ballmer in the summer of 1995 and suggested that Microsoft publish a Webzine. An online magazine, liberated from the production and mailing costs that squeezed general-interest print titles, might actually become profitable. Ballmer and Bill Gates, newly enthralled with the Internet, quickly signed up Kinsley. On Christmas Day, 1995, he moved to Seattle (occasioning a *Newsweek* cover for which he posed in a rain slicker, holding a salmon) and set up shop on the Microsoft campus.

When *Slate* launched six months later, it was both radical and conservative. *Slate* intended to be skeptical about its new medium, Kinsley declared in his opening essay: "We do not start out with the smug assumption that the Internet changes the nature of human thought, or that all the restraints that society imposes on individuals in 'real life' must melt away in cyberia. There is a deadening conformity in the hipness of cyberspace culture in which we don't intend to participate. Part of our mission at *Slate* will be trying to bring cyberspace down to earth."

The early *Slate* was indeed earthbound. At first, *Slate* was essentially a weekly print magazine that happened to be published on the Web—more like a *New Republic* without the lead time than a revolution. Most articles were posted on Friday, and the site was not regularly updated during the week. (The first "issues" even had page numbers.) But we took baby steps toward Webiness with e-mail debates and computer art exhibits. Perhaps the most important editorial accomplishment of our first six months was The *Slate* 60, a roster of the year's most generous charitable donors. The ranking would become an annual tradition.

By year's end, *Slate* was attracting 15,000 readers a day. We had offices in Seattle, New York (home base for culture editor Judith Shulevitz and political correspondent Jacob Weisberg), and Washington (a tiny bureau run by Jodie Allen). *Slate* lost money, of course—our only revenues were a tiny trickle from early banner ads. One creative business scheme went memorably awry. Our first publisher struck a deal with a burgeoning coffee chain called Starbucks to sell copies of a monthly *Slate* compendium in its outlets around the country. It was a disaster. Store managers had no idea what to do with the magazines, which mostly piled up in their storerooms under boxes of Amaretto syrup. So much for Seattle synergy.

Airline English

Why flight attendants talk like that.

BY CULLEN MURPHY

Aug. 28, 1996

IN AN OPENING MONOLOGUE not long ago, *Tonight Show* host Jay Leno told his audience that Air Force One had hit a patch of turbulence during a recent trip, forcing President Clinton to return the flight attendant "to her full upright and locked position."

What social historians of the future may find most notable about Leno's joke is not what it says about popular perceptions of Bill Clinton's sex life, but what it says about the language of air travel, and how its sui-generis vocabulary ("seat pocket," "ground personnel," "emergency flotation"); its stilted constructions ("We are now ready to pre-board those passengers who . . . "); its sometimes counterintuitive rhythms and emphases ("The captain *has* turned off the seat-belt sign. . . . "); its unblinking, look-you-in-the-eye reliance on euphemisms ("In the unlikely event of a water landing . . . "); its blasé invocation of an all-enveloping legal regime ("We remind you that it is a federal offense to tamper with, disable, or destroy any lavatory smoke detector. . . . "); and its utter regularity across corporate and international boundaries—how all these things have become matters of mass familiarity.

Airline English has, in a way, become the linguistic equivalent of the worldwide nonverbal graphic system that conveys such meanings as "ladies' room," "no parking," "first aid," and "information." It is just as streamlined, just as stylized, often in the same oddly archaic sort of way. The worldwide symbol for "cocktail lounge" is a martini glass with olive, even though martinis themselves are a relatively uncommon sight these days. The symbol for "pharmacy" is a mortar and pestle. Airline language is similarly atavistic. Whenever else does one hear the word "stow" being used, except as part of the command to "stow your belongings in the overhead bins"?

Actually, the other place where "stow" is frequently used is onboard boats and ships. One significant element of airline language, including many of its archaisms, derives from the nautical terminology that the pioneers of air travel appropriated—not unnaturally, given the obvious parallels between the two modes of transportation (fragile means of conveyance, built to negotiate a boundless, often turbulent medium of fluid or gas). An airplane is a "craft," and its "crew," including a "captain," "first officer," and "purser," operates from a "deck" inside a "cabin." The aircraft is segmented by "bulkheads." Its kitchens are "galleys." It carries cargo in "holds."

But the compressed time of air travel gives its language a focused, liturgical quality that oceanic travel has never had (at least for passengers), from the initial welcome aboard to the cautionary homily to the ritual meal—on more and more flights, a merely symbolic activity—to the final "Goodbye. Goodbye. Goodbye. Goodbye. Goodbye." The linguistic contours of a typical airline flight are every bit as scripted as those of a religious service. For American carriers, the Nicene Creed of official cabin talk comes in the form of a number of Federal Aviation Administration regulations, such as No. 121.571 ("Briefing passengers before take-off") and No. 121.573 ("Briefing passengers: extended overwater operations"). The subject matter of these dense passages of text, which in their original versions date back to the early 1960s, concerns everything from seat belts and life jackets to emergency exits and oxygen masks. The regulations are distilled by each airline into detailed scripts that are reviewed by company lawyers and must be approved, finally, by the FAA. The scripts are then circulated to in-flight personnel.

Credal formulations aside, airlines have considerable latitude when it comes to routine announcements; again, though, the language is often fastidiously scripted, down to even the most casual remarks. ("Would you like Coke or Sprite?" appears in a script provided by the Association of Professional Flight Attendants.) Most of the dozen or so airlines contacted were reluctant to furnish actual transcripts of approved language manuals, although one veteran pilot (with United) asserted: "You're gonna hear the same thing, but you'll hear it just a bit differently." Southwest Airlines did provide an example of an unusual rap announcement that some of its ground personnel have used. It reads, in part: "We board in groups of thirty,/ According to your card;/ One thru thirty boards first,/ It's really not that hard." And it goes on, "Federal law prohibits smoking/ On most domestic flights./ No smoking is permitted,/ So don't even try to light." Southwest's corporate culture of officially sanctioned iconoclasm, if there can be such a thing, is far from typical.

From time to time, passengers may notice a crew member reading an announcement from a laminated text—changes do get made and are distributed airline-wide—but for the most part the scripts are committed to memory, and the habits born of rigorous training die hard. Not long ago, one of my sisters discovered that she was to be the only passenger on a commercial flight, and settled in for the journey. As she prepared for the plane to push back, a flight attendant materialized for the safety briefing, and in the one concession to the circumstances, sat down in the seat next to my sister instead of standing in the aisle at the front of the cabin. The dull monotone was the same as ever. "As we prepare for take-off," the flight attendant said, looking at my sister from 6 inches away, "please check that your seat belt is fastened"—and here she made the requisite clicking and unclicking movements with the demonstration model—"and *do* take time to look through the safety information in the seat pocket in front of you. Our aircraft is equipped with four emergency exits. . . . "

As you might imagine, my sister, at that point, was ready to use them all.

The Omnivore

Learning to eat everything.

BY JEFFREY STEINGARTEN

Aug. 28, 1996

"MY FIRST IMPULSE WAS to fall upon the cook," wrote Edmondo de Amicis, a 19th-century traveler. "In an instant I understood perfectly how a race who ate such food must necessarily believe in another God and hold essentially different views of human life from our own. . . . There was a suggestion of soap, wax, pomatum, of unguents, dyes, cosmetics; of everything, in short, most unsuited to enter a human mouth."

Though de Amicis was describing his feelings about Moroccan cuisine, this is precisely how I felt about desserts in Indian restaurants until 1989, the year that I, formerly a lawyer, was appointed food critic of *Vogue* magazine. As I contemplated the heavy responsibilities of my new post, I realized how inadequate I was to the honor, for I, like everybody I knew, suffered from a set of strong and arbitrary likes and dislikes regarding food. I feared that I was no better than an art critic who becomes nauseated by the color yellow or suffers from red-green color blindness. At the time, I was friendly with a respected and powerful editor of cookbooks who so detested the flavor of cilantro that she brought a pair of tweezers to Mexican and Indian restaurants and pinched out every last scrap of this herb before she would take a bite. Imagine the dozens of potential Julia Childs and M.F.K. Fishers whose books she pettishly rejected, whose careers she snuffed in their infancy! I vowed not to follow in her footsteps.

It went even deeper than that. Humans were designed to be omnivores. Blessed with all-purpose dentition and digestive systems, we are ready for anything. Unlike those of most other animals, our genes do not tell us what foods we should find tasty or repulsive. We enter the world with a yen for sweets and an aversion to bitterness. (Newborns, it has recently been discovered, can even distinguish among glucose, fructose, lactose, and sucrose—but little else.) After four months, we develop an innate fondness for salt. And that's about it.

The nifty thing about being omnivores is that we can take nourishment from an endless variety of sources and easily adapt to a changing food world—crop failures, droughts, herd migrations, restaurant closings, and the like. Cows will starve in a steakhouse and wolves in a salad bar, but not we.

The tricky part about being omnivorous is that we are always in danger of poisoning ourselves. That is why the most potent cause of food aversions is an attack of nausea after eating. Just one illness will do the trick—even if the food we ate did not actually cause the problem and even if we know it didn't. Hives or rashes may make us rationally avoid a given food in the future, but only a stomachache will result in a lasting, irrational, lifelong sense of disgust. Otherwise, psychologists know very little about the host of powerful likes and dislikes—let's lump them all under the term "food phobias"—that children carry into adulthood.

By shutting ourselves off from the bounties of nature, we become failed omnivores. We let the omnivore team down. And that is only the beginning.

I have always thought that people who keep a long list of certifiably delicious foods that they avoid are at least as troubled as people who avoid sex, except that the latter will probably seek psychiatric help, while food phobics rationalize their problem in the name of genetic inheritance, allergy, vegetarianism, matters of taste, nutrition, food safety, obesity, or a sensitive nature. (True food allergies can be extremely dangerous, but no more than 1 percent or 2 percent of adults suffer from them.) The examples of neurotic food avoidance could take several volumes to fill, but milk is a good one.

Suddenly, everybody has become lactose intolerant. But the truth is that very, very few of us are so seriously afflicted that we cannot drink even a glass of milk a day without trouble. I know several people who have given up cheese to avoid lactose. But fermented cheeses contain no lactose! Lactose is the sugar found in milk; 98 percent of it is drained off with the whey (cheese is made from the curds), and the other 2 percent is quickly consumed by lactic-acid bacteria in the act of fermentation.

I cannot figure out why, but the atmosphere in America today rewards this sort of self-deception. Fear and suspicion of food have nearly become the norm. Civil dinners have become impossible, and with them, the sense of festivity and exchange. We are as pitiable as the poor bushmen of the Kalahari who perish in large numbers during the droughts that afflict them every two or three years because they consider only about a quarter of the 223 animal species that inhabit their world to be edible.

People should be ashamed of the irrational food phobias that keep them from sharing food with each other. Instead, they have become proud and arrogant and aggressively misinformed. But not me. When I donned the heavy mantle of food critic, I sketched out a six-step program to rid myself of all puissant and crippling likes and dislikes.

Step One was to list my food phobias, which ranged from mild to psychotic. They included dill, kimchi (the national pickle of Korea), swordfish, miso, mocha, chutney, raw sea urchins, cinnamon, California chardonnay, falafel (those hard, dry, fried little balls of chickpea flour unaccountably enjoyed in Middle Eastern countries), chickpeas generally, cranberries, kidneys, okra, millet, coffee ice cream, refried beans, and most forms of yogurt.

I was also convinced that "Greek cuisine" was an oxymoron. Nations are like people. Some are good at cooking while others have a talent for music or baseball or manufacturing VCRs. The Greeks are really good at both pre-Socratic philosophy and white sculpture. They have not been good cooks since the fifth century B.C., when Siracusa in Sicily was the gastronomic capital of the world. Typical of the Greeks' modern cuisine are feta cheese and retsina wine. Any country that pickles its national cheese in brine and adulterates its national wine with pine pitch should order dinner at the local Chinese place and save its energies for other things. The British go to Greece for the food, which says volumes to me. You would probably think twice before buying a Russian or Algerian television set. I had thought for 10 years before buying my last Greek meal.

This had to stop.

Step Two was to immerse myself for several weeks in the scientific literature on human food selection. Did you know that babies who are breast-fed will later have less trouble with novel foods than those who are given formula? The reason is found in the variety of flavors that make their way into breast milk from the mother's diet and prepare the infant for the culinary surprises that will follow weaning.

Food phobias can be extinguished in five or six ways, of which I considered only brain surgery, medication, and mere exposure. Bilateral lesions made in the basolateral region of the amygdala seem to do the trick in rats and, I think, monkeys—eliminating old aversions, preventing the formation of new ones, and increasing the animals' acceptance of novel foods. But the literature does not report whether this brain operation also diminishes the ability of these phobia-free animals to, say, watch the entire Republican Convention on C-SPAN or get an external CD-ROM changer to work under Windows 95, key skills I might even value over becoming phobia-free. I am kidding, of course—nobody can do these things.

Administration of the drug chlordiazepoxide also seems to work. According to an old *PDR*, this is nothing but Librium, the once-popular tranquilizer also bottled as "Reposans" and "Sereen." But the label warns you about nausea, depression, and heavy machinery. I just said no.

Bribery does not work. Children who are offered more playtime for eating spinach may temporarily comply. Those who are offered Milky Way bars in return for eating spinach quickly learn to value Milky Way bars.

Step Three was to choose my weapon. Exposure was the only answer. Researchers have found that eating moderate amounts of a novel or hated food at moderate intervals is nearly guaranteed to work. The reason is that omnivores are born with neophobia, a fear of new foods that accompanies our biological need to explore for them—an ambivalence that protects us from unbridled banqueting. Most parents give up trying out novel foods on their weanlings after two or three attempts and then complain to the pediatrician; this may be the most frequent cause of finicky eaters, of omnivores *manqués*. Most babies will accept nearly anything after eight or 10 tries.

Step Four: I immediately made eight or 10 reservations at Korean restaurants, purchased eight or 10 anchovies, searched the Zagat guide for eight or 10 restaurants with the names "Parthenon" or "Olympia" (which I believe are required by statute for Greek restaurants), and brought a pot of water to a boil for cooking eight or 10 chickpeas.

I dedicated the next six months to this effort, and by the time I had finished, nearly every food aversion (along with every positive preference that had kept me from exploring freely) was gone. Now I yearn for miso and am a noted connoisseur of anchovies. Try to find those packed in salt rather than in oil.

Step Five, the final exam and graduation ceremony. I was in Paris, France—a city that my professional duties frequently compel me to visit. I was trying a nice new restaurant, and when the waiter brought the menu, I found myself in a state unlike any I had ever attained—call it Zen-like if you wish. Everything on the menu, every appetizer, hot and cold, every salad, every fish, every bird, and every meat was terrifically alluring, but none more than any other. I had absolutely no way of choosing. Though blissful at the prospect of eating, I was completely unable to order dinner. I was reminded of the medieval church parable of the ass equidistant between two bales of hay, who, because animals lack free will, starves to death. A man, supposedly, would not.

The Catholic Church was dead wrong. I would have starved—if my companion had not saved the day by ordering for both of us. I believe I had a composed salad with slivers of foie gras, a perfect sole meunière, and sweetbreads. Everything was delicious.

Step Six: learning humility. Just because you have become a perfect omnivore does not mean that you must flaunt it. Intoxicated with my accomplishment, I began to misbehave, especially at dinner parties. When seated next to an especially finicky eater, I would amuse myself by going straight for the jugular. Sometimes I began slyly by staring at the food left on her plate and then inquiring about her allergies; sometimes I launched a direct assault by asking how long she had had a fear of bread. And then I would sit back and sagely listen to a neurotic jumble of excuses and explanations: the advice from her personal trainer, her intolerance to wheat gluten, a pathetic faith in Dean Ornish, the exquisite—even painful—sensitivity of her taste buds, hints of childhood abuse.

While it is perfectly all right—even charitable—to practice this kind of tough love on those of one's dinner-party neighbors who are less omnivorous than oneself, the perfect omnivore must always keep in mind that it is an absolute necessity to get invited back.

1997

WE BEGAN THE YEAR by chickening out. Our plan had been to start charging for subscriptions to *Slate* in January. But our payment software was buggy, which gave us the excuse we were looking for to postpone the day of reckoning.

More notable was that *Slate* began to act less like a print magazine and more like a Web site. One prod for this was the death of Princess Diana in August. When the news broke, Web traffic spiked to record levels, and our competitors (notably *Salon*) crammed their sites with news stories, speculation, memorials, poems—anything to capture browsers. *Slate* chose not to interrupt one of its summer "skip weeks"—a tradition inherited from print magazines in which publications shut down and everyone goes to the beach. Diana's death finally made us understand that online journalism is by nature a round-the-clock business. Our publishing pace began to pick up—from weekly to daily to several times a day.

Another mark of our accelerating pace was the launch of "Today's Papers," an early-morning summary of the five national newspapers. Scott Shuger stayed up every night reading the papers on the Web, then posted the column by 6 a.m. and e-mailed it to tens of thousands of subscribers. (Matt Drudge, then an obscure Internet junkie, had been our first choice to write "Today's Papers," but he turned us down and suggested Scott.) Other beginnings: Herb Stein, our 80-year-old economics columnist—and the most rational man you could hope to meet—started writing an agony column called "Dear Prudence." Atul Gawande inaugurated the "Medical Examiner" column; James Surowiecki signed on as our first business writer; and Michael Lewis moved to Silicon Valley and started covering Internet-boom culture for us in a column called "Millionerds."

Go Ahead—Sleep With Your Kids

The urge is natural. Surrender to it.

BY ROBERT WRIGHT

March 28, 1997

EVERY NIGHT THOUSANDS OF PARENTS, following standard child-care advice, engage in a bloodcurdling ritual. They put their several-months-old infant in a crib, leave the room, and studiously ignore its crying. The crying may go on for 20 or 30 minutes before a parent is allowed to return. The baby may then be patted but not picked up, and the parent must quickly leave, after which the crying typically resumes. Eventually sleep comes, but the ritual recurs when the child awakes during the night. The same thing happens the next night, except that the parent must wait five minutes longer before the designated patting. This goes on for a week, two weeks, maybe even a month. If all goes well, the day finally arrives when the child can fall asleep without fuss and go the whole night without being fed. For Mommy and Daddy, it's Miller time.

This is known as "Ferberizing" a child, after Richard Ferber, America's best-known expert on infant sleep. Many parents find his prescribed boot camp for babies agonizing, but they persist because they've been assured it's harmless. Ferber depicts the ritual as the child's natural progress toward nocturnal self-reliance. What sounds to the untrained ear like a baby wailing in desperate protest of abandonment is described by Ferber as a child "learning the new associations."

At this point I should own up to my bias: My wife and I are failed Ferberizers. When our first daughter proved capable of crying for 45 minutes without reloading, we gave up and let her sleep in our bed. When our second daughter showed up three years later, we didn't even bother to set up the crib. She wasn't too vocal and seemed a better candidate for Ferberization, but we'd found we liked sleeping with a baby.

How did we have the hubris to defy the mainstream of current child-care wisdom? That brings me to my second bias (hauntingly familiar to regular readers): Darwinism. For our species, the natural nighttime arrangement is for kids to sleep alongside their mothers for the first few years. At least, that's the norm in hunter-gatherer societies, the closest things we have to a model of the social environment in which humans evolved. Mothers nurse their children to sleep and then nurse on demand through the night. Sounds taxing, but it's not. When the baby cries, the mother starts nursing reflexively, often without really waking up. If she does reach consciousness, she soon fades back to sleep with the child. And the father, as I can personally attest, never leaves Z-town.

So Ferberization, I submit, is unnatural. That doesn't necessarily mean it's bad. The technique may well be harmless (though maybe not, as we'll see below). I don't begrudge Ferber the right to preach Ferberization or parents who prefer sleeping sans child the right to practice it. Live and let live. What's annoying is the refusal of Ferber and other experts to reciprocate my magnanimity. They act as if parents like me are derelict, as if children *need* to fall asleep in a room alone. "Even if you and your child seem happy about his sharing your bed at night," writes Ferber, "and even if he seems to sleep well there, in the long run this habit will probably not be good for either of you." On television I've seen a father sheepishly admit to famous child-care guru T. Berry Brazelton that he likes sleeping with his toddler. You'd think the poor man had committed incest.

Why, exactly, is it bad to sleep with your kids? Learning to sleep alone, says Ferber, lets your child "see himself as an independent individual." I'm puzzled. It isn't obvious to me how a baby would develop a robust sense of autonomy while being confined to a small cubicle with bars on the side and rendered powerless to influence its environment. (Nor is it obvious these days, when many kids spend 40 hours a week in day care, that they need extra autonomy training.) I'd be willing to look at the evidence behind this claim, but there isn't any. Comparing Ferberized with non-Ferberized kids as they grow up would tell us nothing—Ferberizing and non-Ferberizing parents no doubt tend to have broadly different approaches to child-rearing, and they probably have different cultural milieus. We can't control our variables.

Lacking data, people like Ferber and Brazelton make creative assertions about what's going on inside the child's head. Ferber says that if you let a toddler sleep between you and your spouse, "in a sense separating the two of you, he may feel too powerful and become worried." Well, he may, I guess. Or he may just feel cozy. Hard to say (though they certainly *look* cozy). Brazelton tells us that when a child wakes up at night and you refuse to retrieve her from the crib, "she won't like it, but she'll understand." Oh.

According to Ferber, the trouble with letting a child who fears sleeping alone into your bed is that "you are not really solving the problem. There must be a reason why he is so fearful." Yes, there must. Here's one candidate. Maybe your child's brain was designed by natural selection over millions of years during which mothers slept with their babies. Maybe back then if babies found themselves completely alone at night it often meant something horrific had happened—the mother had been eaten by a beast, say. Maybe the young brain is designed to respond to this situation by screaming frantically so that any relatives within earshot will discover the child. Maybe, in short, the reason that kids left alone sound terrified is that kids left alone naturally get terrified. Just a theory.

A few weeks of nightly terror presumably won't scar a child for life. Humans are resilient, by design. If Ferber's gospel harms kids, it's more likely doing so via a second route: the denial of mother's milk to the child at night. Breast milk, researchers are finding, is a kind of "external placenta," loaded with hormones masterfully engineered to assist development. One study found that it boosts IQ.

Presumably most breast-feeding benefits can be delivered via daytime nursing. Still, we certainly don't *know* that an 11-hour nightly gap in the feeding schedule isn't doing harm. And we do know that such a gap isn't part of nature's plan for a 5-month-old child—at least, to judge by hunter-gatherer societies. Or to judge by the milk itself: It is thin and watery—typical of species that nurse frequently. Or to judge by the mothers: Failing to nurse at night can lead to painful engorgement or even breast infection. Meanwhile, as all available evidence suggests that nighttime feeding is natural, Ferber asserts the opposite. If after three months of age your baby wakes at night and wants to be fed, "she is developing a sleep problem."

I don't generally complain about oppressive patriarchal social structures, but Ferberism is a good example of one. As "family bed" boosters have noted, male physicians, who have no idea what motherhood is like, have cowed women for decades into doing unnatural and destructive things. For a while doctors said mothers shouldn't feed more than once every four hours. Now they admit they were wrong. For a while they pushed bottle feeding. Now they admit this was wrong. For a while they told pregnant women to keep weight gains minimal (and some women did so by smoking more cigarettes!). Wrong again. Now they're telling mothers to deny food to infants all night long once the kids are a few months old.

There are signs that yet another well-advised retreat is under way. Though Ferber hasn't put out the white flag, Brazelton is sounding less and less dismissive of parents who sleep with their kids. (Not surprisingly, the least dismissive big-name child-care expert is a woman, Penelope Leach.) Better late than never. But in child care, as in the behavioral sciences generally, we could have saved ourselves a lot of time and trouble by recognizing at the outset that people are animals, and pondering the implications of that fact.

Watching the Couples Go By

Why is this basic woman so valuable to this basic man whose arm she holds?

BY HERBERT STEIN

Friday, June 13, 1997

ONE OF MY PERSISTENT FANTASIES used to be of sitting at a sidewalk table at a cafe in Paris. I would be writing with my pen (*la plume de ma tante*) in a notebook (*un cahier*) while smoking a Gauloise. I would not be writing economics. One cannot write economics while sitting at a sidewalk cafe. Maybe that is why there have been so few distinguished French economists. I would be writing a novel, or perhaps poetry, or even a philosophical treatise. But I would frequently raise my eyes to watch the girls (*les filles*) go by.

I no longer have that fantasy. I do, however, eat from time to time at an outdoor table in front of a small restaurant on the street leading to the Kennedy Center. I don't try to write there. I can't write with *la plume de ma tante*. I am addicted to the word processor. I suppose I could use a laptop computer. But that mechanism would destroy the romantic illusion. Instead, I watch the passers-by.

I am not concentrating on the girls. I am concentrating on the married couples. How do I know that those men and women walking two-by-two up to the Kennedy Center are married to each other? Well, 75 percent of all men between the ages of 30 and 75 are married, so if you see a man in that age group walking with a woman to the Kennedy Center—which is not exactly Club Med—it's a good bet that the two are married, and almost certainly to each other.

I look particularly at the women in those couples. They are not glamorous. There are no Marlene Dietrichs, Marilyn Monroes, or Vivien Leighs among them. (It is a sign of my age that I can't think of the name of a single living glamorous movie actress.) Some of them are pretty, but many would be considered plain. Since they are on their way to the Kennedy Center, presumably to attend a play, an opera, or a concert, one may assume that they are somewhat above average in cultural literacy. But in other respects one must assume that they are, like most people, average.

But to the man whose hand or arm she is holding, she is not "average." She is the whole world to him. They may argue occasionally, or even frequently. He may have an eye for the cute intern in his office. But that is superficial. Fundamentally, she is the most valuable thing in his life.

Genesis says, "And the Lord God said: 'It is not good that the man should be alone; I will make him a help meet for him.'" And so, "made He a woman." It doesn't say that He made a pretty woman, or a witty woman, or an any-kind-of-adjective woman. He made the basic woman.

Why is this basic woman so valuable to the man whose hand or arm she is holding as I see them making their way up to the Kennedy Center? I think there are three simple things.

First, she is a warm body in bed. I don't refer to their sexual activity. That is important but too varied for me to generalize about. I refer to something that is, if possible, even more primitive. It is human contact.

A baby crying in its crib doesn't want conversation or a gold ring. He wants to be picked up, held, and patted. Adults need that physical contact also. They need to cuddle together for warmth and comfort in an indifferent or cold world. At least, they need to be able to do that. The plain woman and plain man I am watching do that for each other.

But conversation is also important. These couples may have been talking to each other for 30 years or more. You might think they have nothing left to say. But still they can talk to each other in ways that they cannot talk to anyone else. He can tell her of something good he has done, or something good that has happened to him, without fearing that she will think he is bragging. He can tell her of something bad that has happened without fearing that she will think he is complaining. He can tell her of the most trivial thing without fearing that she will think he is bothering her. He can count on her interest and understanding.

The primary purpose of this conversation is not to convey any specific information. Its primary purpose is to say, "I am here and I know that you are here."

Third, the woman serves the man's need to be needed. If no one needs you, what good are you, and what are you here for? Other people—employers, students, readers—may say that they need you. But it isn't true. In all such relationships you are replaceable at some price. But to this woman you are not replaceable at any price. And that gives you the self-esteem to go out and meet the world every day.

So this "ordinary" woman—one like about 50 million others in America—has this great value to this man she is going to the theater with. He surely does not make a calculation—doesn't mark her to market. He probably never says how much he values her, to himself or to her. But he acts as if he knows it.

I see that I have written these views entirely from the point of view of the man. That is only natural for me. But I don't for a minute think that the relationship I have been trying to describe is one-sided. On the contrary, I am sure it is reciprocal.

I can hear you saying, "How do you know all this? You are only an economist, practitioner of the dismal science. You aren't Ann Landers." That is all true. But my wife and I walked up that hill to the Kennedy Center many times.

Why I Hate Liberals

A conservative's manifesto.

BY DEBORAH NEEDLEMAN

Sept. 18, 1997

LIKE MOST PEOPLE, gardeners can be categorized as liberal or conservative. It is the liberals who concern me. Their hearts may be in the right place, but, as a result of attachment to dogma and oversimplification of facts, there is much that they fail to understand. Since they are the majority, and their views the predominant ones, I feel compelled to come forward on behalf of my fellow politically incorrect gardening compatriots.

Liberal gardeners are people who feel that, through gardening, we can alleviate our sense of alienation from nature and that, through good gardening, we can repair some of the damage we have done to our environment. The most extreme liberals believe that there is an original or a natural state in which the environment would be if we hadn't shown up on the scene and that we have not only the ability but also a moral imperative to help nature return to this state. Remember the 1970s, when people were turning their suburban lawns loose and allowing them to aspire to being meadows? They were letting the grass express its natural inclination toward longness and reduced greenness, while their neighbors were handing them citations demanding a return to neatness and neighborliness. This liberation of grass struggling to be free was yet another response to the man/nature divide that has worried liberals for centuries. The basic idea is that nature is good, man is not, and the more we can keep the beastly hand of man out of things, the better.

The liberal solution is what has come to be known as a "natural garden." Judging from the looks of it, it might more properly be called a "naturalistic garden." These gardens contain many elements cribbed from nature herself, such as sinuous paths, free-form ponds, curvy clumps of shrubs, and squiggly planting beds. Curvilinearness is believed to be next to godliness. A walk or a drive up to the house or through the garden should bend and wind and provide a "sense of journey," as one might experience on a walk in the woods. Such a garden may even contain a craggy-ledged waterfall or some other wonder of the natural world. Sometimes, if the garden seems very "natural," as Central Park is meant to, people may even mistake their experience for one in nature. But Frederick Law Olmsted, the park's architect, is no hero to our liberals, for he committed the unforgivable sin of using "exotics"—plants of foreign origin come to mingle on our virgin terrain. "Natural gardening" is a strictly regional affair, done with those plants that thrived in a particular area—around say, Des Moines or Dubuque—before the fall of man. (This type of gardening came into vogue in the 1980s as the gardening environmentalists' response to the excesses of that decade. It incorporated the teachings of the organic-gardening movement and spun them not only with lessons about water conservation and ecosystems but also with the promotion of natural-seeming styles and plants.)

So, after setting their turf free, natural gardeners began to regard the chemical- and water-dependent lawn as a villainous expression of suburban man's environmental insensitivity, and turned against it entirely. Grass was yanked out by its roots and tossed onto the compost heap. Those offending areas are now populated by happy natives thriving in their xeroscapes in xenophobic splendor. Presumably these indigenous plants refrain from sending their seed downwind into other areas where they do not belong. But can we be sure that any "native" plant was not merely brought into alien territory on the sandal-sole of an unwitting nomad long ago?

Henry Mitchell, the late, great, and I think, conservative garden writer (he smoked cigarettes in his garden, an act incomprehensible to liberals), poked fun at those who think they garden in "a natural way." That, he claimed, could be seen in "any desert, any swamp, any leech-filled laurel hell." Gardening, on the other hand, was for him the "high defiance of nature herself." Nature has no patience for your garden. She wants to reclaim it, and if you turn your back on it for a moment, she'll be there, with weeds and vines and tangled brush. It is men and women, not gardens, who are found in nature. And because we conservatives view ourselves as part of nature—albeit a quirky, self-conscious bit of it—we feel we have the honor and privilege of tussling with it.

Where liberals are moralists, conservatives are aesthetes. Gardens, particularly flower gardens, serve no real purpose. If gardens must have a higher calling, it is the cause of beauty. Failing to recognize the primacy of aesthetics in gardening, liberals are left vulnerable to all sorts of unnecessary errors, such as using bark mulch as a decorative element. This can lead you down the slippery slope toward plants artlessly plunked down in an unrepentant mishmash, the garden equivalent of an unshaven armpit.

Conservatives like lawns, especially when we call them *tapis verts*. We like topiary, pollarded trees, *allées*, bosques, exotic plants, and formal rigor. Of course, we may also love wildness, meadows, indigenous plants, woods—we are not without our libertarian inclinations—but not exclusively or senselessly. Gardening is ultimately a folly whose goal is to provide delight. A liberal may look at a boxwood bunny frozen in mid-hop and see only a plant in bondage. Conservatives love gardens *because* they are artifice. Dan Kiley, one of the most important landscape architects of the 20th century, creates landscapes based on a grid. His belief is that we should not shy away from geometry in the design and layout of gardens, since the entire cosmos is based on it. To garden in this way is to copy the spirit of nature, not its letter.

The most slanderous thing liberals say about conservatives is that we are not sufficiently concerned about the environment. We, too, are concerned. We just express our concern in a different way. Imagine Nature looking down at what we have made at, say, Versailles, and also at a low-maintenance ornamental grass planting around a boggy pond. Which would it feel was a more fitting testament to its mysteries and strength?

The Cult of Che

Knowing what we know, why do we still celebrate him?

BY PAUL BERMAN

Oct. 30, 1997

So THEY HAVE FINALLY GIVEN Che Guevara a proper burial—the interment took place Oct. 17—in Cuban soil, in the town where he achieved his greatest revolutionary victory. You might suppose that, in these after-days of communism, Che's legendary glamour will soon enough find its way to a similar interment, though perhaps not in Cuba itself, where glamour, like everything else, remains under state control.

Che was not, after all, the best of communists. He was, in his dashing manner, the worst—an extreme dogmatist, instinctively authoritarian, allergic to any democratic or libertarian impulses, quick to order executions, and quicker still to lead his own comrades to their deaths in doomed guerrilla wars. Love of the Soviet Union was his first instinct, and when he evolved a second, more critical instinct, it was only because the Soviet leaders turned out to be less rigidly Marxist-Leninist and less suicidal than himself.

Of the innumerable commentaries on Che that have been published in the last few weeks, Alma Guillermoprieto offered the clearest, in *The New Yorker*. "He was a fanatic," she wrote, "consumed by restlessness and a frightening abstract hatred, who in the end recognized only one moral value as supreme: the willingness to be slaughtered for a cause." But I am struck most by a commentary that appeared in the Mexican weekly *Etcétera*, under the byline Gilberto Guevara Niebla—no relation to Che himself, yet a figure of great importance in the revolutionary history of the 1960s. Gilberto Guevara Niebla was arguably the single most important student leader of the Mexican student uprising of 1968—the uprising that was finally put down in a massacre by the Mexican army in October 1968.

He wrote, "Che offered his life to the cause of the disinherited, but he did it by offering a political method that, in the long run, had disastrous effects on whoever tried to uphold it. Guerrilla war imposed a militarist logic and closed the space for democracy. What Latin America lived since Che launched his slogans was a bloodbath and a wave of destruction and terror. . . . The myth of Che has been a wall impeding the observation of those fatal historical results." Who was Che? A man who "wanted to change the world through the means—always sordid—of killing other men."

Couldn't be clearer. Yet, among the kind of people who once upon a time had admired Che and his cause—a lot of people, especially in the generation that was young in the 1960s—the more typical commentaries have balanced on a "but," as on a fulcrum. Che was wrong; but he was good. His ideas were hopeless; but he remains the embodiment of an ideal. Let me quote the French weekly *Le Nouvel Observateur*, which devoted an issue to Che earlier this month: "That his politico-military theory . . . failed matters little. What remains, on both sides of the Andes, is the example of a man, the child of his continent, who knew how to die for his generous ideas in an unequal struggle." Or last Sunday's *New York Times Book Review*, which concluded, "What is left is simply the man—a rebel who could not part with his dream, and who earned a place in history precisely because he refused to yield to it."

Or a Portuguese writer in *Etcétera*'s special Che issue: "Che Guevara is only the other name of what is most just and dignified in the human spirit." And so forth, one commentator after another, which would be hard to believe, except that right now the world is awash in Che T-shirts, mugs, barroom décor, a Che beer (in England), posters, and utterly pointless editions (let us hope) of Che's military writings. And the mania is not just a matter of mass culture.

Among the books about Che that have just now come out, one by Jorge G. Castañeda, *Compañero: The Life and Death of Che Guevara*, offers an exceptionally lucid analysis of Che's life and doings, based on a tremendous amount of research both in Cuba and in American-government files. (Castañeda knows more about Latin American guerrilla movements than anybody, outside of Castro's secret agencies.) Yet in a few paragraphs at the front and close of his book on Che, even Castañeda, this most intelligent and admirable of historians, extols "the fervent idealism and generational arrogance of 1968" around the world, and then anoints Che as "the one man who most closely embodied its deeper meaning." Régis Debray, Che's comrade, wrote a memoir last year in which he warned against exactly that delusion—"the anti-authoritarian revolt of '68 taking this hardcore partisan of authoritarianism for its emblem." But then, I can understand that particular confusion. A couple of years ago I wrote a piece of my own about Che in *The New Yorker* and, though I knew better, I ended up adding a superfluous nod to the innate "nobility" of this man whose fanaticism and lack of human sympathy brought about so much suffering and death.

Why do people who know better say such things? It is not because of the doctrines of communism. It is because of the doctrines of glory, which are much more primitive. What is glory? This: an absolute commitment to your own principle, whatever it may be—the kind of commitment that expresses itself in only one way, by a willingness to kill other people on its behalf and to be killed in turn. A commitment, finally, to defeat. For victory is always partial and compromised, but defeat and death are total and grand. Victory is secular; defeat is sacred.

A Che who, like any ordinary communist politician, had never killed anyone; a Che who had survived his guerrilla adventures and was today an elderly figure, administering some grim bureaucracy for Fidel Castro or, alternatively, writing books at home in Argentina, surrounded by his anti-communist grandchildren—a Che like that would cause no stir at all today, and writers around the world would not be straining their brains to draw ever-finer distinctions between the man's calamitous influence and some undefinable greatness.

There is a precedent to the Che cult. It was the cult of Napoleon in the 19th century, a young man's craze that went on for generations—the craze that Stendhal described in his character Julien Sorel in *The Red and the Black* and Victor Hugo in his character Marius in *Les Misérables*. In the 19th century, intelligent people in France knew perfectly well that Napoleon had embodied the worst aspects of the French Revolution, had betrayed the revolution's democratic ideals, and had spread death and fire from Spain to Moscow. Yet those same clear-thinking people found ways of separating Napoleon's horrors from his glamour. They would say: He was wrong, but he was great. It was a question of glory—of his having risen in the world, and having killed his thousands, and having failed spectacularly, and not having flinched. It was the appeal of death—doled out, and accepted. And so the cult of Napoleon was, finally, a cult of the tomb.

In 1821 Napoleon was murdered—he was poisoned—while in the hands of his enemies, far away from home, just as Che was murdered in 1967. It took 19 years to bring Napoleon's remains back to France, compared to 30 years for Che. Napoleon's reburial took place on Dec. 15, 1840. People who should have known better found the ceremony moving. Victor Hugo, who stood among the crowd, dutifully recorded, in a poem on the occasion, that

Napoleon had been wrong—that Napoleon had tried to conquer with the sword instead of with the mind. Yet a few lines later, Hugo wrote, his Bonapartist blood pounding:

> May the people forever keep you in their memory, Day as beautiful as glory, Cold as the tomb!

So in the Cuban tropics, too, there has just now been a day as beautiful as glory, cold as the tomb. And because the cult of glory feeds on defeat and not on victory, we can be sure that, like the passion for Napoleon in the last century, the passion for Che will disappear no time soon. Not in this generation, not in the next.

1998

SLATE'S BRIEF, UNFORTUNATE PERIOD as a paid magazine began in February. We figured that readers accustomed to subscribing to paper magazines would readily fork over $19.95 for a year of *Slate* (and the premium of a Seattle-suitable *Slate* umbrella). Michael Kinsley gamely tried to persuade readers that paying for *Slate* was the right, even patriotic, thing to do: "One of *Slate*'s main goals is to demonstrate, if we can, that the economics of cyberspace make it easier for our kind of journalism to pay for itself. Most magazines like *Slate* depend on someone's generosity or vanity or misplaced optimism to pay the bills. But self-supporting journalism is freer journalism," Kinsley wrote in his Readme column. "If the Web can make serious journalism more easily self-supporting, that is a great gift from technology to democracy."

Given how early we were in the development of the medium, signing up more than 20,000 subscribers was hardly a defeat. But do the math—it barely covered our latte bills. And authors who had been reaching a growing and enthusiastic audience suddenly found themselves performing for a tiny circle of readers. Many of us bit our tongues—or didn't—while waiting for the experiment to be pronounced a failure.

The other excitement was the Lewinsky scandal—nicknamed "Flytrap" by *Slate*. Timothy Noah inherited "Chatterbox," a funny, idiosyncratic political column. Several authors collaborated to produce a serialized e-mail novel. Titled *Reply All*, it was very ambitious, and somewhat less successful. We launched

"The Explainer," which became our most popular regular column. And we tweaked the corporate masters with daily coverage of the Microsoft antitrust trial. The dispatches gleefully mocked the stumbling lawyers and implausible executives sent to defend the company. (This tweaking did not seem to bother the big boss: Bill Gates wrote a weeklong "Diary" for us that spring.)

E.R. and the Triple Hex

When a full moon and a lunar eclipse collide with Friday the 13th, do more accidents really happen?

BY ATUL GAWANDE

March 20, 1998

A COUPLE OF MONTHS AGO, when my fellow surgical residents and I went around a table divvying up nights on emergency room duty, one March date sat conspicuously unpicked—Friday the 13th. C'mon, I thought. This is ridiculous. So when it was my turn again, I put my name down for March 13. Rest up, one resident told me. You'll be in for a long night. I laughed and dismissed the thought.

But looking at my calendar a while later, I noticed that the moon would be full that Friday night. When someone noted that a lunar eclipse would be occurring then, too, I felt my skepticism slip a little. Perhaps I would be in for a miserable night, after all. Trained scientists such as myself, however, do not succumb easily to superstition. Like any self-respecting rationalist, I asked the obvious question: Isn't there a study on this?

It turns out there is one reputable study that has tried to assess whether or not luck actually does go bad on Friday the 13th. (I'm not sure which is more surprising: that someone actually spent time researching this or that I could find only one such study. This is, after all, a world that has studied even how chewing gum distributes saliva around the mouth.) The 1993 study, published in the *British Medical Journal*, compared hospital admissions for traffic accidents on a Friday the 13th with those on a Friday the 6th in a community outside London. Despite a lower highway traffic volume on the 13th than on the 6th, admissions for traffic accident victims increased 52 percent on the 13th. "Friday the 13th is unlucky for some," the authors concluded. "Staying at home is recommended." How you escape the bad luck at home they didn't explain.

You really can't make much of one study of one Friday the 13th in one town. Lots of other factors could have caused that surge of crashes. Still, Friday the 13th phobia is widespread. Donald Dossey, a North Carolina behavioral scientist, has coined a term for it: *paraskevidekatriaphobia*, which he derived from the Greek for fear of Friday the 13th. He estimates that between 17 million and 21 million Americans suffer mild to severe anxiety or change their activities—performing rituals before leaving the house, calling in sick to work, or postponing flights or major purchases—and that businesses lose $750 million in revenues because of these fears.

Superstitions about the moon may be taken even more seriously. For centuries, and in disparate civilizations around the world, people have suspected that the cycles of the moon have a powerful influence over us. A 1995 poll found that 43 percent of people still believed the moon alters individual behavior. And mental health professionals believed it more often than anybody else. The centuries-old word "lunatic" derives from the connection thought to exist between the full moon and madness.

The idea of lunar human cycles seems more plausible than a Friday the 13th effect. Scientists once dismissed daily biological cycles as preposterous, but they now widely accept that body temperature, alertness, memory, and mood all fluctuate according to a predictable "circadian" rhythm. Evidence also shows seasonal effects on mood and behavior.

I found some 100 studies testing for "circalunidian" cycles. My favorite is a five-year study of self-poisoning at a hospital in New South Wales, Australia, published in the *Medical Journal of Australia*. From 1988 to 1993, the hospital admitted 2,215 patients for overdosing on drugs or poisoning themselves with toxic substances. The researchers checked to see whether peaks in such events occurred not just according to the phase of the moon but also according to one's zodiac sign or numerological readings (as "calculated according to the formulas contained in Zolar's *Encyclopedia of Ancient and Forbidden Knowledge*"). To no one's surprise, self-poisoning rates were not affected by whether a patient was born a Virgo or a Libra. Nor did Zolar's "Name Number," "Month Number," or "Birth Path Number" for a person make any difference. However, women (but not men) were about 25 percent less likely to overdose around the time of a full moon than around a new moon.

That self-poisonings decrease at the full moon actually correlates with the results of other studies. If any link between psychology and the full moon exists, it seems to be protective. The authors of a 1996 study of 10 years of suicides in Dordogne, France, concluded, in charmingly ungrammatical English, that "the French dies less in Full Moon, and more in New Moon period." Studies in Cuyahoga County, Ohio, and Dade County, Fla., also found a drop in suicides at the full moon. These studies don't quite clinch the full moon's happy effect, however. More than 10 other studies have been done, and they have not confirmed a lunar cycle for suicide.

As for other forms of craziness, the moon seems to have no effect. Researchers have reviewed logs for calls to police stations, consultations to psychiatrists, homicides, emergency room visits, and other measures of our daily burden of madness. They found no consistent relationship, one way or another, with the moon.

Somehow, however, the moon does have an effect on human beings—at least on women. Menstruation typically occurs on the

28-day lunar cycle. And even the phase of the moon matters. In a study of 826 women, 28 percent began menstruating during the four days around the new moon, whereas no more than 13 percent did so during any other four-day period. This puts the peak of ovulation at the full moon. (Could this provide an evolutionary explanation for the romantic associations we have with the moon? I'll leave that to Robert Wright, Slate's resident Darwinian, to sort out.) How this happens is baffling. The lone hypothesis I've found proposes that the moon generates tidal forces on the 50 percent to 60 percent of our bodies that is water. But that only raises more questions—such as how tides are supposed to make women menstruate.

The evidence satisfied me that neither the full moon nor the inauspicious date threatened my night. Nonetheless, I came on duty that evening to find the resident from whom I was taking over swamped with patients. He stayed late to help me catch up. Just after he left, a new trauma victim rolled in—a 28-year-old who had been knocked unconscious in a high-speed head-on collision. The police and paramedics said he had been stalking his girlfriend with gun in hand. He fled in his car when cops arrived and led them on a chase that ended in the massive crash. The rest of the night was no better. I was, as we say, "slammed." It's full-moon Friday the 13th, a nurse explained. I was about to say that studies showed no connection. But my pager went off before I could start. I had a new patient coming in.

The Breakfast Table

BY TIMOTHY NOAH AND MARJORIE WILLIAMS

July 1998

From: Marjorie Williams
Subject: Red Skelton Just Died Again?
Dear Tim,

Let's not hurt each other. If you know what I mean. Nice little marriage you got there; shame if something happened to it.

That out of the way, it's exciting to be launching into this breakfast-table chat with you. Talk around our real breakfast table, as any parents of two small children could attest, concerns the merits of Lucky Charms versus Frosted Flakes, and whether Tiny Alice can be taught not to wipe her hands on my bathrobe, and where Willie's [expletive] sandals are, lest the Efficient Mother we share carpool with turns up to find him once again unshod. At these times, your game tries at discussing the news of the day tend to come at me as simply another layer of the morning din. I've had entire months in which it seems like you're trying to tell me, every morning, that Red Skelton just died.

Timothy Noah and Marjorie Williams were married until Marjorie's death in 2005.

From: Timothy Noah
Subject: Prosperity
Dear Marjorie,

I'm back to my morning routine—up at 6, read the papers while wife and children sleep, then assume my place at the Actual Breakfast Table (which this morning meant scurrying around the kitchen to feed our children a nutritious breakfast of lemonade and Lucky Charms—I really must get to the supermarket today).

Am I callous for not caring about the Secret Service's worry that Ken Starr is endangering the safety of presidents by making their Secret Service agents testify about them? It seems to me there's a social contract that goes along with Secret Service protection: We, the people of the United States, will go to extraordinary lengths to protect you, the president, from would-be assassins. You, the President of the United States, will in turn refrain from doing anything in the Secret Service's presence that might lead to your indictment or impeachment. If you must engage in such shenanigans, understand that the Secret Service agent will drop a dime on you. If that's unacceptable to you, then confine your misbehavior to moments when the Secret Service isn't within listening or viewing distance—but also know at such moments that your physical protection will be compromised.

Administering Tough Love to the Oval Office,
Tim

P.S. Forgot to mention the most important thing in today's paper: the showtimes for *Out of Sight*, which you promised you'd sneak off with me to see this afternoon. (I don't intend to be a bum for long, but while I am a bum I want to get the most out of it.) It's at 1:20 at the Wisconsin Ave. Cineplex Odious. That leaves us plenty of time to get back and file more Breakfast Table dispatches about the size and appeal of Jennifer Lopez's butt. (I didn't start this; *Salon* ran a piece a few days ago arguing that Lopez is giving mainstream white-bread America a new and welcome appreciation for the virtues of Big Ethnic Butts.)

From: Marjorie Williams
Subject: Hmmph
Dear Tim,

If *Salon* jumped off the Empire State Building, would you do it too? Your invitation to discuss Jennifer Lopez's endowments was ugly and, come to think of it, unappetizing. I'm female, remember? This is what you have *Slate* No. 2 editor Jack Shafer for. I'll spare you the lecture on feminism (especially because you are at the Safeway, even as we speak, and this morning you actually Hoovered up the crumbs under the kitchen table—a blight that I had formerly thought was completely invisible to the naked male eye), but really. . . .

On the Secret Service: As I wrote last week, I'm with you all the way here. With one exception: If it's really true that Ken Starr is trying to get the chief of Clinton's security detail to relate the President's conversation with his own lawyer in the limo right after Clinton's deposition in the Paula Jones case (which is where he may have committed the perjury Starr is pursuing), that's a clear and pretty sleazy effort to circumvent the attorney-client privilege. If this is so, Starr will have done it again: taken an observer (me) whose every sinew is inclined to believe the worst of Clinton's behavior vis-à-vis Lewinsky, and offended even me with his overreaching. I used to think that Clinton had created the enemies he deserves; lately, I've come around to thinking he has lucked into the enemies he needs.

Bullishly,
Marjorie

From: Timothy Noah
Subject: But, But, But
Marjorie,

"[U]gly and . . . unappetizing"? Oh, please. Let's break this argument down into its three constituent parts:

"Butt" is an inappropriate word.

I disagree. It is short for "buttocks," which I believe is the term most favored by our Official Culture. It has a friendly, Midwestern ring that I like. It is evocative (it ends abruptly, just like most Actual Butts). It is certainly better than the arch "derrière" or "caboose" or the indisputably crass "can" or "tail." It is less bland than "behind" or "bottom." (And here I'd like to point out that the British, who favor "bottom," have a much greater tendency to leer and otherwise obsess about butts than Americans do.)

Our lefty friend Marie, who works for a union and volunteers for a battered women's shelter, refers to the posterior by using the term "butt." I have heard her do so many times. So does her similarly left-leaning and sensitive cohabitant, Paul, and their daughter, Zoe.

Our children use the word "butt" from time to time, and I really don't mind (provided the context isn't puerile bathroom talk, or calling someone a "butthead," which isn't nice, or calling someone a "butthole," which is beyond the pale for child or adult).

So "butt" is fine with me.

"Butt" is an OK word, but it isn't appropriate for a man to discuss a woman's butt in public.

I'd agree with you if Jennifer Lopez were a data processor, or a nuclear physicist, or a bagger at the local Safeway, or anybody I work with. But her occupation is Sexpot Actress. People are *supposed* to look at her butt. *Vanity Fair*, the magazine you work for, ran a photograph of Jennifer Lopez recently that inspired the *Salon* essay in the first place. It was a rear, topless shot, and its caption might as well have been, "Check out Jennifer Lopez's ample butt."

I wouldn't talk about her butt at an elegant social gathering, or around the water cooler at work, but surely it's OK to discuss within the (sort-of) intimacy of our Breakfast Table. . . .

"Butt" is an OK word, and it's OK to discuss Jennifer Lopez's highly public butt, but it's inappropriate to discuss big butts as an ethnic trait.

I agree, we're drifting into the danger zone when we talk about physical attributes of various ethnic groups. But I liked the boldness and humor of the *Salon* writer, a self-described "black woman with a similar (all right, bigger) endowment," who sees Lopez's ascent to Sex Goddess as a source of pride. Indeed, her main complaint in the piece is that Lopez's butt isn't big enough or shown off enough in *Out of Sight*. Yes, I hear you saying, but that doesn't mean you, Tim Noah, enjoy similar license to carry on about big butts. But wait a minute. I am of Jewish descent. Jews aren't exactly known for having small butts.

There. I think I just whipped your butt.

You're right about the caveat on the Secret Service and Starr: The prosecutor shouldn't be allowed to use the Secret Service to violate attorney-client confidentiality. I'm trying to figure out whether it's OK for the newspapers to pass up Tim Russert's apparently irresponsible scoop but also OK for you to pass it along in our Breakfast Table.

Fondly,
Tim

From: Marjorie Williams
Subject: Tim, Tim, Tim
Honey, it's really OK with me if you don't get a job for a while. But you need to get a life.

Worriedly,
Marjorie

From: Marjorie Williams
Subject: The Last Word
Dear Tim,

Now that we've been to the movies and back, I wanted to amplify slightly on my last response. You missed the totally obvious point, which was the difference between you and Erin J. Aubrey, who wrote the *Salon* piece cleverly pegged to Jennifer Lopez's buttocks:

Aubrey: used this provocative image for a nobler reason, which was to write a very interesting piece about how confining the roles awarded to black and Hispanic actresses remain.

Tim: just wanted to leer.

But I will credit your sincerity enough to meditate further on one item in your sick self-defense. I'm really interested in your last point about whether it's acceptable for nonmembers of some social group to make observations—even simple ones—that members of that group would readily make about themselves. (The common example, of course, being the way some blacks feel comfortable with certain uses of the N-word but reasonably report being enraged to hear whites saying it.) This question, I think, marks one of the most fluid areas in our otherwise ice-locked conversation about race.

It makes me think of my father, who died two months ago. I happened to ride along in the ambulance when he left the hospital to go home to die. Here we are, bumping along the Manhattan potholes in the back with a young, black, female emergency medical technician. My father is bundled and strapped to a gurney like Hannibal Lecter. Although he has only a few days to live (two, as it turns out), the EMT's stupid rules say that she has to take a medical history during the ride and check to make sure he's really OK to be released; if she doesn't think he's good to go, she'll route him right back to NYU Hospital. Imagine his anxiety: If he doesn't pass this test, he will lose his chance to die at home. So finally she gets to the point on her checklist where she asks questions to test his alertness: What day is it, who's the president, and so on. "What," she asks him, "was the first thing you noticed about me?"

I see panic on his face—the face of a lifelong liberal who thinks the best things went out of politics with Adlai Stevenson. The obvious answer is her very dark skin. Yet he rouses himself and says in his most sort of humbly gallant manner, "That you're so . . . trim."

Later we all sat around his bed, drinking strawberry daiquiris (him too) and laughing until we wept at this crystallization of his himness. But to this day I'm awed by the scene, its evidence that the social taboos around acknowledging racial difference—the suspicion that terrible bruises can bloom from the simplest truth—could be so important that we would carry them, literally, to the end.

I was raised in that liberal tradition of respecting racial difference, the kind of respect that says it's too electric even to mention. It's obviously better to try to muddle into the mess, giving offense here but making a connection there; sure is scary, though. Which may be a very long way of saying I admire you a little bit for wading into the whole subject of ethnic butts. But don't tell anyone I said so.

Love,
Marjorie

From: Timothy Noah
Subject: My Last Word
Dear Marjorie,

Erin Aubrey was making more than just the Socially Acceptable point that black and Hispanic actresses don't get enough good roles in Hollywood (a sentiment I heartily, if somewhat perfunctorily, endorse). That's why her *Salon* piece was so good. But I'll leave it at that. What a sweet story about your father.

It was really fun going to the movies with you. *Out of Sight* is a really good movie. And Jennifer Lopez has a very large and attractive butt.

Love,
Tim

When Gross Stuff Happens to Good People

The bottom-of-the-barrel genius of the Farrelly brothers.

BY DAVID EDELSTEIN

July 19, 1998

A FEW YEARS AGO, during an especially grim Sundance Film Festival (the top prize went to *The Brothers McMullen*), a parade of black-turtlenecked independent filmmakers bemoaned the crass state of mainstream American cinema. "How much room is there for us," whined one indie auteur, "when the year's most popular movie is *Dumb & Dumber*?" I thought, Pal, you should make a movie as smart as *Dumb & Dumber*.

OK, some of its scenes looked as if they'd been lit with a desk lamp, and the bit where the hero ignites his fart like a blowtorch lacked a certain élan. But fashionable as it was to dismiss the picture as a puerile Jim Carrey vehicle, *Dumb & Dumber* was tirelessly inventive, riding in on a wave of gross-out sight gags: not mere fart jokes but expulsive diarrhea jokes, blind-child jokes, decapitated pet-bird jokes, kung-fu dismemberment jokes, plus wall-to-wall jokes on the theme of "How stupid can these morons actually be?" What held those jokes together—apart from Carrey's resourceful clowning and Jeff Daniels' sweetness—was an elusive combination of professional discipline and feces-hurling infantilism, reinforced by the conviction that the tastiest cuisine is whatever you can scrape off the bottom of the barrel. That, plus a kind of tenderness, a joy in all things scatological, rendered outrage spurious. Clever monkeys, these filmmakers.

They were brothers from Rhode Island named Peter and Bobby Farrelly, who seemed like a coarse variation on Joel and Ethan Coen: If the Coens took junky premises and turned them into film-school (even postdoctoral) exercises, the Farrellys remained pre-kindergarten, arrested at Eriksonian levels of anal and oral fixation. Their next film, *Kingpin* (1996), was a slobbish takeoff on *The Color of Money* in which dissolute ex-champ Woody Harrelson propels raw Amish prodigy Randy Quaid to the top of the bowling leagues. It was a commercial flop, but I roared at everything—even the zoophilic jokes—until its terrible tag line. Am I the only one who caught the quotation from the 1965 Don Knotts classic *The Ghost and Mr. Chicken*? The Farrellys' heroes are dweebish losers like Knotts with the post-John Waters burden of uncontrollable bowels and sexual fluids. To call them "pathetic" would be to romanticize them.

Losers competing against one another (and even bigger losers) for a dishy woman: That's the setup for their wrackingly funny new farce *There's Something About Mary*, maybe the ultimate nerd masochistic fantasy. For two hours, a procession of dweebs humiliate themselves and one another to attract the attention of the smart, friendly, coltish, blond goddess Cameron Diaz, who's like a tall drink of water—no, a tall milkshake—a tall ice cream sundae . . . wow, she's just . . . wow. Over here, Cameron! Read this dweeb's review!

Sorry. But what a distracting presence: a creamy beauty with the bearing of a Swede but larger, friendlier, more clownlike features and an irresistibly sunny disposition. Around this gossamer vision the Farrellys have built their grossest comedy yet. Rarely have I sat with an audience that literally *screamed* at a gag as if it were watching a grisly hack-'em-up. Come to think of it, the brothers have a hack-'em-up way with a joke, comedy and horror being joined for them like Siamese twins at the crotch. Every action generates the most hideous, degrading consequences; the universe is littered with castrating land mines.

As a pimpled, brace-faced high-school senior, diminutive hero Ben Stiller hopes to impress his unlikely date (Diaz) by charming her mentally challenged (read: retarded) brother—who responds with a pummeling that drives him into the bathroom to wash his bloody nose and urinate—whereupon he's sighted through the window by his date and her mom, who think he's masturbating—whereupon he pulls his zipper up *through* his testicles—whereupon the entire neighborhood descends to watch police and firefighters attempt to free his private parts—whereupon they discover he's a *big* bleeder . . . .

I won't spoil the subsequent slapstick set pieces, which are even more ghastly. The bulk of the film happens 16 years later, when Stiller, still dreaming of the girl (whom he never saw again), is urged by his vaguely satanic buddy, played by Chris Elliot, to hire a private detective to locate her. This turns out to be Matt Dillon with a greasy caterpillar of a mustache, a con artist who travels to Miami and himself falls for the still-unmarried Diaz—now an orthopedist who brings apples to old neighbors, greets everyone with a smile, and romps in her spare time with the physically and mentally challenged. It's no wonder her world abounds with stalkers, each cretin bent on fooling her into thinking he's whatever she wants in her Prince Charming.

Stiller, with his Mr. Potato Head ears and homuncular demeanor, regards the world with a dopey, loping innocence. His hellish trek to Florida and war of wits with Dillon—a gung-ho physical comedian—give the picture all the narrative it needs. But the real stars of *There's Something About Mary* are the humiliations themselves—the masturbation travesties, drug disasters, pustule eruptions, and dead-pet crises that dog each character like Fate. Even when you're able to guess the next calamity, it's still a shock in its ejaculatory intensity. The Farrellys never throw in the towel. Pretentious Sundance independents could learn a lot from such pistols.

Baby-Sitting the Economy

The baby-sitting co-op that went bust teaches us something that could save the world.

BY PAUL KRUGMAN

Aug. 14, 1998

TWENTY YEARS AGO I read a story that changed my life. I think about that story often; it helps me to stay calm in the face of crisis, to remain hopeful in times of depression, and to resist the pull of fatalism and pessimism. At this gloomy moment, when Asia's woes seem to threaten the world economy as a whole, the lessons of that inspirational tale are more important than ever.

The story is told in an article titled "Monetary Theory and the Great Capitol Hill Baby-Sitting Co-op Crisis." Joan and Richard Sweeney published it in the *Journal of Money, Credit, and Banking* in 1978. I've used their story in two of my books, *Peddling Prosper-*

ity and *The Accidental Theorist*, but it bears retelling, this time with an Asian twist.

The Sweeneys tell the story of—you guessed it—a baby-sitting co-op, one to which they belonged in the early 1970s. Such co-ops are quite common: A group of people (in this case about 150 young couples with congressional connections) agrees to baby-sit for one another, obviating the need for cash payments to adolescents. It's a mutually beneficial arrangement: A couple that already has children around may find that watching another couple's kids for an evening is not that much of an additional burden, certainly compared with the benefit of receiving the same service some other evening. But there must be a system for making sure each couple does its fair share.

The Capitol Hill co-op adopted one fairly natural solution. It issued scrip—pieces of paper equivalent to one hour of baby-sitting time. Baby sitters would receive the appropriate number of coupons directly from the baby sittees. This made the system self-enforcing: Over time, each couple would automatically do as much baby-sitting as it received in return. As long as the people were reliable—and these young professionals certainly were—what could go wrong?

Well, it turned out that there was a small technical problem. Think about the coupon holdings of a typical couple. During periods when it had few occasions to go out, a couple would probably try to build up a reserve—then run that reserve down when the occasions arose. There would be an averaging out of these demands. One couple would be going out when another was staying at home. But since many couples would be holding reserves of coupons at any given time, the co-op needed to have a fairly large amount of scrip in circulation.

Now what happened in the Sweeneys' co-op was that, for complicated reasons involving the collection and use of dues (paid in scrip), the number of coupons in circulation became quite low. As a result, most couples were anxious to add to their reserves by baby-sitting, reluctant to run them down by going out. But one couple's decision to go out was another's chance to baby-sit; so it became difficult to earn coupons. Knowing this, couples became even more reluctant to use their reserves except on special occasions, reducing baby-sitting opportunities still further.

In short, the co-op had fallen into a recession.

Since most of the co-op's members were lawyers, it was difficult to convince them the problem was monetary. They tried to legislate recovery—passing a rule requiring each couple to go out at least twice a month. But eventually the economists prevailed. More coupons were issued, couples became more willing to go out, opportunities to baby-sit multiplied, and everyone was happy. Eventually, of course, the co-op issued too *much* scrip, leading to different problems . . .

If you think this is a silly story, a waste of your time, shame on you. What the Capitol Hill Baby-Sitting Co-op experienced was a real recession. Its story tells you more about what economic slumps are and why they happen than you will get from reading 500 pages of William Greider and a year's worth of *Wall Street Journal* editorials. And if you are willing to really wrap your mind around the co-op's story, to play with it and draw out its implications, it will change the way you think about the world.

For example, suppose that the U.S. stock market was to crash, threatening to undermine consumer confidence. Would this inevitably mean a disastrous recession? Think of it this way: When consumer confidence declines, it is as if, for some reason, the typical member of the co-op had become less willing to go out, more anxious to accumulate coupons for a rainy day. This could indeed lead to a slump—but need not if the management were alert and responded by simply issuing more coupons. That is exactly what our head coupon issuer Alan Greenspan did in 1987— and what I believe he would do again. So as I said at the beginning, the story of the baby-sitting co-op helps me to remain calm in the face of crisis.

Or suppose Greenspan did not respond quickly enough and that the economy did indeed fall into a slump. Don't panic. Even if the head coupon issuer has fallen temporarily behind the curve, he can still ordinarily turn the situation around by issuing more coupons—that is, with a vigorous monetary expansion like the ones that ended the recessions of 1981–82 and 1990–91. So as I said, the story of the baby-sitting co-op helps me remain hopeful in times of depression.

Above all, the story of the co-op tells you that economic slumps are not punishments for our sins, pains that we are fated to suffer. The Capitol Hill co-op did not get into trouble because its members were bad, inefficient baby sitters; its troubles did not reveal the fundamental flaws of "Capitol Hill values" or "crony baby-sittingism." It had a technical problem—too many people chasing too little scrip—which could be, and was, solved with a little clear thinking. And so, as I said, the co-op's story helps me to resist the pull of fatalism and pessimism.

But if it's all so easy, how can a large part of the world be in the mess it's in? How, for example, can Japan be stuck in a seemingly intractable slump—one that it does not seem able to get out of simply by printing coupons? Well, if we extend the co-op's story a little bit, it is not hard to generate something that looks a lot like Japan's problems—and to see the outline of a solution.

First, we have to imagine a co-op with members that realized there was an unnecessary inconvenience in their system. There would be occasions when a couple found itself needing to go out several times in a row, which would cause it to run out of coupons—and therefore be unable to get its babies sat—even though it was entirely willing to do lots of compensatory baby-sitting at a later date. To resolve this problem, the co-op allowed members to *borrow* extra coupons from the management in times of need—repaying with the coupons received from subsequent baby-sitting. To prevent members from abusing this privilege, however, the management would probably need to impose some penalty—requiring borrowers to repay more coupons than they borrowed.

Under this new system, couples would hold smaller reserves of coupons than before, knowing they could borrow more if necessary. The co-op's officers would, however, have acquired a new tool of management. If members of the co-op reported it was easy to find baby sitters and hard to find opportunities to baby-sit, the terms under which members could borrow coupons could be made more favorable, encouraging more people to go out. If baby sitters were scarce, those terms could be worsened, encouraging people to go out less.

In other words, this more sophisticated co-op would have a central bank that could stimulate a depressed economy by reducing the interest rate and cool off an overheated one by raising it.

But what about Japan—where the economy slumps despite interest rates having fallen almost to zero? Has the baby-sitting metaphor finally found a situation it cannot handle?

Well, imagine there is a seasonality in the demand and supply for baby-sitting. During the winter, when it's cold and dark, couples don't want to go out much but are quite willing to stay home and look after other people's children—thereby accumulating points they can use on balmy summer evenings. If this seasonality isn't too pronounced, the co-op could still keep the supply and demand for baby-sitting in balance by charging low interest rates in the winter months, higher rates in the summer. But suppose that the seasonality is very strong indeed. Then in the winter, even at a zero interest rate, there will be more couples seeking opportunities to baby-sit than there are couples going out, which will mean that baby-sitting opportunities will be hard to find, which means that couples seeking to build up reserves for summer fun will be even less willing to use those points in the winter, meaning even fewer opportunities to baby-sit . . . and the co-op will slide into a recession even at a zero interest rate.

And this is the winter of Japan's discontent. Perhaps because of its aging population, perhaps also because of a general nervousness about the future, the Japanese public does not appear willing to spend enough to use the economy's capacity, even at a zero interest rate. Japan, say the economists, has fallen into the dread "liquidity trap." Well, what you have just read is an infantile explanation of what a liquidity trap is and how it can happen. And once you understand that this is what has gone wrong, the answer to Japan's problems is, of course, quite obvious.

So the story of the baby-sitting co-op is not a mere amusement. If people would only take it seriously—if they could only understand that when great economic issues are at stake, whimsical parables are not a waste of time but the key to enlightenment—it is a story that could save the world.

1999

OUR EXPERIMENT AS A PAID SITE ended abjectly on Valentine's Day, less than a year after it had begun. Wry political analysis, it turned out, was different from porn. A few would pay for it, but not enough to cover our costs. *Slate*'s new publisher, Scott Moore, brought us a new business plan: No subscriptions = more readers. More readers = more advertisers. More advertisers = more revenue.

One of our signal achievements of 1999 wasn't recognized at the time. *Slate* started running Mickey Kaus' musings and linkings under the rubric "Kausfiles." There was as yet no name for what Mickey was writing—a casual, first-person, frequently updated, obsessive, link-heavy journal. Only several years later was it recognized that Mickey had been writing what was probably the first political blog. Our favorite Canadian arrived, too: Dahlia Lithwick began covering the Supreme Court, and her hilarious, eagle-eyed dispatches soon became required reading for every lawyer in Washington—and many elsewhere around the country.

Regular contributor Herb Stein died in September. And in what would become a regular pattern, the *New York Times* started poaching *Slate* writers. Paul Krugman was the first to go, lured away with an op-ed column. The *Times* soon nabbed Virginia Heffernan, Judith Shulevitz, and Jodi Kantor as well.

The Cartoon Closet

Tinky Winky is gay. Who else?

BY JACOB WEISBERG

Feb. 21, 1999

THE REACTION TO the Rev. Jerry Falwell's outing of Tinky Winky, the purple Teletubby, was widespread scorn and hilarity. Comedians and column writers mercilessly ridiculed Falwell for his paranoia in seeing gays under the crib.

Three comments in defense of Falwell: First, he didn't write the article in question, which appeared unsigned in *National Liberty Journal*, a magazine he publishes. When asked about the charge, Falwell said he had never seen *Teletubbies* and didn't know whether Tinky Winky was homosexual or not. The notion of Falwell attacking a cartoon character is too appealing to liberal prejudices to be easily abandoned.

Second, if you've ever watched *Teletubbies*, you might well suspect some kind of subliminal messaging. The four tubbies have aerials coming out of their spacesuit hoods, which receive programming that's broadcast on TV screens in their tummies. As they prance out of their bunker and around the strange, apocalyptic landscape where they live, periscope speakers pop out of the ground and feed them orders. It's both cute and creepy.

Third, the folks at Liberty College apparently got their idea about Tinky Winky not from watching the program but from reading such publications as the *Washington Post* and *People*. On Jan. 1, the *Post* included "TINKY WINKY, THE GAY TELETUBBY" in its annual list of what's "in" for the New Year. No one got excited. The press, including the *Post*, then mocked Falwell as a reactionary hick obsessed with the sexuality of puppets. Seems like a bit of a trap.

Is Tinky Winky gay? He is not the first cartoon character to be outed. More often than not it is homosexuals who claim a character as one of their own—which also puts the Falwell fuss in perspective. At the level of the creators' stated intentions, the Teletubbies have no sexual orientation. The program tries to recreate the world of toddlers, which does not involve any level of sexual understanding. But TV programs are group products, and it's not impossible that references—Tinky Winky's handbag, his purple triangle antenna, and the tutu he sometimes wears—are bits of code included for the benefit of adults. If Tinky Winky has a bit more spring in his step than Dipsy, the other male tubby, it may be because the actor who originally inhabited his costume added that dimension. Gays in Britain love Tinky Winky, and some protested outside the BBC when the actor who played him was fired.

Sexual signals can be received without being consciously sent. The first cartoon characters to be accused of aberrant sexual practices were Batman and Robin. In a 1954 book titled *Seduction of the Innocent*, a psychologist named Fred Wertham attacked the sadistic violence and sexual deviance portrayed in comic books. Batman and Robin, he noted, were two men living together who liked to wear capes and tights. Back home at stately Wayne Manor, they lounged about in dressing gowns. Wertham was a student of Freud who discovered a message that Bob Kane, Batman's creator, probably never consciously intended. But that doesn't mean it wasn't there.

Wertham's book led to the adoption of a code of standards by the comic book industry, which included, among other things, an admonition that "sex perversion or any inference to same is strictly forbidden." After this history, the *Batman* TV series, which was made in the mid- to late 1960s, couldn't plead the same innocence. Post-Wertham, the producers were well aware of the gay take on Batman and Robin. Rather than resist it, they gave a camp tenor to the whole series. In the 1960s, even most adult viewers interpreted the program as broad parody. But once the idea of a gay subtext has been planted, Louie the Lilac (as played by Milton Berle) isn't just a villain who likes to wear purple.

In a curious way, gays, their friends, and their enemies have all collaborated in destroying the sexual innocence of cartoon characters by making an issue out of it. When trying to elude Elmer Fudd or Yosemite Sam, Bugs Bunny is liable to dress up as a woman, vamp around, or imitate Katharine Hepburn. Is this meant to indicate that he likes other boy bunnies? Many of these antics were borrowed from vaudeville comedy, where a man dressing up as a woman didn't necessarily imply homosexuality (although the same questions arise in retrospect). The Warner Bros. studio, where these cartoons were created in the 1940s and 1950s, was an aggressively heterosexual milieu. Chuck Jones and other illustrators were mocking stereotyped homosexual behavior, not winking at homosexuals in a friendly way. But while a man dressing up as a woman may not have "meant" anything in the 1940s, it does mean something in the late 1990s. What has sexualized these cartoon characters is the change in the culture, which in the last few decades has become not just aware of homosexuality but increasingly open about and tolerant of it.

Ernie and Bert are another good example of this process. When *Sesame Street* was created in the early 1970s, no one meant for them to be taken as lovers. But consider two men living together, sleeping in the same room, and taking great interest in each other's baths. Predictably, the "urban legend" that Ernie and Bert were gay began to spread. In 1994, a Southern preacher named Joseph Chambers tried to get them banned under an old North

Carolina anti-sodomy law. (He said they had "blatantly effeminate characteristics.") The Children's Television Workshop eventually had to deny the rumors, which have included an impending same-sex union. But the gay read on Ernie and Bert isn't wrong because the creators don't endorse it. The same goes for the *Peanuts* characters Peppermint Patty and her tomboy friend Marcie, who always refers to her as "Sir." When Charles M. Schulz created the strip, he never imagined that Patty and Marcie would be claimed as proto-lesbians.

In recent years, children's entertainment has contained an increasing number of apparently intentional or even obviously intentional gay references. In *The Lion King,* Simba leaves home and is more or less adopted by Timon and Pumbaa, a male meerkat and a male warthog who live together as a couple in the jungle. In the 1994 Disney film, the actor Nathan Lane supplied the voice of Timon in much the same style as his flamboyantly gay character in *The Birdcage.* When I saw the Broadway version of the musical, the audience roared at Timon's even more exaggerated gay mannerisms.

Or consider *Pee-wee's Playhouse.* Pee-wee Herman minces about and becomes obviously infatuated with other male characters who conform to gay archetypes. While parents may pick up this gay semaphore, kids aren't likely to. To them, Timon, Pumbaa, and Pee-wee are just goofy characters.

Elsewhere, the implicit has become explicit. On *The Simpsons,* Smithers, the bow-tie-wearing toady who trails around after Mr. Burns, has become increasingly gay. According to Larry Doyle, who writes for the show, Smithers was originally just a sycophant in love with the boss. But lately he has taken to cruising college campuses in his Miata, looking for "recruits." In last week's episode, Apu, the Indian convenience store owner, goes down to the docks to donate porno magazines to sailors. The sea captain calls out to thank him: "Thank you for the *Jugs* magazines. They'll keep my men from resorting to homosexuality . . . for about 10 minutes!" The sailors all laugh, and one calls out, "Look who's talking!"

It isn't absurd for anyone, including Falwell, to notice these hints, inferences, and references. But it is ridiculous to object to them. There's no scientific or psychological basis for believing that children are affected in their sexual development or eventual sexual orientation by exposure to homosexuality—on television or in real life. If the creators of cartoons are intentionally or unintentionally giving children the idea that gay people are part of the big, happy human family, that's a good thing, not a bad one. (If it weren't for gay people, there would be no *Lion King*—or much else on the all-American cultural front.) The conservative paranoia about recruiting, which leads them to think that gay school teachers and Boy Scout leaders present a hazard to the young, is pure prejudice.

Anyway, for the religious right, this battle is pointless because the war is already lost. Gay themes are everywhere. *Pee-wee's Playhouse* runs every day on the Fox Family Channel, the cable network Pat Robertson recently sold to Rupert Murdoch. It's just a couple of hours ahead of *The 700 Club*.

I, Antichrist?

I'm Jewish. I'm male. I'm alive. By Jerry Falwell's standards, that puts me on the shortlist of candidates.

BY JEFFREY GOLDBERG

Friday, Nov. 5, 1999

EARLY ONE SHINY AUTUMN MORNING, I got in my car and drove to Lynchburg, Va., in order to find out whether or not I am the Antichrist. You know: the Beast, the Worthless Shepherd, the Little Horn, the Abomination, the linchpin of the Diabolical Trinity. That Antichrist.

I had my suspicions. Nowhere on my body could I find the mark of the Beast—666—but I do have a freckle that's shaped like Bermuda. And though I have never been seized by a desire to lead the armies of Satan in a final, bloody confrontation with the forces of God on the plain of Armageddon, I do suffer from aggravated dyspepsia, as well as chronic malaise, conditions that I'm sure afflict the Antichrist.

The surest suspicion I had about my pivotal role in Christian eschatology grew from the fact that I am Jewish, male, and alive. These are the qualifications for the job of Antichrist as specified by Lynchburg's most famous preacher, Jerry Falwell, in a speech he made earlier this year.

I was actually going to see the Rev. Falwell on a different matter, the future of Jerusalem, but I thought I might just slip this question—the one about me maybe being the Antichrist—into the stream of the interview. Falwell, I guessed, wouldn't be happy to discuss his views on the identity of the Antichrist—he had apologized for the remark but took quite a load of grief for it anyway.

As it turned out, though, Falwell was eager to talk about the Antichrist. And, as it also turned out, he didn't really feel bad for saying what he said. In fact, he was more convinced than ever that the Antichrist is a Jew who walks among us.

Let me pause for a moment to give three concise reasons why I'm so curious about the identity of the Antichrist:

1. I think I speak for all the approximately 4.5 million adult male Jews in the world when I say that we get a little antsy when Christians start looking at us like we're the devil. This is on account of Christian behavior over the past 2,000 years, by which I mean blood libels and pogroms and inquisitions—those sorts of things.

2. I've always been possessed by the delusional notion that I am to play a major role in world history, so why not a role in the End of Days? And I don't mean the Schwarzenegger movie.

3. Now that we stand on the lip of the millennium, much of the evangelical Christian world is in the grip of Armageddon fever, and, according to the evangelical interpretation of the books of Daniel and Revelation, the Antichrist will make his appearance before Christ makes his, and his is looking kinda imminent. The Antichrist, in this reading, will be a world leader who strikes a peace deal with Israel,

only to betray the Jewish state and make war on it, until Jesus comes to the rescue. The thankful Jews, those who are still alive, will then become Christians and live happily ever after. These beliefs, held by tens of millions of Christians are, journalistically speaking, worthy of note.

The day before my visit with the Rev. Falwell, I had just finished reading a novelistic treatment of these events, *Assassins*, which is subtitled *Assignment: Jerusalem, Target: Antichrist*. *Assassins* is the sixth book in the "Left Behind" series, "left behind" referring to those unfortunate nonevangelical Christians who are not taken up to heaven in the Rapture—the opening act in God's end days plan—and are forced to contend with the Antichrist's evil reign on Earth. The "Left Behind" series, co-written by Tim LaHaye, the prominent right-wing screwball and husband of Beverly LaHaye, the even more prominent right-wing screwball, and Jerry B. Jenkins, who, his biography states, is the author of 130 books, which is a lot of books for one guy to write, is a phenomenon. Ten million copies of the series have sold already—hundreds in my local PriceClub alone. "Left Behind" is the Harry Potter of the Armageddon set.

The notable thing for me about the "Left Behind" series—besides the fact that few in the secular media have noticed that millions of Americans are busy reading books warning about the imminence of one-world government, mass death, and the return of the Messiah—is that all the Jewish characters are Christian. LaHaye and Jenkins are both active participants in the absurd and feverish campaign by some evangelical Christians to redefine Judaism in a way that allows for belief in Jesus.

Jews (and again, I feel comfortable speaking for all of us here) find this sort of Christian imperialism just a wee bit offensive. Just imagine if Jews began an official campaign calling Muhammad irrelevant to Islam—can you imagine the *fatwas* that would produce?

But evangelical leaders, who are, in my experience, uniformly kind and generous in their personal relations, can also be terribly obnoxious in their relations with Jews.

There is only one road to salvation for Jews, and that road runs through Jesus, LaHaye told me. To his credit, though, LaHaye doesn't believe that the Antichrist will be Jewish. He will be a European gentile, who will kill lots of Jews. "The Jews will be forced to accept the idolatry of the Antichrist or be beheaded," he said. This will take place during the seven-year Tribulation.

Jewish suffering, though, is divinely ordained. Even though the Antichrist will not be Jewish, Jews are still capable of great evil and have often been punished for their evil, LaHaye explained. "Some of the greatest evil in the history of the world was concocted in the Jewish mind," LaHaye told me, for reasons that aren't entirely clear—he knew what the name "Goldberg" generally signifies. "Sigmund Freud, Marx, these were Jewish minds that were infected with atheism."

I asked LaHaye to tell me more about the Jewish mind.

"The Jewish brain also has the capacity for great good," he explained. "God gave the Jews great intelligence. He didn't give them great size or physical power—you don't see too many Jews in the NFL—but he gave them great minds."

Of all the evangelical leaders I have interviewed, LaHaye is capable of some of the most anti-Semitic utterances, which is troublesome, because he is also the most popular author in the evangelical world.

The Rev. Falwell is smoother than LaHaye. He acknowledges "where the sensitivity comes from," though he shows no understanding of the role the myth of the Antichrist played in the history of anti-Semitism, and he refuses to back away from his opinion that somewhere in Great Neck or West L.A. or Shaker Heights is living Satan's agent.

"In my opinion," he told me, "the Antichrist will be a counterfeit of the true Christ, which means that he will be male and Jewish, since Jesus was male and Jewish."

I asked him if he understood that such statements strip Jews of their humanity, which is the first step anti-Semites take before they kill them. He responded, "All the Jewish people we do business with on a daily basis, not one has ever got upset over this." It is not Jews who picked this most recent fight, he said, it is supporters of President Clinton.

"Billy Graham made the same statement a dozen times last year, but there was no comment about that," Falwell said. "But Billy Graham was not calling for the resignation of the president." Falwell, you'll recall, is no fan of Clinton's; he has even peddled a video accusing the president of murder.

Falwell is right: Evangelical preachers are constantly accusing the Jews of harboring the Antichrist.

I asked Falwell if he knew the actual identity of the Antichrist. No, he said. "People might say, it's a certain person, it's Henry Kissinger, like that, but the Lord does not let us know that."

So there's a chance, then, that I'm the Antichrist?

Falwell chuckled a condescending chuckle. "It's almost amusing, that question. Of course not. I know that you're not."

Why?

"The Antichrist will be a world leader, he'll have supernatural powers," he said.

He got me there—I have no supernatural powers. I can't even drive a stick shift.

I pressed him further on the identity of the Antichrist, but Falwell wouldn't play. "We'll know the Antichrist when he arrives," he said.

Most evangelical leaders, in fact, refuse to publicly guess the name of the Antichrist—though, as Falwell suggests, Kissinger is a perennial favorite, at least among those evangelicals who believe the Antichrist will be Jewish. For most of their history, Christian leaders had been content to ascribe the characteristics of the Antichrist to the Jewish people as a whole. "Ever since the second century C.E., the very beginning of the Antichrist legend, Christians have associated Jews with everything unholy," Andrew Gow, who teaches Christian history at the University of Alberta, told me. In the minds of early Christian leaders, the church was the new Israel; God's covenant with the Jews was obsolete. Therefore, the Jews who remained on Earth were there to serve devilish purposes, Gow explained.

There are plenty of evangelical thinkers who differ with Falwell, who believe, like LaHaye, that the Antichrist will be a gentile who rises out of Europe. "The Antichrist is supposed to make a peace treaty with Israel," Ed Hindson, the author of *Is the Antichrist Alive and Well?*, explained. "Why would a Jew make a peace treaty with a Jewish state?"

Hindson suggested that Satan will make the Antichrist the leader of the European Union—the revived Roman Empire, eternal enemy of Israel—though Hindson disputed one popular idea advocated by Monte Judah, an Oklahoma-based prophecy-teacher, that Prince Charles is the Antichrist.

"There's no way Prince Charles is the Antichrist," Hindson said. "Satan can do better than that."

In his book, Hindson runs through a list of potential candidates. Bill Clinton is there, of course, as well as Saddam Hussein and Ronald Wilson Reagan (six letters in each of his three names. Get it?).

Of course, none of these men is gay.

"It says in the Bible that the Antichrist will have 'no regard for women,' and so many evangelicals interpret that to mean that he will be a homosexual," Hindson said, though he added that he's not entirely convinced.

This idea—the Antichrist as gay—strikes a chord with many evangelicals, just as the idea that the Antichrist is Jewish strikes a chord.

I gradually came to see how far-fetched it was to think that I might be the Antichrist. I'm not gay, I'm not famous, I wouldn't know a euro if I found one in my wallet.

Then it struck me: Barry Diller is the Antichrist.

There's no way to know for sure. But if you wake up one morning to read that Barry Diller is the head of the European Union (and that David Geffen is his deputy), well, remember where you read it first.

Stripper Bingo at the Supreme Court

BY DAHLIA LITHWICK

Nov. 11, 1999

THE ORDINANCE UNDER SCRUTINY in the U.S. Supreme Court this morning is a piece of anti-naked-dancing legislation coming out of Erie, Pa.: *City of Erie v. Pap's A.M.*, Kandyland. Because the ordinance in question is principally concerned with such things as "nipples, genitals, pubic hair, anal regions and buttocks," I immediately array these words along the top of my notebook. I then crayon the names of all nine Supreme Court justices down a y-axis and presto! Justice Bingo. Points to the first justice to say "nipple." And if Justice Thomas says "pubic hair," players must stand and shout "Bingo!"—risking lifetime expulsion from the highest court in the land, but worth it, I think.

You may play along at home.

The Supreme Court decided its G-string/pasties case in 1991 in *Barnes v. Glen Theatre*, when an Indiana public-indecency statute was challenged on First Amendment grounds by two strippers and two girlie bars. In *Barnes*, the court ruled in a fractious 5–4 plurality opinion that the Indiana statute requiring exotic dancers to wear G-strings and "pasties" (I gather pasties are some sort of nipple-beret) was constitutionally permissible. The problem with the *Barnes* opinion was that no five justices could agree on *why* the statute was constitutional, and drafted a Frankensteinian opinion comprising four separate opinions, with concurrences from the dissenters and dissents from the plurality.

After *Barnes*, depending on whose opinion you read, a city's effort to suppress nude dancing is either a content-neutral regulation of morality (Rehnquist, O'Connor, Kennedy); a content-neutral regulation justified by dangerous "secondary effects" of nude dancing—such as prostitution and sexual assault (Souter); or an impermissible content-based suppression of communicative speech (White, Marshall, Blackmun, Stevens). And Justice Scalia, who joined the majority in upholding the statute, wrote a separate concurrence urging that nude dancing does not constitute "speech" at all and thus warrants no constitutional protection.

You may not care a whit about any of this, but you might if you were a stripper. Or the 6th Circuit, who—in trying to winnow out a distinct majority holding in *Barnes*—likened it to "reading tea leaves." And so the Pennsylvania Supreme Court, when faced with an ordinance remarkably similar to the one in Indiana, but with no interest in persecuting innocent strippers, elected to upend the teacup and go home. The Pennsylvania court, calling the *Barnes* decision "hopelessly fragmented" in five different ways, thus ignored the majority/plurality altogether and applied the law as laid out by Justice White in the dissent and found the Erie naked law unconstitutional.

The U.S. Supreme Court took the *Pap's* case despite the fact that the nudie bar filed a motion to dismiss based on the fact that the 70-year-old owner had sold the business, rendering the case moot. Nothing doing, the Supremes voted to hear *Pap's* anyway—ostensibly to clear up the mess after *Barnes* into which lower courts are slippy-sliding all over the land.

This is why it's a bit surprising when Justice Scalia's first question to Gregory Karle, the city solicitor from Erie, is why isn't this case moot? Karle explains that although Kandyland has been sold, the corporation is still active and may just resume business any day now (also, maybe it's a little chilly for strippers in Erie in the wintertime). The court chews on this awhile and Justice Scalia actually does a pretty creditable impression of a 70-year-old nudie-bar operator crowing: "I'm getting out of the rust belt and moving to Florida!" When it begins to look as if none of the justices can recall why this case isn't void for mootness, Justice Ginsberg supplies the possible explanation that Kandyland's operator closed the place down after his crushing victory in the Pennsylvania Supreme Court precisely to stave off further scrutiny in the Supreme Court. Karle agrees enthusiastically.

First Amendment Law for Cocktail Parties holds that the state can regulate some speech and expressive conduct if it does so in a "content-neutral" fashion. That means that if Kenosha wants to prohibit women from dancing naked, it should draft legislation prohibiting women from also being naked—at least in public. After *Barnes*, cities can't suppress erotic dancing just because they don't like the erotic message of the dancers. But they can prohibit all public nudity—from Aurora Borealis in the Kage at Kandyland, to me on the Mall in Washington, D.C. (Or, as Dr. Seuss would say it: "Hooters are hooters no matter how small . . . ")

The problem with the Erie ordinance is that it claims to be a content-neutral prohibition on all public nudity but expressly says in its preamble that it was enacted "for the purpose of limiting a recent increase in live nude entertainment." Note to ordinance drafters: It's generally a bad idea to draft your content-neutral legislation in such a way as to persecute only strippers.

The other problem, picked up by Justice Souter at oral argument today, is that the Erie naked law was not applied to prosecute the naked performers in a performance of *Equus*. Oh, and Karle indicated at the trial court that it would not be used to prosecute performers in productions such as *Hair, Oh! Calcutta!*, or *Equus*. When questioned on this point by Justice Souter, Karle explains enthusiastically that he was not telling the truth about that at the trial court.

Justice Scalia, who is now doing a better job than Karle of answering questions put to Karle, offers a possible reason to regulate strippers but not *Hair*. Karle looks relieved. Scalia also does a nice job of convincing the court—when Karle cannot—that just because the trigger for the ordinance was the targeting of nude dancing only, the law itself is neutral on its face. Karle looks relieved.

John Weston, representing the nudie bar, does a breathtaking job of answering the questions Karle couldn't answer, without Scalia's intercession. Nevertheless, Weston has a tough time explaining why the case isn't moot, since he is the one who urged the court to dismiss it on those grounds in the first place. The gist of his answer—"Because you say it isn't moot"—is masterful.

This brings us to Scalia's point from *Barnes*—not addressed today—about whether naked dancing is "expressive conduct" worthy of First Amendment protection. Not that I plan to make it a practice to agree with Scalia on stuff, but I read his dissent in *Barnes* with grudging admiration. My own feeling is that writhing around topless on the lap of a sweaty guy in an acrylic sweater is no more expressive of an "erotic message" than a prostitute's hour with her John is expressive of a "romantic" one. If the strippers' lobby has some eloquent defense on this issue, however, I am keeping an open mind.

The question the Supreme Court was meant to reach in *Pap's* was: What do lower courts do with an impenetrable plurality opinion that cannot be applied consistently? The court cannot possibly want to encourage Pennsylvania's insolent shunting aside of its holding. But based on oral argument today, I don't think the court plans to rewrite *Barnes*. Too bad, that. Hockey games go into overtime when tied, and hung juries are chased back into the jury room to try again to come up with a majority. Ties suck. The Supreme Court should definitely clear this one up, if for no other reason than to allow the owner of Kandyland to retire to Florida in peace.

2000

THE YEAR BEGAN with a pointless, mean-spirited, and highly enjoyable spat with *Salon*, which had made a public stock offering and dramatically expanded its staff. *Slate*'s rather different response to the Internet bubble involved hunkering down and controlling costs. The competition culminated with Michael Kinsley and *Salon* editor David Talbot slinging insults at each other. Talbot charged that Kinsley was "not the sexiest guy in the world." Kinsley responded by gleefully dissecting *Salon*'s dismal balance sheet.

Slate's traffic surged around our 2000 election coverage. We also made news by flouting two silly election-year conventions. During presidential primaries, we posted leaked exit-poll results that other publications were withholding until they were prepared to declare a winner. And just before Election Day, more than 40 *Slate* staffers disclosed whom they were voting for and why. (Gore trounced Bush at *Slate*, for all the good it did him.) The eventual winner gave *Slate* a great present. Jacob Weisberg began tracking George W. Bush's malapropisms and publishing them as "Bushisms," which also became a series of popular books.

Edith Wharton for President

Even in 2000, blue blood still helps.

BY MICHAEL KINSLEY

Feb. 4, 2000

IN THEORY, ANYONE can grow up to be president. In practice, the next president is going to be a graduate of Harvard, Yale, Princeton, or the Naval Academy. Chances are he will also be a graduate of either St. Albans School or Phillips Academy Andover. He will be either the son of a senator, the son of a president and grandson of a senator, the son and grandson of an admiral, or—the humblest background and longest shot in the group—the son of a Midwestern banker.

Given the small slice of the population these privileged backgrounds represent, we have here a spectacular breakdown in the law of averages. Either that or an interesting perspective on American society. To be sure, you don't have to be an aristo to become president. For one thing, George W. Bush is the only full blue blood in the lot. For another, poor white trash defeated Andover-and-Yale Sr. eight years ago. But even in supposedly class-bound Britain it would be considered shocking if the two politicians battling for the top job both had attended hoity private schools.

For decades now we've been hearing about the decline or death of the Protestant Establishment (or the Episcopacy or the WASP Ascendancy or just the Upper Class). In fact, in America we're not supposed to have had an inherited class system. Even left-wing critiques of power in American society tend to emphasize the role of money, not bloodlines.

What is supposed to have replaced the Protestant Establishment is something called meritocracy. Enthusiasts celebrate meritocracy as the perfect human-resources policy for democracy and capitalism: a system in which everyone has equal opportunity to thrive based on his or her own talents and efforts. Skeptics, such as Nicholas Lemann in his current book *The Big Test*, see an aristocracy of bloodlines being replaced by an aristocracy of test scores. Even meritocracy is already dead, according to many social critics, mainly conservative. They mourn that meritocracy was killed by affirmative action and political correctness, and succeeded by a social order based on government fiat.

Yet it seems that bloodlines remain remarkably powerful, even in a political culture where denunciation of "elites" is as routine as "God bless America." And it's not just in politics. Even at the cutting edge of the economy, the place where everything is new, where success can strike anyone and failure can too, where capitalism sorts and sifts with blind efficiency, where what you do matters and where you're from doesn't, and blah blah blah—in cyberspace, that is—the law of averages seems to have broken down.

In the mid-1970s I was a "tutor" (precious term for resident adviser) in a "house" (dormitory) at Harvard. Scott McNealy was there. Now, as founder and CEO of Sun Microsystems, he is one of the biggest cyberbigshots. George Bell was there too, and he's now also a cyberbigshot, CEO of Excite@home, the Web portal and cable access company. The other day I was trying to remember the name of that woman who got hired as CEO of eBay, the auction site, and almost immediately became an IPO billionaire. Was it something like "Meg Whitman"? No, that was Ann Whitman's sister who dated that premed guy from Kirkland House and went to Harvard Business School, then moved to San Francisco, and oh my gosh! Steve Ballmer, now CEO of Microsoft (and therefore my boss), was not in K-House but had friends there and was around a lot. Bill Gates? Maybe he was around too. Who noticed?

All this future royalty of cyberspace in one dorm at one university. Coincidence? Or is there some other explanation? Like almost all dorms at all universities back then—and unlike almost all dorms at all universities now—Kirkland House was definitely not a fertile culture of entrepreneurialism, let alone of computer studies. So that's not the explanation. A Harvard education is good, but not that good. And to get into Harvard you have to be reasonably bright, but you don't have to be a genius. So those possible explanations don't wash either. Among the Harvard students, these folks did not stand out as especially brilliant or promising. You would have liked them, found them intelligent, and predicted happiness and success. But you would not have predicted that they would be among the very top leaders of a new economy that is transforming America.

If these individuals have anything in common, beyond Kirkland House, it's that they're from a group that was already a small minority even at Harvard a generation ago: prep-school WASPs. Whitman and Bell are classic East Coast American blue bloods out of Henry James or Edith Wharton: full members of the club. The others only qualify for various levels of associate membership. McNealy and Ballmer both attended private schools in Detroit, as did Gates in Seattle. McNealy's father was an auto company CEO, Gates's a prominent lawyer.

As in politics, you don't need to be a blue blood to make it in cyberspace. Silicon World probably is as wide open as any place in history to talent and energy from any social background, ethnic heritage, citizenship, table manners, or sanitary habits. This isn't investment banking. That's what makes it so interesting that bloodlines and elite institutions still seem to count.

Money can't explain it. The WASP establishment no longer dominates this country financially. None of the cyberpioneers comes from a huge fortune. All four of the leading presidential candidates are rich, but none is impressively rich by current standards. Far richer men have tried using their own fortunes to run for president, so far without success.

Of course, the notion of Ivy League universities as bastions of bloodlines is half a century out of date. Harvard, Yale, and Princeton—and the Naval Academy—all claim to be loyal servants of meritocracy now. And that's pretty much true. However, as it happens, each of the four top presidential candidates had—as a senator's son, an alumni son, an admiral's son, or a star athlete—a substantial exemption from the meritocratic rigors of the admission process. So meritocracy can't explain it either.

No, it's not money, and it's not merit in any conventional or at least observable sense. I think it must be genuine moral superiority. What other explanation could there be?

How the Grinch Stole Election Day

BY FRANK CAMMUSO AND HART SEELY

Nov. 21, 2000

(With respects to Theodor S. Geisel.)

Every Chad
Down in Chad-ville
Liked voting a lot . . .
But the Grinch,
Who lived just north of Chad-ville
Did NOT!

The Grinch hated voting! He thought it a bore.
Now, please don't ask why. Could be Bush, could be Gore.
It could be his heart bled with liberal mush.
It could be, perhaps, that he listened to Rush.
But I think the real reason his trust was so shattered
Was the great Grinchy view that his vote never mattered.

BUT
Whatever the reason,
Lack of trust, lack of goals,

The Grinch dreaded that day when Chads went to the polls.
He just hated those speeches and negative ads,
And when push came to shove, he just hated the Chads.
He just hated their theme parks, their football-team rooters,
He just hated their gun laws, their barmaids at Hooters.
He just hated their weather, even hated their hate.
And he hated that they were a battleground state.

"So they're making their choices," he snarled with a sneer.
"This 'Decision Two Thousand' is practically here!
"They'll struggle to choose 'tween a crumb and a bum,
" 'Cause a voter's a voter, no matter how dumb."
Then he growled, his Grinch fingers nervously drumming,
"I MUST find a way to keep outcomes from coming!"

For tomorrow, he knew . . .
All the flag-waving souls,
Would again waste their efforts on Clintons or Doles.
And by then, oh, the polls! Oh, the polls! Polls! Polls! Polls!
That's the one thing he hated! The POLLS! POLLS! POLLS!
POLLS!

So the Chads, rich and poor, and by bus, car, or boat,
They would vote! And they'd vote!
And they'd VOTE! VOTE! VOTE! VOTE!
They would vote to ban smoking or clearing your throat.
They would even vote laws in for curbing your goat.

And THEN . . .
They'd sing that anthem. It always came later.
Be they Bush-ites or Gore-ites or ites of Ralph Nader.
They'd stand close together, and though still full of fight,
They'd stand and they'd sing, by that dawn's early light.

And the more the Grinch thought of Election Day's ring,
The more the Grinch thought, "I must stop this whole thing!
"Why, for two hundred years I've put up with it now!
"I MUST stop these outcomes from coming!
". . . But HOW?"

Then he got an idea!
Yes, a legal idea!
THE GRINCH
GOT AN AWFUL BUT LEGAL IDEA!

"I know just what to do!" The Grinch laughed with a jig.
And he wove from his goat a Sam Donaldson wig.
And into the mirror he spoke with grand rancor,
"With this helmet of hair, they'll all think I'm an anchor!"

"All I need are some ballots . . . "
The Grinch looked around.
But since ballots were private, there were none to be found.
So he made his own ballot, printing letters quite little,
And he scattered the names, running holes down the middle,
And he stuck it together with Chad-berry spittle.
And he said, "They'll need Einstein to figure this riddle!"

THEN
He loaded his boxes, and without looking nervous
Put a sign on his van that said "Voter News Service."
THEN
The Grinch pulled away in his van with a screech
Toward the pads of the Chads in a place called "Palm Beach."

When he came to the first polling place in the square,
All the lines were quite long. Thoughtful talk filled the air,

As the Chads chatted merits of managed health care.
"Vote early and often," the Grinch said with a grin.
And he marched to the front of the line and stepped in.

There he left all his ballots, the strange ones with punches,
And instructions that said, "Please punch punches in bunches."
As he slunk out the door toward the nearest Grand Hyatt,
He could hear what you'd think was an Elián riot.
The Cohens—sisters Esther, Mitzi, and Shannon,
Just realized that their votes had all gone to Buchanan!

At a place in Dade County near a middle-school yard,
The Grinch donned a shirt that said, "Polling Place Guard."
And he eyeballed each Chad and said, "Where is your card?
"Voter card? Motor card? Credit card? Diner's?
"Face card? Race card? Baseball card? Shriners?"
And he turned them away. Then the Grinch, like a fox,
Stuffed all of his ballots and locked the lockbox!

Then old Grinch returned home to go "LIVE" on TV.
He had waited quite late: (It was now eight-oh-three.)
So the Grinch Network News first projected a score:
"Now with one percent in, we pick Chad-ville for GORE."
Every Gore-ite in Chad-ville said, "GIVE US SOME MORE!"

So he pulled more projections straight out of his stack.
Then, "Oh, dear!" said the Grinch, "I must take it all back!"
So the Grinch Network News, in grand fairness to all
Now reported that Chad-ville was "TOO CLOSE TO CALL."

"Don't be mad, all you Chads, for this isn't a scandal,
"It was just," the Grinch said, "we forgot the Panhandle.
"The science of sampling can leave one out-simpled."

So the Chads were left hanging and pregnant and dimpled.
And the stress of it all put George Bush among the pimpled!
Then the Grinch raised a finger for the night's final push.

"Election Day's done, and the winner is BUSH."
After all, George was leading at least by a dozen.
(And whenever it's close, always go with your cousin.)
"Play the music, the songs, pop the corks, sing the praises,
" 'Cause with Bush as the winner, you're all getting raises!"
And then the Grinch yawned, "This election stuff's hokey,
Good-bye 'till next year! And now back to you, Cokie."

And the Grinch, he went back to his old Grinchy pad.
But en route, he was nabbed by a little Chad lad
Who had stayed up all night (quite ignoring his dad).
He stared at the Grinch and said, "Sir, who's our leader?
"Is it Bush? Is it Gore? Or, my choice, Derek Jeter?"
And the Grinch simply smiled: This day couldn't be sweeter.

They were finding out now that no outcome was coming!
They were seeing it now, all their dumbness and dumbing.
"They're just waking up!" he said. "Here's what they'll do!
"Their mouths will hang open a minute or two
"And the Chads down in Chad-ville will all cry, 'WE'LL SUE!' "

As he stared down at Chad-ville, the Grinch popped his eyes,
But the scene that he saw brought a shocking surprise.
All the Chads down in Chad-ville, Chad lads and Chad dads,
They were counting the votes, they were counting the chads!
He hadn't stopped an outcome from coming.
IT CAME!
SOMEHOW OR ANOTHER, IT CAME JUST THE SAME!

As the Grinch with his head buried deep in the sand
Sat puzzling and puzzling, "They will count them by hand?"
Yes, it came with the lawsuits, it came with the lawyers,
It came with Tim Russert, it came with Bill Moyers.
When the ballots were plucked and the counting was done
The last margin of victory turned out to be . . . ONE!
And if the Grinch had just voted,
. . . HIS GUY WOULD HAVE WON!
And what happened then . . .
Well . . .
In Chad-ville they say
That the Grinch's small district
Grew three sizes that day.

'Cause the minute his mood had come out of its slump,
The Grinch said, "Hmm! I could be running this dump!"
So he formed a committee to do all the work
And he . . .
HE HIMSELF!
The Grinch ran for town clerk!

Diary

BY TOBY CECCHINI

Dec. 12, 2000

EARLY ON WHILE IT'S STILL QUIET a couple sweeps in whooping and laughing. I eye them peripherally as they loudly storm two seats at the far end of the bar. The guy isn't actually being raucous, I realize, he's just along for the ride, with bright-red dyed hair and the requisite tattoos and piercings.

It's the chick who's hellbent and wanting the whole bar to know about it. She's a lot of girl, stuffed precariously into a pair of red leather pants and some godawful black lycra top, with large oval cutouts both above and below her breasts, which are clearly otherwise untethered. She's also got a black cowboy hat on, always a discouraging sign on this side of the Mississippi. I know the type entirely too well; she's a party gal, a man-eating tigress, five miles of bad road. Or so she desperately wants you to think.

Immediately they are asking my name and trying to buy me a shot, with an aggressive friendliness that sets off my alarms like a hot doorknob. I coolly tell them my name is Ezra and inform them I don't drink while behind the bar, which is nearly true. Finding the fishing poor with me, they decide to chat up three amped-up French boys who have been trolling for girls for three-quarters of an hour. Shots are ordered all around, and almost instantaneously Miss Outrageous is shaking her ample groove thing in a painfully ostentatious bump-and-grind, poorly disguised as a private lap dance for her dolt of a boyfriend, whose head is bobbing up and down like one of those backseat Goofys in a car. The French kids are mesmerized as well. I occupy myself cutting limes at the other end of the bar until I hear roars and look up to find Miss O exaggeratedly miming a "Whoops-a-daisy!" as she tucks a naughtily AWOL udder back into place. "Ye gods!" I mutter, turning back to my limes.

When next I turn around, a few minutes later, the boyfriend is gone, perhaps to buy cigarettes, which I don't sell at the bar in an effort to, well, piss off smokers, mainly. Miss O has moved to a table with the French boys and is getting into some kind of contest over who has more piercings or maybe just who's a bigger moron. One of the Gauls is hiking up his shirt to show he has rings in both of his nipples, while another of them has his hand in Miss O's chemise and is rooting around in there for lucre. I'm trying to decide if it's time I step in here and enforce some decorum when I notice Boyfriend stopped dead in his tracks on the other side of the glass door leading to the entrance hallway, taking in the spectacle before us both with great wonder leaking from his face and a pack of smokes being strangled in his paw. It isn't until he pushes through the door and has been standing agape in the bar proper for 30 more seconds that Miss O finally rouses herself from the languor of her gropings and leaps up with the fervor reserved for those pinched in *flagrant délit*. In a hop she's all over Boyfriend, who stands stonily receiving her frantic cooings and caresses. He turns, opens the door, and shuffles out like a mummy, with her wrapped around him pleading. Her coat is still lying on the bar stool.

2001

SLATE PRODUCED SOME of its smartest, and most moving, work in the days and months after the Sept. 11 attacks. Navy veteran Scott Shuger left "Today's Papers" to cover the war on terror full-time, and handed off the feature to its current writer, Eric Umansky.

The year had its goofier side, too. As *The Sopranos* exploded as a cultural phenomenon, we enlisted psychiatrists and therapists to conduct a weekly dialogue about the show and Tony Soprano's therapy. Virginia Heffernan became our first regular TV critic. David Plotz's Seed project, an investigation into the mysterious Nobel Prize sperm bank, played with a new kind of Internet journalism—open-source, collaborative reporting. By using readers as his sources, Plotz dug out the buried history of this strange eugenic experiment in a series of stories that would lead to his 2005 book, *The Genius Factory.*

Extroverted Like Me

How a month and a half on Paxil taught me to love being shy.

BY SETH STEVENSON

Jan. 2, 2001

I DREAD PUBLIC SPEAKING. I get nervous on first dates. I hate to be called on in classes or meetings. In short, I'm shy. Not debilitatingly so. I'm guessing many of you are no different.

I've often wondered what it's like to be outgoing—a social butterfly, an extrovert. That's why TV ads for Paxil caught my eye. You've seen them: They promise ease in a pill. An end to social anxiety. Does my degree of shyness warrant medication? It was enough to make me want to see what life was like without being shy. I wondered what Paxil could do for me. Was a smoother, suaver Seth just 20 milligrams away?

Skimming my insurance company's list, I found a nearby general practitioner and made an appointment.

I. The Transformation

Day 1: After taking my blood pressure, the doc sits me down and asks a few questions. Am I shy? Yes, I'm uncomfortable speaking in groups. Have I suffered from depression? I've been blue but nothing serious. I tell him I've taken the self-test at Paxil.com (example: "I avoid having to give speeches—Not at all, A little bit, Somewhat, Very much, or Extremely") and it said, "Your score suggests that you may be experiencing the symptoms of social anxiety disorder." Of course, it wouldn't surprise me if it always said that.

He lists Paxil's side effects—headache, nausea, tremor, etc. "The most universal side effect," he says, "is delayed orgasm. For some people, that's a good thing." I nod. He explains a little about the drug itself (it's a Prozac-type antidepressant that later got approved for social anxiety treatment) but concludes, "No matter what anyone says, we basically have no clue how this works." And that's that. He writes out the prescription, for 20 milligrams a day. "If you'd like, we've got some counselors upstairs you can talk to, but it sounds like you just want the drug," he says, and hands over the slip. "It could take a couple of weeks to kick in. Be patient."

I walk around the corner to CVS. Boom: Fifteen minutes with a doctor, $15 at the pharmacy, and I've scored a month's supply of a powerful, mood-altering substance. Back home, I pop my first pill and wait.

Day 2: I'm lying on the couch, wrapped in a blanket, staring at the wall. My head is buzzing. My eyes won't focus. My stomach hurts and I'm shaking. I feel like a slo-mo version of Dr. Jekyll's violent transformation.

I do not feel outgoing.

Day 3: Ditto.

Day 4: No longer confined to the couch, but head still buzzing. Feeling totally detached from my surroundings. There's a constant lump in my throat (apparently a common side effect), and the shaking is getting worse. Eating cereal, I spill milk from the spoon before it reaches my mouth. When the doc said tremor, I thought it could be cool—give me a little Katharine Hepburn style. Turns out tremors are not so cool.

Day 8: Delayed orgasm, beyond a reasonable point, is not a good thing. I will say nothing further about this.

Day 11: Side effects have mostly faded out, save for the orgasm thing, which is in for the long haul. I'm not seeing any personality changes, though. At a party a few nights ago (among good friends, so not a worthy testing ground), I did notice one thing: After a few drinks, I began to discourse freely on my Paxil experience.

Generally, talking about myself, even with close friends, is my least favorite thing to do (writing about myself is clearly a different [2,000-word] story). So this was odd. But was it the Paxil? The alcohol? Or just that, for a change, I had something to talk about?

II. The Unexamined Life

Day 16: Still no visible change. However, I can't get a lick of work done. Unfinished articles are lying around, waiting for my attention. Motivation has dried up. Coincidence?

Day 25: A pattern is emerging. Since starting on Paxil, I've been drinking like a fish. For some reason, vitamin P combines incredibly well with alcohol. It's more fun to drink than it was before. I want to be drunk every night. I don't get hung-over now, and I remain pretty lucid even when sloshed.

Day 27: Paxil is messing with my livelihood. I'm still not getting any work done. Could it be Paxil's antidepressant effects? Perhaps I'm too content to be motivated. Do I require bile and unhappiness to write? I could clearly go the rest of my life on this stuff and never feel down again.

Another scary part: Before Paxil, while working on stories, turns of phrase would pop into my head, fully formed. Lying awake at night, or riding on the subway, *poof*—a neat arrangement of words would appear from nowhere. And would often show up in the article. It's part of what makes writing fun and surprising. On Paxil, it's gone. The words just aren't coming.

Also, the last few days I've considered cutting down on freelancing and getting a regular job—consulting or something. Previously, I couldn't imagine a job like this. Regular hours and no creative outlet sounded like a nightmare. All wrong for me. But now, stability, routine, and boredom sounds A-OK. Pleasant, even. An easy way to make a buck and just live my life.

Day 29: A literati book party. My first real test, and it's basically a failure. Upon meeting a gaggle of strangers, I still sprout flop sweat all over my torso, just like before. I still can't introduce myself to people I'd like to meet. I still don't know how to talk in big groups.

But then something magical happens. After deciding Paxil is worthless and downing three glasses of wine, I find I want to talk to people. No, it wasn't the alcohol. I drink at parties all the time—and go from standing alone in the corner to standing drunk and alone in the corner. This time, I'm craving conversation. In fact, I want to talk about myself. And in the midst of a lively monologue delivered to a group of four people (previously unimaginable for me), I recognize the feeling: It's like being on ecstasy! Relaxed, exceedingly comfortable with strangers, completely open. It makes some sense—both drugs noodle with your serotonin. Paxil, like Prozac and Zoloft, is a selective serotonin reuptake inhibitor. SSRIs block reabsorption of serotonin—a neurotransmitter—by your nerve endings, boosting serotonin levels in your brain. Ecstasy tweaks up your serotonin, too. But instead of paying $20 for a night on E, I paid $15 for a month on P. The catch: I seem to require alcohol as a trigger. Not sure why, and I doubt my doc could explain it.

Day 35: Drinking a lot, several nights a week. Liquor + Paxil = Wow!

Pre-Paxil, I was a social drinker. Now I'm walking a mile in someone else's brain chemistry. I can see why some of you like to drink so much, maybe even need to drink so much. It's fun for me now, in a way it just wasn't before. On liquor and Paxil, strangers mean novelty, not fear. Group conversations are a chance to play raconteur, not a chance to smile weakly and shut up.

And it's so much better than sobriety. Sober for me these days means *extreme* detachment. Movies, once a favorite hobby, do nothing for me now. Likewise books—I just don't connect with the plots or characters. I can't recall laughing (while sober) in the past couple of weeks. I'm never sad, but never happy. Why *wouldn't* I drink?

Day 38: I spent the first semester of my freshman year of college in a haze. During the Southern California evenings, I often played tennis, pulling bong hits between games. I distilled homemade rum in my dorm room, using Sterno cans and plastic tubing. My roommate grew 6 ounces of weed in our closet. It was more fun than I'd ever had in my life. The day after I got home for Christmas break, I decided to transfer.

It occurs to me that the past month has been a bit like that semester. I'm living the unexamined life. It's fantastic. I'm about ready to transfer.

Day 45: I stop my treatment. I had planned elaborate tests for myself—crashing formal parties, giving a dinner toast to a full restaurant, singing jazz standards in subway stations—but I decide these will prove nothing. Also, my lack of engagement with life is freaking out my girlfriend. And my seismic personality shift when drunk is freaking out me.

My day-to-day, sober interactions with people are unchanged by Paxil. A crisis along the lines of a public speaking engagement would still send sweat coursing down my spine (unless I downed a few scotch-and-sodas first). As best I can tell, Paxil works by creating massive detachment from your own emotions. If your social anxiety verges on looniness, detachment from those emotions is a good thing. For me, a milder case, hard-core detachment is just spooky. So, no more pills.

III. The Withdrawal

Day 46: At dinner, I feel the onset of mutation. While staring at a plate of artichoke hearts, my focus suddenly shifts, like the track-out/zoom-in camera trick in *Vertigo*. My brain is shifting out of Paxil gear and back to normal. It's like coming down off a hallucinogen. Later in the evening, it happens a few more times.

Day 47: Cannot get out of bed. Pounding headache. Extreme intestinal unhappiness. Dizzy all day.

Day 48: More of the same. I'm exhibiting classic withdrawal, which I've read about on some anti-Paxil Web sites. The dizziness and lightheadedness are overwhelming and far scarier than mere stomach distress. I leave the house but have to sit down every 10 minutes for fear of keeling over.

Day 49: Not much better. I can't describe how awful it is to be lightheaded for 72 straight hours. I try to lift my blood sugar by eating, but it makes no difference. Nothing helps. More alarmingly, the dreaded "zaps" have arrived. I'd read about these on the Paxil Database, a site for self-proclaimed Paxil victims, but I thought they were made up—there are so many hypochondriacs on the Web.

Turns out the zaps are for real. They're hard to describe. Imagine low-level electrical shocks all over your head, as though someone removed the top of your skull and dragged a staticky blanket across your brain. Zaps come in waves that last about 15 minutes then go away for a few hours. They do not hurt but are unnerving, to say the least.

Day 50: Zap waves all day. Have now been dizzy and burping for four days.

Day 51: Intestines happier. Dizziness comes and goes. Zaps still there.

Day 52: It's mercifully over. But a new phenomenon has taken hold. When I get teary-eyed watching a horrid chick-flick on a cross-country flight, I recognize it: feelings. On Paxil, I barely noticed they were gone. Now that they're back, even overcompensating, I never want to lose them again. Bitterness, anger, jealousy, sadness: They all make me happy.

IV. Epilogue

In retrospect, it was a bad idea to screw with my brain chemistry and possibly inflict lifelong damage just for the sake of experiment. I would not do something like this again. At the height of my withdrawal I was seriously terrified, thought it might never end, and repeatedly cursed my own stupidity. The fact that I considered a wholesale career change under the drug's effects, and couldn't complete any work, is alarming. Also, the zaps are for real. Fear them.

At the same time, I admit it was fascinating to try out a different personality. He only came out when I drank, but I caught a glimpse of an alternate me, and he wasn't such a bad guy—if a little gabby. I think I gained some empathy for other types of folk and maybe got an idea of how alcohol can mean different things to different people. I also sort of discovered what emotions are for and decided being shy isn't so bad after all. Thanks, Paxil!

O'Reilly Among the Snobs

It takes one to know one.

BY MICHAEL KINSLEY

March 2, 2001

DO YOU BELIEVE THIS STORY?

Bill O'Reilly, the Fox News talk-show host, is in the capital for the Bush inauguration. He is invited to a fancy dinner party. Reluctantly, he accepts, although it is not his kind of thing. According to *Newsweek*, "O'Reilly said he could feel the socialites and bigwigs 'measuring' him. 'They're saying, "What's he doing here?" One couple even got up to leave,' O'Reilly later recalled."

Two people left a Washington dinner party rather than share a table with a prole like Bill O'Reilly? Although I wasn't there, I state baldly: It never happened. That kind of snobbery barely exists in America. (Wednesday's *Wall Street Journal* had a front-page feature on country clubs that exclude Jews, treating the matter—correctly—as an odd cultural cul-de-sac, like a town where everyone plays hopscotch or a Web site devoted to whistling.) Certainly, traditional snobbery cannot hope to compete with today's most powerful social ordering principle: celebrity. O'Reilly, as he himself has been known to admit, has the most popular news show on cable. His book, *The O'Reilly Factor* (named after the show), was a No. 1 best seller. When he appears at an "A-list"

(*Newsweek*'s label) social function, nobody wonders, "What's he doing here?"

Yet O'Reilly, like many other people, clings to the fantasy that he is a stiff among the swells. He plays this chord repeatedly in the book, a potpourri of anecdotes and opinions about life in general and his in particular. He had a very strange experience as a graduate student at Harvard's Kennedy School of Government (which let the likes of Bill O'Reilly through its ivy-covered gates, he is careful to note, "in an effort to bring all sorts of people together"). Other Kennedy School students, he says, insisted on being called by three names, none of which could be "Vinny, Stevie, or Serge." Their "clothing was understated but top quality . . . and their rooms hinted of exotic vacations and sprawling family property. Winter skiing in Grindelwald? No problem." They tried to be nice, but Bill was nevertheless humiliated, in a Thai restaurant, to be "the only one who didn't know how to order my meal in Thai."

I should explain this last one to those who may not have been aware that Thai is the lingua franca of the American WASP upper class. The explanation is simple. American Jewish parents only one or two generations off the boat often spoke in Yiddish when they didn't want their children to understand. Italian-Americans used Italian, and so on. But WASPs only had English. (They tried Latin but tended to forget the declensions after the second martini.) So they adopted Thai, which they use in front of the servants and the O'Reillys of the world as well. (At least it sounds like Thai after the second martini.) When they turn 18, upper-class children attend a secret Thai language school, disguised as a ski resort, in Grindelwald.

The notion that the Kennedy School of Government, populated by swells out of P.G. Wodehouse, reached out to O'Reilly, a poor orphan out of Dickens, as representing the opposite pole of the human experience, would be remarkable enough. But O'Reilly's chapter on "The Class Factor" (Chapter 1, luckily for me) contains some puzzling counterevidence. "I'm working-class Irish American

Bill O'Reilly . . . pretty far down the social totem pole," he says. Growing up in the 1960s, he watched his father "exhausting himself commuting from Levittown" to work as an accountant for an oil company. Dad "never made more than $35,000"—which would be $100,000 or more in today's money.

Oh, the shame of it! O'Reilly has been downward social climbing. He is actually—and I wish I could say this in Thai, to avoid humiliating him with the children—m-i-d-d-l-e c-l-a-s-s. He apparently regards that status with just as much horror as do the toffs of his fevered imagination.

Why fake a humble background? Partly for business reasons: Joe Sixpack versus the elitists is a good posture for any talk-show host, especially one on Fox. Partly out of vanity: It makes the climb to your current perch more impressive. Partly for political reasons: Under our system, even conservatives need some plausible theory to qualify for victim status, from which all blessings flow. But mainly out of sheer snobbery. And it's the only kind of snobbery with any real power in America today: reverse snobbery. Bill O'Reilly pretends (or maybe sincerely imagines) that he feels the sting of status from above. But he unintentionally reveals that he actually fears it more from below. Like most of us.

This is not a terrible thing. Reverse snobbery, unlike the traditional kind, is a tribute to democracy—it's egalitarianism overshooting the mark. And it is a countervailing social force against growing economic disparity. But when you're faking it, if you're not careful, reverse snobbery can look a lot like the traditional kind. Bill O'Reilly told *Newsweek* he would never patronize a Starbucks because he prefers a Long Island coffee shop "where cops and firemen hang out." Guess what, Bill? Cops and firemen like good coffee too! And they can afford it. Starbucks is one of the great democratizing institutions of our time. You'd know that if you went in there occasionally. You snob.

Shag the Dog

BY WILLIAM SALETAN

April 5, 2001

Years ago, advocates of sexual abstinence came up with a clever motto to instill chastity in youngsters. "Pet your dog, not your date," they preached. They may live to regret those words. The love that dare not bark its name is now a front-page topic, raised at White House news conferences and in state legislatures, thanks largely to philosopher Peter Singer. In an essay titled "Heavy Petting," Singer asks, What's wrong with fondling Fido? The essay, coupled with two scandals involving sex with dogs—one confirmed in Maine and the other alleged by investigators in California—has elicited cries of outrage and disgust. But the outcry has been largely thoughtless. It's easy to say that becoming more than friendly with man's best friend is wrong. What's hard is backing up that statement with a principle and reconciling that principle with your beliefs about meat-eating, sexual orientation, or, in Singer's case, pedophilia.

Singer's essay tackles a series of objections to doggie-style intimacy. The first is that it's unnatural. If nature had wanted you to mate with your pet, the argument goes, you'd be able to procreate together. Singer points out, however, that we've come to tolerate other nonprocreative practices, such as contraception, masturbation, oral gratification, and homosexuality. But isn't sex with animals a uniquely radical affront to tradition? Nope. Dog-bites-man is the oldest story around. Singer cites literary and anthropological evidence that humans throughout history have been attracted to animals—swans, horses, dogs, satyrs, calves—and some have acted on that attraction. OK, but aren't these acts cruel and harmful? Not necessarily, says Singer: "Sex with animals does not always involve cruelty."

So why the taboo? According to Singer, it's because we think we're intrinsically and categorically superior to other species. This is the dogma that Singer really wants to penetrate. "We are animals," he writes. "This does not make sex across the species barrier normal, or natural, whatever those much-misused words may mean, but it does imply that it ceases to be an offence to our status and dignity as human beings."

Conservative editorialists have doggedly denounced and ridiculed Singer's argument. None of them, however, has explained what's wrong with it. The answer matters, because the principle that makes sex with animals immoral—whatever that principle is—must apply to other issues as well. The *Weekly Standard*, for instance, faults Singer's nonchalant reaction to an incident in which a lusty, "powerful" orangutan seized a woman "like a drunken frat boy." Is the *Standard* saying that this incident amounts to a kind of sexual harassment? Is Singer a cad for tolerating it? Then why does the *Standard* publish articles brushing aside "hypersensitivity to 'harassment' and 'date rape'"?

Or take the *Wall Street Journal* editorial page. The *Journal* derides Singer for condoning puppy love while his animal rights buddies demand "intolerable paperwork" from researchers who use animals in lab experiments. But if we want rules about what's done to animals by their owners, why not make rules about what's done to them in labs? The same logic applies to mockery of Singer's vegetarianism. "You could say Singer's take on animal rights is: You can have sex with them, but don't eat them," jokes conservative columnist Debra Saunders. That's funny. But you could just as easily ask those of us who eat meat why, if it's wrong to rape animals, it's OK to kill them.

Liberals have a different problem. Most of them want to say that sex with your dog is wrong, but sex with a human of your own gender isn't. The trouble is, Singer explicitly connects the two practices (both are nonprocreative), and people who advocate sex with animals—"zoophiles," as they prefer to be called—borrow the language of gay liberation. "I'm the first out-of-the-closet 'zoo' to be attacked because of my sexual orientation," Philip Buble, a zoophile, told the *Bangor Daily News* four months ago. Buble says the "relationship" between man and beast "can develop to be a sexual one." Testifying before a Maine legislative committee a week ago, Buble accused proponents of a ban on animal sexual abuse of trying "to force morality on a minority. It will be a disservice to zoo couples and would keep zoo couples from coming out of the closet and drive us deeper underground." Commenting on *Dearest Pet*, the book that inspired Singer's essay, other zoophiles articulate an "alternative sexual lifestyle" defined by "loving relationships with their animal lovers."

Then there's the case of the killer dogs in San Francisco. Last week, Marjorie Knoller and her husband, Robert Noel, were collared on manslaughter charges because two dogs in their care mauled to death their neighbor, Diane Whipple. Knoller and Noel, who are lawyers, claim they were taking care of the dogs on behalf of Paul "Cornfed" Schneider, a client whom they have adopted as their son while he serves a life sentence for attempted murder. According to a prison guard's affidavit, documents found in Schneider's possession include a photo of a male dog's genitals, "numerous photos of Knoller posing nude with fighting dog drawings," and a letter from the couple that discusses "sexual activity between Noel, Knoller and the dog" that subsequently killed Whipple. When the first vague report of the photos surfaced, Noel told the *San Francisco Chronicle*, "I'm not going to confirm it or deny it," adding, "There used to be a time when guy-on-guy or woman-on-woman relationships were looked at as unnatural acts. What concern is it to anybody if there is or isn't a personal relationship?"

The last thing liberals want is to see homosexuality equated with this kind of animal husbandry. While portraying Whipple and her lesbian partner as a loving couple, they dismiss the Noel-Knoller-Schneider-dog "family" as a twisted sham. But what makes one family real and the other fake? Is it monogamy? Fidelity? Commitment? Effort? A *New Republic* article suggests as much: "[A] fundamental reason for prohibiting sex with animals is the human desire to join sex [with love] and our recognition of the complexity of that joining, the care with which it must be nurtured and disciplined, the ease with which it is disrupted and led astray."

Strange as it may seem, however, it's hard to prove that Philip Buble doesn't nurture and discipline his love for the canine companion he calls "Lady Buble." He's a one-dog man. A month ago, when Buble's father was sentenced to jail for attacking him with a crowbar—in part out of disgust with Buble's "lifestyle"—Buble sent a formal request to the judge. "I'd like my significant other to attend by my side if possible as she was present in the house during the attack, though not an eyewitness to it, thank goodness," Buble wrote. "I've been informed your personal permission is needed given that my wife is not human." In his legislative testimony a week ago, Buble declared that he and Lady "live together as a married couple. In the eyes of God we are truly married."

Let's try another criterion. How about harm? Many animal rights activists say this is what's wrong with human-animal copulation, as opposed to gay sex. But that dog won't hunt, either. Singer points out that some sex acts between humans and animals "don't seem to do harm to animals." Is Buble harming the dog for whose emotional well-being he expressed such concern in his letter to the judge? Good luck proving it. In last week's testimony,

Buble said zoophiles are born to care for animals. He denied that their physical interaction with their pets includes abuse. And he added that zoophiles do far less harm to animals than hunters, meat-eaters, and medical experiments do. It's hard to argue with that.

How about consent? *Village Voice* columnist Norah Vincent argues that homosexuality is permissible because "sexual acts between consenting adults should be beyond the prurient reach of the state." However,

> When someone has sex with an animal, he foists himself on a creature that has the mental and emotional capacity of a child. Thus, it is no more capable than a child of giving meaningful consent. . . . [I]f you have had sex with someone who is constitutionally incapable of giving anything that might constitute meaningful consent, you have committed rape. At the very least you have taken advantage of a creature over which you exercise considerable power.

Now we're onto something. The evidence that consent is morally essential—and that animals don't really give it—comes from zoophiles themselves. *Dearest Pet* reportedly suggests that many artistic images of male animals penetrating women are fantasies projected by men. The usual scenario, according to more reliable records cited in the book, is a man penetrating an animal for his own satisfaction. Singer essentially concedes his vulnerability on the consent issue by ducking it. He defends one scenario in which a dog tries to mount a human visitor's leg, and another in which an orangutan grabs a female attendant. Each scenario presumes the animal's initiative. Likewise, Buble goes through a dog-and-pony show to persuade people that his pet consents to their putative marriage. His letter to the judge included, next to his signature, a paw print purporting to represent the signature of "Lady Buble." But in forging his partner's consent, Buble screwed the pooch. Readers of the letter recognized that the paw print had been drawn by hand, and a *Daily News* reader discerned another discrediting detail: "I also noticed in the picture of Buble and his Lady that the Ms. wears a choke collar. A willing participant indeed."

So one mystery is solved. If you want to say that contraception, sodomy, and homosexuality are OK but sex with animals isn't, you can stipulate that sex is permissible only if both parties consent to it. This still leaves you with the problem of explaining why it's OK to kill and eat animals. But two other mysteries remain. One is Singer's position on consent. Does he think sex without consent is immoral? What mental capacities are necessary to give consent? Do animals have those capacities? Who else has those capacities? This line of questioning converges with the other mystery. "One by one, the taboos have fallen," Singer writes in his review of *Dearest Pet*, building up to the subject of zoophilia. The book's publisher calls sex with animals "the last taboo." But it can't be the last taboo, because there's another subject on which Singer, while freely discussing the charms and merits of zoophilia, seems strangely muzzled. The telling issue—the dog that didn't bark—is pedophilia.

A philosopher's duty is to clarify his principles and defend their consistent application. Those who embrace the principle of consent, and who agree that an animal "is no more capable than a child of giving meaningful consent," have done both. They have stated their principle and applied it to sex with children. What about Singer? He has often compared the mental ability of higher animals to that of children. Does he think this level of comprehension is sufficient to give consent to sex? If the answer is no, isn't zoophilia wrong? If the answer is yes, isn't pedophilia OK? Dog paddling, an old dog's new tricks, dog-eat-dog, a three-dog night—that's kid stuff. You want to take on a real taboo, Professor Singer? Stand up and be a man.

2002

A YEAR OF UPHEAVAL at *Slate*. Michael Kinsley announced he was stepping down as *Slate's* editor, though he would stay on as a weekly columnist. In April, chief political correspondent Jacob Weisberg succeeded Mike and shifted the base of *Slate's* operations from Seattle to New York. Christopher Hitchens, fresh from quitting *The Nation* over political differences, began writing a weekly column titled "Fighting Words." In June, Scott Shuger died in a scuba-diving accident at age 50. Fred Kaplan, who had just left the *Boston Globe*, took over the military-affairs column Scott had been writing, "War Stories." Jack Shafer began writing "Press Box" regularly. William Saletan became chief political correspondent. Daniel Gross took over the "Moneybox" column. Meghan O'Rourke, a recent arrival from the *New Yorker*, succeeded Jodi Kantor as *Slate's* culture editor. On the business side, publisher Scott Moore got kicked upstairs to a high-powered executive job, and Cyrus Krohn—who had been Kinsley's first *Slate* hire back in 1995—replaced him.

Choking at the Bowl

Why do men have trouble urinating at ballparks?

BY BRYAN CURTIS

May 13, 2002

A SLATE EMPLOYEE—we'll call him "Thad"—asks the sports department to solve a problem that has been vexing him: Why does he have trouble urinating at ballparks? His testimony, worded as delicately as possible, goes like this: At a Seattle Mariners game, Thad slugged down several ballpark beverages. Later, he shuffled into the restroom, angled toward the urinals, unzipped his trousers, and then . . . nothing. Not a drop. Embarrassed and in acute pain, he waddled back to his seat, where he spent the remaining innings swaying like Stevie Wonder in front of a piano.

After polling some of the country's pre-eminent urologists, we discovered that, surprise, Thad isn't alone. Men experience stage fright at ballpark urinals all the time. In fact, the problem is so common that urologists have a reassuring, pat-on-the-butt-sounding name for it: choking at the bowl.

There are three reasons why ballparks cause men to choke—two physical, one psychological. First, some men spend their time at the ballpark slugging down a beer every half-inning. Alcohol causes the prostate gland to swell, which impedes the flow of urine from the bladder to the urinal channel. Thus, when the man reaches the urinal, nothing happens. Dr. Rodney Appell, a urologist at the Baylor College of Medicine in Houston, says the problem occurs most frequently with older men who have enlarged prostates to begin with.

Other times men choke at the bowl because they guzzle too many beverages, alcoholic or not, and overstretch their bladders. A normal-sized bladder will contract when full, allowing urine to flow out of the body. But an overstretched bladder—distended by four or five souvenir-cup sodas—is slow to contract, and sometimes urination stalls.

But most of the men who choke at the bowl suffer from an anxiety disorder called paruresis, or Shy Bladder Syndrome. These men, quite simply, are embarrassed to bare all in the presence of strangers. Steve Soifer, a professor of social work who founded the International Paruresis Association, estimates that 17 million Americans suffer from some form of Shy Bladder Syndrome, about 7 percent of the population.

When a man with a shy bladder enters the ballpark restroom, the crowds, long lines, and stadium noise make him sweat. So does the ballpark restroom's infamous trough urinal, a knee-high, stainless steel gutter that forces men to urinate while standing elbow-to-elbow. (Some stadiums built before the Trough Era have gutters carved directly into the floor.) If the shy bladder even makes it to the trough—some flee the restroom at this point—his nervousness causes him to clamp down on his sphincter muscle, which prevents his bladder from contracting.

Soifer, a recovering paruretic himself, offers a three-day workshop for shy bladders, held monthly in cities in the United States, Canada, and Great Britain. It costs $300 to attend. The first day is a group counseling session. During the second day, attendees gorge themselves on water and then, in pairs, practice voiding in their hotel bathrooms. In this exercise, one man stands at the toilet while his partner stands a comfortable distance behind him. As the first man begins to urinate, his partner inches closer, eventually standing directly behind the man, sometimes touching or razzing him as he urinates, to re-create the feel of a busy public restroom. The closing event of the workshop, which Soifer calls the "graduation ceremony," is held in a bathroom at a train station, airport, or, occasionally, a ballpark.

Even with therapy, will a shy bladder ever feel at ease at the ballpark trough? "I've suffered from paruresis for 30 years," Soifer says, "and I've been in recovery for the last six. I'm not cured. It's a lot like alcoholism. You can recover close to 100 percent, but it can get set off again in certain situations. That's why I don't talk about a cure."

Flag on the Field

Soccer, the last acceptable form of nationalism.

BY ANNE APPLEBAUM

June 18, 2002

ONCE, AND ONLY ONCE, have I attended a world-class—not quite World Cup—soccer game: England was playing Germany in London in the semifinals of the European championships. I'd previously been to a Super Bowl and one or two Redskins' games, but nothing really prepared me for the decibel level of Wembley Stadium. Over and over again, the fans sang "Football's Coming Home," a weirdly catchy tune, with lyrics predicated on the mystical notion that football (soccer), a game the English invented, was finally "coming home"—and that the chronically weak English team would once again become great. They also chanted. The night I watched England play, they mostly chanted, "Here we go, here we go, here we go," but sometimes the chants are more original. During the England-Argentina World Cup match last week, for example, they chanted, "Where is your navy? At the bottom of the sea"—a not terribly subtle reference to the Falklands War. About once a year, a British anthropologist is trotted out to analyze the chants as a vestigial form of primitive cult religions.

Outside the stadium that day, soccer mania had gripped the nation—and it is a mistake to imagine that only the hooligans temporarily turn into chauvinistic nationalists on the day of an England match. Otherwise well-behaved friends of mine were genuinely outraged that I, a mere foreigner, had received a press ticket. Germany jokes, usually involving the Nazis, were all the rage. One was attributed to Mrs. Thatcher, who upon being told that Germany had defeated England (which they did, of course) had allegedly replied, "They may have beat us at our national game, but we beat them twice at their national game in the 20th century."

And everyone laughed. In the context of soccer, flag-waving nationalism—even chauvinistic, anti-foreigner, flag-waving nationalism—is acceptable in Britain. Which is odd, given that it isn't acceptable in other contexts, not in Britain and not anywhere in Western Europe, where most countries' political elites, at least, are ideologically dedicated to diluting their national identities into the broader European Union—as quickly as possible.

In Britain, even what Americans would consider to be ordinary patriotism is often suspect. When Tony Blair first entered the prime minister's residence in Downing Street, in 1997, he staged a little parade of well-wishers, all of whom were waving the British flag, the Union Jack. The British chattering classes howled their disapproval of this unsightly show of nationalism—one friend told me that the Union Jack always made him think of right-wing extremists—just as they had earlier howled their disapproval of the Blair campaign's brief (and quickly withdrawn) use of the traditional British bulldog. This summer's

Jubilee, the 50th-anniversary celebration of the queen's reign, has been accompanied by some flag-waving—but some opposition, too. One *Independent* columnist wrote that her friends are "studiously ignoring the event," since national symbols such as the queen and the flag "bear uncomfortable overtones of racism and colonialism." Patriotism, she went on, is seen as "profoundly down-market, like doilies and bad diets."

The attitudes vary in other countries—unlike the Union Jack, the French tricolor flies from just about every public building in France—but the general rule of thumb holds true. Certainly there isn't anywhere in Germany you can go to shout, "Deutschland! Deutschland!" except a soccer stadium, for example. Perhaps as a result, feelings run so high in Germany following a soccer match that no incumbent German chancellor has ever lost an election in the wake of a major German victory. The re-election of Helmut Kohl in 1990 was widely attributed to Germany's victory in that year's World Cup. Perhaps it was all a coincidence, but the current German chancellor, Gerhard Schröder, is taking no chances. He has made a point of halting all his current, tight election campaigning for 90 minutes every time Germany plays a World Cup match.

In part, reverse snobbery explains this strange phenomenon. Soccer is the man-on-the-street's game in Europe, and the politicians, academics, and high-end journalists who would normally shun exhibitionist patriotism support their national teams as a means of proving they are really men-on-the-street themselves. But it may also be that high national emotions are permissible when a soccer team is playing precisely because they are impermissible at most other times. There simply aren't many other places where you can sing your national anthem until you lose your voice without causing a riot.

And the implications are broad-ranging. The somewhat strange fact that the British have four international teams (England, Scotland, Wales, and Northern Ireland) instead of one, for example, may well have contributed to the recent revival of Scottish and Welsh separatism. If the England team really did become successful, it might even create some serious English separatism, a previously unknown phenomenon. Certainly the rise in middle-class support for the England team has contributed to the revival of the English flag—a red cross on a white field—which now flies from fans' cars on the days of big matches, and sometimes gets painted on their faces.

But the significance of the American team's weakness has always been underrated, too. Particularly now that the Olympics have been spoiled by total American dominance, it is nice for everybody else that the United States always loses at the only game the rest of the world really cares about. Now that the United States has started to do a bit better, the future looks darker. Hearing the score of this morning's Mexico game—and the rumors that riots might start in Mexico City—I immediately worried: If the United States started to dominate soccer the way it dominates basketball, then anti-Americanism might really start to get ugly.

As it stands, the relationship between the United States and soccer is perfect. Americans—citizens of a modern state—have plenty of opportunities to show their patriotism, on inaugurations and at school assemblies and on the Fourth of July. They don't need to do it in soccer stadiums as well. Europeans, on the other hand—citizens of postmodern states—have fewer and fewer, and need those soccer highs badly as a result. Cheer for the American soccer players if you will—but keep your fingers crossed, and hope the U.S. team doesn't upset the balance by winning too many more matches.

The Pledge of Allegiance

Why we're not one nation "under God."

BY DAVID GREENBERG

June 28, 2002

Poor ALFRED GOODWIN! So torrential was the flood of condemnation that followed his opinion—which held that it's unconstitutional for public schools to require students to recite "under God" as part of the Pledge of Allegiance—that the beleaguered appellate-court judge suspended his own ruling until the whole 9th Circuit Court has a chance to review the case.

Not one major political figure summoned the courage to rebut the spurious claims that America's founders wished to make God a part of public life. It's an old shibboleth of those who want to inject religion into public life that they're honoring the spirit of the nation's founders. In fact, the founders opposed the institutionalization of religion. They kept the Constitution free of references to God. The document mentions religion only to guarantee that godly belief would never be used as a qualification for holding office—a departure from many existing state constitutions. That the founders made erecting a church-state wall their first priority when they added the Bill of Rights to the Constitution reveals the importance they placed on maintaining what Isaac Kramnick and R. Laurence Moore have called a "godless Constitution." When Benjamin Franklin proposed during the Constitutional Convention that the founders begin each day of their labors with a prayer to God for guidance, his suggestion was defeated.

Given this tradition, it's not surprising that the original Pledge of Allegiance—meant as an expression of patriotism, not religious faith—also made no mention of God. The pledge was written in 1892 by the socialist Francis Bellamy, a cousin of the famous radical writer Edward Bellamy. He devised it for the popular magazine *Youth's Companion* on the occasion of the nation's first celebration of Columbus Day. Its wording omitted reference not only to God but also, interestingly, to the United States:

> *"I pledge allegiance to my flag and the republic for which it stands, one nation indivisible, with liberty and justice for all."*

The key words for Bellamy were "indivisible," which recalled the Civil War and the triumph of federal union over states' rights, and "liberty and justice for all," which was supposed to strike a balance between equality and individual freedom. By the 1920s, reciting the pledge had become a ritual in many public schools.

Since the founding, critics of America's secularism have repeatedly sought to break down the church-state wall. After the Civil War, for example, some clergymen argued that the war's carnage was divine retribution for the founders' refusal to declare the United States a Christian nation, and tried to amend the Constitution to do so.

The efforts to bring God into the state reached their peak during the so-called "religious revival" of the 1950s. It was a time when Norman Vincent Peale grafted religion onto the era's feel-good consumerism in his best-selling *The Power of Positive Thinking*; when Billy Graham rose to fame as a Red-baiter who warned that Americans would perish in a nuclear holocaust unless they embraced Jesus Christ; when Secretary of State John Foster Dulles believed that the United States should oppose communism not because the Soviet Union was a totalitarian regime but because its leaders were atheists.

Hand in hand with the Red Scare, to which it was inextricably linked, the new religiosity overran Washington. Politicians outbid one another to prove their piety. President Eisenhower inaugurated that Washington staple: the prayer breakfast. Congress created a prayer room in the Capitol. In 1955, with Ike's support, Congress added the words "In God We Trust" on all paper money. In 1956 it made the same four words the nation's official motto, replacing "*E Pluribus Unum.*" Legislators introduced constitutional amendments to state that Americans obeyed "the authority and law of Jesus Christ."

The campaign to add "under God" to the Pledge of Allegiance was part of this movement. It's unclear precisely where the idea originated, but one driving force was the Catholic fraternal society the Knights of Columbus. In the early 1950s the Knights themselves adopted the God-infused pledge for use in their own meetings, and members bombarded Congress with calls for the United States to do the same. Other fraternal, religious, and veterans' clubs backed the idea. In April 1953, Rep. Louis Rabaut, D-Mich., formally proposed the alteration of the pledge in a bill he introduced to Congress.

The "under God" movement didn't take off, however, until the next year, when it was endorsed by the Rev. George M. Docherty, the pastor of the Presbyterian church in Washington that Eisenhower attended. In February 1954, Docherty gave a sermon—with the president in the pew before him—arguing that apart from "the United States of America," the pledge "could be the pledge of any country." He added, "I could hear little Moscovites [*sic*] repeat a similar pledge to their hammer-and-sickle flag with equal solemnity." Perhaps forgetting that "liberty and justice for all" was not the norm in Moscow, Docherty urged the inclusion of "under God" in the pledge to denote what he felt was special about the United States.

The ensuing congressional speechifying—*debate* would be a misnomer, given the near-unanimity of opinion—offered more proof that the point of the bill was to promote religion. The legislative history of the 1954 act stated that the hope was to "acknowledge the dependence of our people and our Government upon . . . the Creator . . . [and] deny the atheistic and materialistic concept of communism." In signing the bill on June 14, 1954, Flag Day, Eisenhower delighted in the fact that from then on, "millions of our schoolchildren will daily proclaim in every city and town . . . the dedication of our nation and our people to the Almighty." That the nation, constitutionally speaking, was in fact dedicated to the opposite proposition seemed to escape the president.

In recent times, controversies over the pledge have centered on the wisdom of enforcing patriotism more than on its corruption from a secular oath into a religious one. In the 1988 presidential race, as many readers will recall, George Bush bludgeoned Democratic nominee Michael Dukakis for vetoing a mandatory-pledge bill when he was governor of Massachusetts, even though the state Supreme Court had ruled the bill unconstitutional. Surely one reason for the current cravenness of Democratic leaders is a fear of undergoing Dukakis' fate in 2002 or 2004 at the hands of another Bush.

The history of the pledge supports Goodwin's decision. The record of the 1954 act shows that, far from a "*de minimis*" reference or a mere "backdrop" devoid of meaning, the words "under God" were inserted in the pledge for the express purpose of endorsing religion—which the U.S. Supreme Court itself ruled in 1971 was unconstitutional. Also according to the Supreme Court's own rulings, it doesn't matter that students are allowed to refrain from saying the pledge; a 2000 high court opinion held that voluntary, student-led prayers at school football games are unconstitutionally "coercive" because they force students into an unacceptable position of either proclaiming religious beliefs they don't share or publicly protesting.

The appeals court decision came almost 40 years to the day after the Supreme Court decision in *Engel* v. *Vitale*. In that case, the court ruled it unconstitutional for public schools to allow prayer, even though the prayer was nondenominational and students were allowed to abstain from the exercise. When asked about the unpopular decision, President John F. Kennedy replied coolly that he knew many people were angry but that the decisions of the court had to be respected. He added that there was "a very easy remedy"—not a constitutional amendment but a renewed commitment by Americans to pray at home, in their churches, and with their families.

Lewis and Clark

Stop celebrating. They don't matter.

BY DAVID PLOTZ

Aug. 16, 2002

THE AMERICAN INFATUATION with Lewis and Clark grows more fervent with every passing year. The adventurers have become our Extreme Founding Fathers, as essential to American history as George Washington and Thomas Jefferson but a lot more fun. Last month, President Bush announced the Lewis and Clark bicentennial celebration, a three-year, 15-state pageant that begins Jan. 18 in Virginia and could draw as many as 25 million tourists to the Lewis and Clark trail by the time it wraps up in 2006. The same week as Bush's speech, *Time* devoted a special issue to the expedition, 42 salivary pages of Lewis and Clark.

Bookstores have been stuffed with Lewis and Clark volumes since the publication of Stephen Ambrose's in 1996. There are scores of trail guides, multivolume editions of the explorers' journals, a dozen books about Sacagawea, three histories of Fort Clatsop, a Lewis and Clark cookbook, and at least three books about Meriwether Lewis' dog, Seaman.

Our Lewis and Clark have something for everyone—a catalog of 21st-century virtues. They're multicultural: An Indian woman, French-Indians, French-Canadians, and a black slave all contributed to the expedition's success. They're environmental: Lewis and Clark kept prodigious records of plants and animals and were enthralled by the vast, mysterious landscape they traveled through. They're tolerant: They didn't kill Indians (much) but did negotiate with them. They're patriotic: They discovered new land so the United States could grow into a great nation. Lewis and Clark, it's claimed, opened the West and launched the American empire.

Except they didn't. "If Lewis and Clark had died on the trail, it wouldn't have mattered a bit," says Notre Dame University historian Thomas Slaughter, author of the forthcoming *Exploring Lewis and Clark: Reflections on Men and Wilderness*.

Like the moon landing, the Lewis and Clark expedition was inspiring, poetic, metaphorical, and ultimately insignificant. First of all, Lewis and Clark were not first of all. The members of the Corps of Discovery were not the first people to see the land they traveled. Indians had been everywhere, of course, but the corps members were not even the first whites. Trappers and traders had covered the land before them, and though Lewis and Clark may have been the first whites to cross the Rockies in the United States, explorer Alexander MacKenzie had traversed the Canadian Rockies a decade before them.

After the celebration of their safe return, Lewis and Clark quickly sank into obscurity, and for good reason. They failed at their primary mission. Jefferson had dispatched them to find a water route across the continent—the fabled Northwest Passage—but they discovered that water transport from coast to coast was impossible. Jefferson, chagrined, never bragged much about the expedition he had fathered.

Not discovering something that didn't exist was hardly Lewis and Clark's fault, but the expedition also failed in a much more important way. It produced nothing useful. Meriwether Lewis was supposed to distill his notes into a gripping narrative, but he had writer's block and killed himself in 1809 without ever writing a word. The captains' journals weren't published until almost 10 years after the duo's return; only 1,400 copies were printed, they appeared when the country was distracted by the War of 1812, and they had no impact. The narrative was well told, but it ignored the most valuable information collected by Lewis and Clark, their mountains of scientific and anthropological data about the plants, animals, and Indians of the West. That material wasn't published for a century, long after it could have helped pioneers.

Lewis and Clark didn't matter for other reasons. At the time of the journey, the Corps of Discovery "leapfrogged Americans' concerns," says American University historian Andrew Lewis (no relation to Meriwether). "They were exploring the far Missouri at a time when the frontier was the Ohio River. They were irrelevant."

When the country did start catching up, decades later, the Lewis and Clark route didn't help. William Clark told President Jefferson that they had discovered the best route across the continent, but he could hardly have been more wrong. Lewis and Clark took the Missouri through Kansas, Iowa, Nebraska, the Dakotas, and Montana before crossing the Rockies in northern Idaho. Their route was way too far north to be practical. No one could follow it. Other explorers located better, southerly shortcuts across the Continental Divide, and that's where Western settlers went. Lewis and Clark aficionados delight today in the unspoiled scenery along the trail. The reason the trail remains scenic and unspoiled is that it was so useless.

In a few years, Lewis and Clark disappeared from the American imagination and the American project. Lewis was dead, and Clark spent the rest of his life on the frontier, supervising relations with Indians—an important job but not one that gave him any say over government policy. Meanwhile, other daredevils captured the popular fancy, especially during the great wave of exploration in the mid-19th century. John C. Frémont enthralled the country with his bold Western trips. John Wesley Powell—the one-armed Civil War veteran—made his name by rafting the Colorado River through the Grand Canyon. The mid-century explorers provided information that was vastly more productive than anything Lewis and Clark offered.

By the late 19th century, Lewis and Clark were negligible figures. They weren't found in textbooks, according to the University of Tulsa's James Ronda, a leading scholar of the expedition. Americans didn't hearken back to the adventure. It was so unimportant that Henry Adams could dismiss it in no time flat in his history of the Jefferson administration as having "added little to the stock of science and wealth."

The first Lewis and Clark revival occurred at the turn of the 20th century, when the journals were published again after an 80-year hiatus. Americans were remembering the trip only *after* the West had been settled, the Indians had been wiped out, and the frontier closed. During the years that the empire was actually being built, at the time of settlement and conquest, Americans hadn't cared at all about Lewis and Clark.

After World War I, says Ronda, the expedition was ignored again. University of Texas historian William Goetzmann says that when he was writing his Pulitzer Prize-winning *Exploration and Empire: The Explorer and the Scientist in the Winning of the American West* in the mid-1960s, he wasn't even going to include Lewis and Clark, but "my publisher talked me into it."

But by the late 1960s, Americans had rediscovered Lewis and Clark, and their fervor has not flagged since. The creation of the 3,700-mile Lewis and Clark National Historic Trail in 1978 made the story accessible in a way that history rarely is. Millions of people have followed Lewis and Clark's footsteps and oar-swings since the trail opened. Ambrose's book attracted tens of thousands of new fans to the tale. The expedition's various appeal—ecological, patriotic, diverse, literary, thrill-seeking—gives it traction. More and more Americans read directly from the captains' journals, whose blunt, direct, and oddly beautiful language makes the story live. And the United States, as Ronda notes, is a country that loves road stories, and there is none more vivid or exciting than Lewis and Clark's.

But our fascination with Lewis and Clark is much more about us than about them. The expedition is a useful American mythology: how a pair of hardy souls and their happy-go-lucky multiculti flotilla discovered Eden, befriended the Indian, and invented the American West. The myth of Lewis and Clark papers over the grittier story of how the United States conquered the land, tribe by slaughtered, betrayed tribe.

Lewis and Clark didn't give Americans any of the tools they required to settle the continent—not new technology, not a popular narrative, not a good route, not arable land. It didn't matter. Nineteenth-century pioneers were bound to take the great West, with or without Lewis and Clark. Their own greed, ambition, bravery, and desperation guaranteed it. They did not need Lewis and Clark to conquer and build the West. But we do need Lewis and Clark to justify having done it.

An Unlikely Hero

The Marine who found two WTC survivors.

BY REBECCA LISS

Sept. 10, 2002

ONLY 12 SURVIVORS were pulled from the rubble of the World Trade Center after the towers fell on Sept. 11, despite intense rescue efforts. Two of the last three to be located and saved were Port Authority police officers. They were not discovered by a heroic firefighter, or a rescue worker, or a cop. They were discovered by Dave Karnes.

Karnes hadn't been near the World Trade Center. He wasn't even in New York when the planes hit the towers. He was in Wilton, Conn., working in his job as a senior accountant with Deloitte Touche. When the second plane hit, Karnes told his colleagues, "We're at war." He had spent 23 years in the Marine Corps infantry and felt it was his duty to help. Karnes told his boss he might not see him for a while.

Then he went to get a haircut.

The small barbershop in Stamford, Conn., near his home, was deserted. "Give me a good Marine Corps squared-off haircut," he told the barber. When it was done, he drove home to put on his uniform. Karnes always kept two sets of Marine fatigues hanging in his closet, pressed and starched. "It's kind of weird to do, but it comes in handy," he says. Next Karnes stopped by the storage facility where he kept his equipment—he'd need rappelling gear, ropes, canteens of water, his Marine Corps K-Bar knife, and a flashlight, at least. Then he drove to church. He asked the pastor and parishioners to say a prayer that God would lead him to survivors. A devout Christian, Karnes often turned to God when faced with decisions.

Finally, Karnes lowered the convertible top on his Porsche. This would make it easier for the authorities to look in and see a Marine, he reasoned. If they could see who he was, he'd be able to zip past checkpoints and more easily gain access to the site. For Karnes, it was a "God thing" that he was in the Porsche—a Porsche 911—that day. He'd only purchased it a month earlier—it had been a stretch, financially. But he decided to buy it after his pastor suggested that he "pray on it." He had no choice but to take it that day because his Mercury was in the shop. Driving the Porsche at speeds of up to 120 miles per hour, he reached Manhattan—after stopping at McDonald's for a hamburger—in the late afternoon.

His plan worked. With the top off, the cops could see his pressed fatigues, his neatly cropped hair, and his gear up front. They waved him past the barricades. He arrived at the site—"the pile"—at about 5:30. Seven World Trade Center, a 47-story office structure adjacent to the fallen twin towers, had just dramatically collapsed. Rescue workers had been ordered off the pile—it was too unsafe to let them continue. Flames were bursting from a number of buildings, and the whole site was considered unstable. Standing on the edge of the burning pile, Karnes spotted . . . another Marine dressed in camouflage. His name was Sgt. Thomas. Karnes never learned his first name, and he's never come forward in the time since.

Together Karnes and Thomas walked around the pile looking for a point of entry farther from the burning buildings. They also wanted to move away from officials trying to keep rescue workers off the pile. Thick, black smoke blanketed the site. The two Marines couldn't see where to enter. But then "the smoke just opened up." The sun was setting and through the opening Karnes, for the first time, saw clearly the massive destruction. "I just said, 'Oh, my God, it's totally gone.'" With the sudden parting of the smoke, Karnes and Thomas entered the pile. "We just disappeared into the smoke—and we ran."

They climbed over the tangled steel and began looking into voids. They saw no one else searching the pile—the rescue workers having obeyed the order to leave the area. "United States Marines," Karnes began shouting. "If you can hear us, yell or tap!"

Over and over, Karnes shouted the words. Then he would pause and listen. Debris was shifting and parts of the building were collapsing further. Fires burned all around. "I just had a sense, an overwhelming sense come over me that we were walking on hallowed ground, that tens of thousands of people could be trapped and dead beneath us," he said.

After about an hour of searching and yelling, Karnes stopped. "Be quiet," he told Thomas, "I think I can hear something."

He yelled again: "We can hear you. Yell louder." He heard a faint muffled sound in the distance.

"Keep yelling. We can hear you." Karnes and Thomas zeroed in on the sound.

"We're over here," they heard.

Two Port Authority police officers, Will Jimeno and Sgt. John McLoughlin, were buried in the middle of the World Trade Center ruins, 20 feet below the surface. They could be heard but not seen. By jumping into a larger opening, Karnes could hear Jimeno better. But he still couldn't see him. Karnes sent Thomas to look for help. Then he used his cell phone to call his wife, Rosemary, in Stamford and his sister Joy in Pittsburgh. (He thought they could work the phones and get through to New York police headquarters.)

"Don't leave us," Officer Jimeno pleaded. He later said he feared Karnes' voice would trail away, as had that of another potential rescuer hours earlier. It was now about 7 p.m. and Jimeno and McLoughlin had been trapped for roughly nine hours. Karnes stayed with them, talking to them until help arrived, in the form of Chuck Sereika, a former paramedic with an expired license who pulled his old uniform out of his closet and came to the site. Ten minutes later, Scott Strauss and Paddy McGee, officers with the elite Emergency Service Unit of the NYPD, also arrived.

The story of how Strauss and Sereika spent three hours digging Jimeno out of the debris, which constantly threatened to collapse, has been well told in the *New York Times* and elsewhere. At one point, all they had with which to dig out Jimeno were a pair of handcuffs. Karnes stood by, helping pass tools to Strauss, offering his Marine K-Bar knife when it looked as if they might have to amputate Jimeno's leg to free him. (After Jimeno was finally pulled out, another team of cops worked for six more hours to free McLoughlin, who was buried deeper in the pile.)

Karnes left the site that night when Jimeno was rescued and went with him to the hospital. While doctors treated the injured cop, Karnes grabbed a few hours sleep on an empty bed in the hospital psychiatric ward. While he slept, the hospital cleaned and pressed his uniform.

Today, on the anniversary of the attack and the rescue, officers Jimeno and Strauss will be part of the formal "Top Cop" ceremony at the New York City Center Theater. Earlier the two appeared on a nationally televised episode of *America's Most Wanted*. Jimeno and McLoughlin appeared this week on the *Today* show. They are heroes.

Today, Dave Karnes will be speaking at the Maranatha Bible Baptist Church in Wilkinsburg, Penn., near where he grew up. He sounds excited, over the phone, talking about the upcoming ceremony. Karnes is a hero, too.

But it's also clear Karnes is a hero in a smaller, less national, less public, less publicized way than the cops and firefighters are heroes. He's hardly been overlooked—the program I work for, *60 Minutes II*, interviewed him as part of a piece on Jimeno's rescue—but the great televised glory machine has so far not picked him. Why? One reason seems obvious—the cops and firefighters are part of big, respected, institutional support networks. Americans are grateful for the sacrifices their entire organizations made a year ago. Plus, the police and firefighting institutions are tribal brotherhoods. The firefighters help and support and console each other; the cops do the same. They find it harder to make room for outsiders like Karnes (or Chuck Sereika). And, it must be said, at some macho level it's vaguely embarrassing that the professional rescuers weren't the ones who found the two survivors. While the pros were pulled back out of legitimate caution, the job fell to an outsider, who drove down from Connecticut and just walked onto the burning pile.

Columnist Stewart Alsop once famously identified two rare types of soldiers, the "crazy brave" and the "phony tough." The professionals at Ground Zero—I interviewed dozens in my work as a producer for CBS—were in no way phony toughs. But Karnes does seem a bit "crazy brave." You'd have to be slightly abnormal—abnormally selfless, abnormally patriotic—to do what he did. And some of the same qualities that led Karnes to make himself a hero when it counted may make him less perfect as the image of a hero today.

Officer Strauss tells a story that gets at this. When he was out on the pile a year ago, trying to pull Officer Jimeno free, Strauss shouted orders to his volunteer helpers—"Medic, I need air," or "Marine, get me some water." At one point, in the middle of this exhausting work, Strauss, asked if he could call them by their names to facilitate the process. The medic said he was "Chuck."

Karnes said: "You can call me 'staff sergeant.'"

"That's three syllables!" said Strauss, who needed every bit of energy and every second of time. "Isn't there something shorter?"

Karnes replied: "You can call me 'staff sergeant.'"

Cold Shower

How to spit with the wine pros.

BY MIKE STEINBERGER

Oct. 1, 2002

SPIT OR SWALLOW? For wine aficionados, the choice is usually dic-
tated by circumstance: At meals you swallow, at tastings you spit
(unless the wines being tasted are liquid gold; it would be criminal
to cough up even a drop of the 1989 Haut-Brion, for instance).
But as with so many other wine-related rituals, spitting is no simple matter. Proper technique and correct form count for a lot
more in wine circles than you might think.

My method of spitting has always been more or less indistin-
guishable from my approach to vomiting—place my head above
the bucket, open my mouth, and let gravity pretty much handle

the rest. It took me a long time to realize the damage this artless splattering was doing to my credibility as a part-time wine journalist. I was certainly aware that there were world-class spitters: Shortly after catching the wine bug, I had come across a priceless photo of Len Evans, a popular Australian wine writer, vintner, and raconteur. In it, Evans is expectorating a laser beam of purple spittle while wearing a suit and tie (with a white shirt!). For weeks thereafter, I kept returning to the picture, gazing at it worshipfully.

Still, I saw no need to emulate Evans; I assumed that projectile spitting was simply a flourish. My opinion did not change even after I started regularly visiting wineries. Several years ago, I paid a call on a Burgundian estate of some renown. The proprietor took me to the cellar, where he poured and I tasted. Knowing that he was watching made me self-conscious, which only made my spitting worse. At one point, as I was dabbing my chin with a tissue while trying to rub the stains out of my khakis, I caught him with an arched eyebrow and an expression that seemed to say, Who sent you here?

Thereafter, I got into the habit of spending a few minutes practicing spitting before heading off to wine country; usually, this involved taking a glass of water, standing in the doorway of the shower, and attempting to blast a cohesive stream out of my mouth. I never succeeded, but that didn't bother me: I had confidence in my palate and figured that as long as I showed myself to be a competent taster, my disposal problem would be forgiven.

Turns out I was wrong. A few weeks ago, I was thumbing through the British wine writer Jancis Robinson's latest book, *How To Taste*, and discovered that she devotes an entire page and then some to the topic of spitting. One sentence in particular struck a nerve: " 'Spit with pride' might well be the wine taster's motto." It dawned on me that spitting was perhaps more important than I had imagined. I immediately placed a call to Daniel Johnnes, the wine director at Montrachet, who is widely considered the dean of New York sommeliers. He confirmed it: Spitting really is a big deal. I asked Johnnes if he would help spare me any more embarrassment and give me some tips. He graciously agreed and invited me to his office in Tribeca for a lesson.

Johnnes is affable, energetic, and a little cheeky—perfect sommelier material. Within minutes of my arrival, it became clear that this would be a mutually beneficial exercise: He would give me pointers, I would give him a good laugh. As Johnnes fetched a bucket and a bottle of red, the 1999 Chateau de Lascaux from the Languedoc region in France, he explained to me that "there are three types of spitters: droolers, dribblers, and beeline spitters. Dribbling usually becomes spray before it becomes a bead."

I asked him to name some of the more esteemed wine-hockers. "Jancis Robinson is excellent. Robert Parker is a great spitter. But the most famous is probably [New York wine writer] Alex Bespaloff. He has incredible accuracy and distance."

What is considered good distance? "Two feet is standard. Three feet—that's competition spit."

So, how competitive does this stuff get? "Very. When I'm tasting with other sommeliers, we all look out of the corner of the eye to check the other guy's spitting ability. It's noticed, and any sommelier who tells you otherwise is not telling the whole story."

By that point, Johnnes had uncorked the wine and put a generous pour in his glass. Perhaps feeling some performance anxiety himself, he advised me that he was a bit tired and might be off his game that day. With that, he took a swig of wine, held it in his mouth for a few seconds, and then rifled what looked to be a fairly compact effluence into the bucket.

"Better than I expected," he said. "But if you noticed, I lost my form at the end. The finish is the one flaw in my spitting; the pressure drops, and I get just a little dribble at the end. I'm working on it."

Now it was my turn. I gathered my thoughts, took a good sized sip, and let it fly. As I pulled my head away from the bucket, wiping my mouth with my fingers, Johnnes handed me a paper towel.

"I think you just created a new category—cascade spitter," he said, chortling. "That was awful. You get a D. But I've seen worse, if it's any consolation."

It wasn't. As I set my glass down, Johnnes began a step-by-step explanation of how to spit like a pro. It is essential, he said, to put the right amount of wine in your mouth; he recommends between one-quarter and one-half ounce. Once you have tasted the wine and are ready to expel it, you pucker your lips, tighten your cheeks, and press your tongue up against your top teeth, broadening the tongue so that it extends past the molars on each side. This pools the wine between the top of your tongue and the roof of your mouth. The key, Johnnes says, is muscle control and force: You need to generate sufficient power to push the wine out while maintaining your form throughout the process.

With his instructions in my mind, I refilled my glass and gave it another try, struggling to keep all the parts in place. "Better," Johnnes reported. "A little spray, but tighter, better." Feeling emboldened, I poured some more wine and repeated the drill. Johnnes shook his head. "Bad. You're really going to have to practice. To be honest, the way you are spitting right now, I personally wouldn't want to go into too many cellars." I asked him if it was hopeless.

"You are never going to be great, but you are clearly willing to work on it, and that's half the battle."

I am working on it, every chance I get. Even spitting out mouthwash has become an opportunity to practice. If all this strikes you as a bit asinine and pathetic, you may have a point. After all, stylish spitting does not improve your ability to appraise wine; it only keeps your clothes clean and the floor dry. But the wine world is a clubby, often catty one, with its own rites of passage. If you want to be seen as legit by the Crips, it helps to have a drive-by shooting to your credit. If you want be seen as legit by wine geeks, you need to be able to shoot a mouthful of Chardonnay in a clean, straight line.

No doubt, spitting's importance is amplified by the fact that so much else about wine is subjective. One man's elegant Cabernet is another man's tannic beast. There is no accounting for taste, nor is there much sense in arguing over it. Among the few aspects of wine that can be assessed with some degree of objectivity is spitting. The wine is expunged either in a tidy package or a centrifugal mess—and the tablecloth never lies.

Fifty/Fifty Forever

Why we shouldn't expect America's political "tie" to be broken anytime soon.

BY MICKEY KAUS

Nov. 29, 2002

THE MASS MARKET NEWSWEEKLIES (*Time, Newsweek, U.S. News*) can't be seen as taking sides in political campaigns—imagine *Time* writing a cover story on "Bush's Dangerous Iraq Policy" or "Why the Democrats Can't Be Trusted." It would be a commercial disaster. Yet the weeklies are also expected to deliver more in the way of bold, dramatic analysis than can be found in your daily paper. As a result, every two years they glom on to some sweeping, seemingly-biting-but-also-neutral story line through which to tell the story of the election. When I wrote for *Newsweek* in 1988, our Neutral Story Line was "Is This Any Way To Pick a President?" More recently, the favorite NSLs have been along the lines of "Oh, What a Negative Campaign" or "Money Talks: The Influence of Campaign Fund Raising." Yet these story lines have by now been worked so hard even the weeklies can't pretend that they're fresh anymore.

What to do? This week, *Newsweek*'s Howard Fineman makes a good try at casting the campaign as a giant family feud between the Clintons and Bushes. (Fineman's a genius at coming up with plausible NSLs and fleshing them out, one reason he's anchored *Newsweek*'s political coverage for decades.) As a believer in cheap Darwinian analysis, I find the Family Feud line—with its mixture of genetic solidarity and status-seeking—highly useful. (Ann Bardach's new book *Cuba Confidential*, to pick another example, plausibly and entertainingly describes all of U.S.-Cuba relations since 1959 as a big family feud.)

But neither *Newsweek* nor *Time*, as far as I know, has showcased the most obvious Neutral Story Line for 2002—the idea that the nation is, for the second election in a row, split right down the middle by virtually every national political measure. Columnist Michael Barone did advance this notion after the 2000 Florida recount—Barone notes that Clinton was elected in '96 with 49 percent of the vote, Bush in 2000 with 48 percent, that the popular vote for the House splits about evenly between the two parties, each with either 49 or 48 percent, etc. etc. Barone calls his NSL "The 49 Percent Nation," though I tend to think the phrase "50/50 Nation," used elsewhere, is more instantly accessible.

Barone's big 50/50 essay, which appeared in the *National Journal* of June 9, 2001—in other words, before 9/11—subtly describes how a split along religious and urban/rural lines led to the current deadlock. Barone holds out hope, however, that the deadlock will be broken in Bush's favor for reasons of demography (the "Americans of the Bush nation tend to have more children . . . and the communities of the Bush nation tend to welcome growth") and substance (voters will like Bush's plans on education and Social Security that "provide citizens with more choice [and] rely less on centralized authority").

But why should we expect the deadlock to be broken at all? Think of it in . . . well, cheap Darwinian terms. Imagine that we have a two-party system, and each party is a collection of status-seeking individuals looking for power by winning a greater "market share" of the vote. Imagine that they each have their ideological principles—one is more to the left, one more to the right—but these principles are quite flexible in the face of imminent or repeated failure at the polls. Over time, as each party crafts its message to maximize its appeal—and adjusts its message after each election to regain any lost share of the votes —*wouldn't one expect the system to reach a roughly 50/50 equilibrium, in which every election was a cliffhanger?*

Surely, you say, this 50/50 equilibrium couldn't last. Wouldn't demographic shifts push one party into the lead? Yes, but only temporarily. Suppose, as Barone argues, that more families are moving from the pro-Gore cities to the pro-Bush rural areas. Also assume, somewhat implausibly, that, rather than making these counties more liberal, these yuppie migrants are assimilated into the rural, God-fearing, gun-loving, anti-abortion red-state culture. Does that mean Republicans will gain a permanent edge? No. It means Democrats will have to adjust to become more pro-gun and anti-abortion, which is exactly what is happening in elections like the current Arkansas Senate race. Likewise, if the growth of the Hispanic vote currently favors Democrats, Republicans can be expected to counter with elaborate and not-very-principled efforts to appeal to Hispanics. That, too, is exactly what's happening.

Even large substantive trends can be fairly easily countered. I'm not convinced by Barone's wishful thinking regarding the pro-GOP tie-breaking power of "individual investment accounts" or Medicare "choice." But I've often argued myself that the need for some sort of universal health coverage offers a similar tie-breaking advantage to the Democrats—and maybe I was just as wrong about that. What's to stop Republicans, if a wave of support for a rationalized, secure national insurance system materializes, from shifting to accommodate it? It won't be because Republicans are too tied to corporate interests. Corporations are pragmatic. Once they see that the demand for universal health insurance is unstoppable, they'll adjust and figure out how to maximize profits within that constraint.

In other words, our politics may drift either to the left or to the right. (I still expect them to drift to the left, thanks to the health-care issue.) But this ideological drift *won't translate into political dominance by one party or the other.* Both parties will simply move toward the new popular center of gravity, as poll-driven pols are wont to do. We'll still have a tie between Coke and Pepsi—between the more-left party and the more-right party.

What about external shocks or epochal domestic events? Couldn't they alter the 50/50 equilibrium? Sure. It took a long time after the Civil War for Southern conservatives to even consider switching to the Republicans. But it happened. We've just had about as big an external shock as can be imagined—the 9/11 attacks, which profoundly altered our idea of our place in the world. But 9/11 is an argument *for* the permanence of the current stalemate, not an argument against it. After all, 9/11 was a year ago, and we're still stuck at 50/50! If the nation can endure that sort of external shock and still not be jogged out of its political deadlock, it's frightening to imagine what it might take to disrupt the stalemate. Invasion by an overwhelming force of space aliens who demand repeal of the Davis-Bacon Act or the Second Amendment—something along those lines might force one party or the other out of contention. Anything short of that seems insufficient, however.

Viewed in this light, the important developments of the past few decades have been, not the substantive and demographic changes that more or less *accidentally* combined to produce the *current* deadlock (just as they produced one in the late 1880s), but the changes that made American politics more like the cheap, cynical, flexible two-player Darwinian system that might *inevitably* tend toward a *permanent* deadlock. Those changes include:

A. The *convergence of both parties' ideologies*. Democrats and Republicans were never as far apart, ideologically, as parties in Europe, where socialism was until recently a live alternative. But now our parties are *really* not far apart. Both endorse a form of democratic market capitalism. Both endorse a fairly robust welfare state. The differences are at the far margins. As in faculty politics, these relatively small stakes make for vicious fights. But they also mean that adjustments don't really involve abandoning grand principles—principles like, say, government ownership of the means of production. Instead, adjustment means agreeing to a prescription drug benefit *within* the existing Medicare system instead of outside it. This ideological compression means adjustments are easier—and each party has more flexibility to pursue its 50 percent market share.

B. The *withering away of interest groups* that inhibit party flexibility. For the Democrats, unions inhibit ideological adjustment in a way that pragmatic corporations don't—one reason Clinton's successful realignment of the Democrats as a free-trade, business-friendly, welfare-reform party hasn't "taken." But the unions are withering away, increasing the Democrats' flexibility. The declining power of the Christian Right has a similar freeing-up effect on the Republicans.

C. The *dimming of historic memories* that tie large segments of the population to one party or the other. Southern whites, as mentioned, took decades to get over their post-Civil War allergy to Republicans. Similarly, as Barone documents, African-Americans and Jews are still loyal to Democrats. But, eventually, time will dilute those loyalties too. California's Hispanics may even forget Pete Wilson!

The "50/50 Forever" theory suggests a possible near-future that's both exciting and depressing—exciting because close races are exciting; depressing because close races, as we learned in 2000, tend to end in so much acrimony, litigation, and uncertainty that they undermine democratic legitimacy.

I'm not sure I even buy the theory myself. Maybe Barone could rip it apart. But it's plausible enough that I'm not counting on being able to take a vacation on Nov. 6. Or the day after Election Day in 2004 and 2008. One, two, many Floridas—that's the American prospect. We'd better get used to it.

2003

WE JOINED FORCES with two media powerhouses in 2003. In May, *Slate* began distributing Garry Trudeau's *Doonesbury* strip on the Web, along with *Doonesbury*'s archives, special polls, and contests. In the summer, *Slate* and National Public Radio began producing *Day to Day*, an hour-long midday news magazine. *Day to Day* became the fastest-growing show in NPR's history, airing on more than 100 stations by year's end. Seth Stevenson took over the "Ad Report Card" column from Rob Walker. Emily Yoffe began writing her hilarious, masochistic "Human Guinea Pig" column. We won the National Magazine Award for General Excellence Online, the first time a Web-only publication had nabbed the prize.

Motherhood Lost

A Dialogue on Miscarriage.

BY EMILY BAZELON AND DAHLIA LITHWICK

Jan. 22, 2003

Dear Dahlia,

Mis-carry: The word itself creeps with guilty error, as if you've carelessly dropped something you were meant to hold. In the 14th week of my pregnancy, my midwife couldn't detect a fetal heartbeat at a routine checkup and sent me for an ultrasound. I knew from the technician's expression before she said a word. I asked to see the baby—I'm pretty sure I used that word, since to me that's what it was. The technician said gently that, well, there were two. In the space of a breath I'd gone from buoyantly carrying the beginnings of one child to heavily bearing the endings of twins.

I couldn't quite believe my midwife when she said it wasn't my fault. I kept replaying what I'd said a week or two earlier when a friend asked me whether I might be carrying twins. "God, I hope not," I'd said, daunted by the challenge of caring for one new child. "What if they knew?" I whispered to my husband. "What if they felt like I didn't want them?" I know, I know, it's crazy. But it still troubles me. In the days after I miscarried, I worried over what had happened to my babies' souls—even though I couldn't tell you exactly what I think souls are.

I wonder about the common assumption that it's better, or in better taste, to grieve for the loss of a pregnancy in private. Have the politics of reproduction made feminists lose sight of the effect a miscarriage has on many women's psyches? Pro-choice women have trained themselves to think that life begins at viability; when we miscarry, we're disturbed to find ourselves mourning a child rather than a mass of developing cells.

Between 20 percent and 25 percent of pregnancies end in miscarriage, 3 percent of them after 16 weeks. That's a lot of awkward hush. Shouldn't we be talking openly about this much more often so that we're better prepared for the grief when it hits us?

Yours,
Emily

Dear Emily,

I miscarried at 12 weeks last winter, just after we'd announced the news to anything with a pulse on this planet. Like you, I couldn't help blaming myself. I think ours is a generation of women who are uniquely captive to the illusion of control: If you study for the test, you do well. If you drink your V–8, the baby will be fine. There are no rituals, no expectations, no Hallmark cards for miscarriage—as there are in abundance for illness, death, or the loss of a pet. "My Own Private Elba," I called it, as I lay in bed after my D and C, wondering why I was being doubly punished: first by the death of this baby we already loved so desperately, then by all the people working so hard to erase all traces of it.

After the miscarriage, I spent seven months in the liminal space of not-motherhood. I was nearly debilitated by the No. 1 symptom of life after miscarriage: blinding jealousy of anyone pregnant, recently delivered, or who appeared to be ovulating. (Don't ask how I could tell who was ovulating. Miscarriage-related insanity is a terrifying thing.) A friend who'd miscarried warned me candidly that you really never are quite OK until you get pregnant again, and, at least in my case, she was right. Which probably answers your question about whether my sense of self was assaulted. My sense of self was flattened. I became unrecognizable to me.

As I write to you, my No. 2 baby is doing that garbage-can lid scene from Stomp against my rib cage. And I can't help but wonder: Could you and I have written even one line of this dialogue if we hadn't managed to become pregnant again? I wrote letters to both my babies through each pregnancy. The first book is jolly and silly and ends abruptly. The second is spare and fearful and cautious. I don't think you ever go back.

Best,
Dahlia

Dear Dahlia,

I have one small, unprofound suggestion for the medical profession. Until doctors have better scientific tools at their disposal, they should use the basic tool they do have: human kindness. The rest of us can also try to pick up on the cues that women give when they've recently lost a pregnancy or suffered a fertility disappointment. I didn't equate my miscarriage with a death—the longing I felt for my not-to-be-born babies, however real, wasn't like missing someone I'd known and loved. But I took comfort from this line in the Book of Ruth: "I went out full, but empty has God returned me." Naomi says that to the women of Bethlehem when she returns to their city after a long absence. She's not talking about a miscarriage: She has lost her husband and two grown sons. But she could be.

In fact, the image of being "returned empty" speaks to a lot of life's worst moments, I think. It means beginning again the hard work of filling ourselves up, in whatever way we can. You and I are blessed to be filling again with babies. And despite our previous losses, with hope.

Dahlia, I wish for you all the joys of motherhood—the salt with the honey, the vinegar with the wine. Thank you for writing to me.

Yours,
Emily

Dear Emily,

One of the wisest things said to me about pregnancy loss came from a rabbi. He talked to me for a very long time about how this loss would change the way Aaron and I viewed fertility and pregnancy and children forever. He talked about a newfound reverence we would feel, and that has proved true. There isn't much of the levity and fearlessness left—the goofiness that marked our first pregnancy. But it's been replaced by something very sweet and—as you put it—full. I don't feel entitled to this baby, but I do feel blessed by it.

In the days after my loss, my wonderful cousin called from Paris to tell me that she had dreamt that night of our baby and that she was now certain that there had been some purpose to its short life. And my agent—from whom I just don't expect sentimentality—told me shortly after, that this was one lucky little baby to have chosen us for parents, even for just a few weeks. I don't know why such comments healed us as much as they did. Maybe because it spoke to the possibility of something eternal, of baby souls, or some purpose beyond what felt at the time to be simply pain without bottom.

I thank you so much, Emily, for your kind wishes. You know that with the birth of a healthy baby comes a lifetime of yet more fear and worry—about electrical sockets and defective car seats and (heaven help us) those Sigma Chi keg sucks of 2020. Still, I wish you some small amount of peace and great buckets of unvarnished joy in the coming weeks and years. And I thank you for carving out, in this tiny corner of cyberspace, a place to share sad secrets.

Yours,
Dahlia

Marching Orders

Goose-stepping, the dance craze of tyrants.

BY MARK SCHEFFLER

Wednesday, Jan. 29, 2003

MUCH OF THE TV FOOTAGE used these days to shed light on the bizarre, hermetically sealed regime of North Korea features its massive army parading through the streets of Pyongyang in extremely tightknit, highly synchronized marching formations. A prominent and chilling feature of these marches is the goose-step, in which thousands and thousands of troops kick their legs up like belligerent, robotic Rockettes. North Korean dictator Kim Jong-il ("Dear Leader") is just the latest in a long line of vicious rulers whose soldiers have stepped the goose. Where and when did the goose-step originate, and why has it been so common among recent history's most sadistic tyrants?

Norman Davies, author of *Europe: A History*, traces the origins of the march back to the Prussian army in the 17th century. The body language of goose-stepping, he wrote, transmitted a clear set of messages. To Prussia's generals, it said that the discipline and athleticism of their men would withstand all orders, no matter how painful or ludicrous. To Prussian civilians, it said that all insubordination would be ruthlessly crushed. To Prussia's enemies it said that the Prussian army was not made up just of lads in uniform, but regimented supermen. To the world at large, it announced that Prussia was not just strong, but arrogant.

The marching mode proved so effective that it became a prime feature of German and Prussian parades well into the 20th century. It was also adopted by the Russian army and later, after the Bolshevik Revolution in 1917, by the Red Army. Even after the Soviet Union's collapse in 1991, honor guards could still be seen goose-stepping around Lenin's tomb in Moscow. But for many people the step is most closely associated with the Nazis. Hitler believed that tighter bonds of solidarity could be achieved through gestures that demonstrated loyalty in a physical sense (the stiff-armed salute falls into this category, too).

George Orwell, who knew totalitarianism when he saw it, succinctly articulated the menacing nature of the goose-step in his wartime essay "The Lion and the Unicorn: Socialism and the English Genius" (1941). Sitting in Britain, while "highly civilized human beings are flying overhead, trying to kill me," he wrote:

> One rapid but fairly sure guide to the social atmosphere of a country is the parade-step of its army. . . . The goose-step, for instance, is one of the most horrible sights in the world, far more terrifying than a dive-bomber. It is simply an affirmation of naked power; contained in it, quite consciously and intentionally, is the vision of a boot crashing down on a face. Its ugliness is part of its essence, for what it is saying is, "Yes, I am ugly, and you daren't laugh at me." . . . Beyond a certain point, military display is only possible in countries where the common people dare not laugh at the army.

North of the 38th parallel, Kim's vainglorious propaganda parades are clearly designed to evoke Hitler's gargantuan Nuremberg rallies of the 1920s and 1930s. North Korea's sinister, macro-scaled, Vegas-on-acid shows—which involve incredibly choreographed mass games, acrobatic displays, and the aforementioned goose-stepping troops—top even the Nazis' efforts to visually convey the toxic grandeur of mass ideology.

Goose-stepping is the ultimate tactical anachronism—yet another sign that Kim is stuck in the delusional global-domination schemes of yesteryear. Though he clearly intends his marches to be shows of prowess (and though he claims to have the nuclear weapons to back it up), the whole notion of conveying military might by way of a rigid march seems almost quaint in a world where smart weapons, special operations units, and state-of-the-art air forces are steadily supplanting large-scale ground forces.

And though the association between the goose-step and authoritarian regimes is permanently sealed in the collective cultural consciousness, the march today is mostly viewed as an obsolescent remnant of a maniacal past. "Since World War II," writes William McNeill, author of *Keeping Together in Time: Dance and Drill in Human History*, "widespread revulsion against everything associated with the Nazis has discredited mass muscular manifestations of political attachments." Except in North Korea, apparently.

Where there isn't revulsion, there's humor. Years of sarcastic derision—both in the popular culture at large and by comedians such as Mel Brooks and ex-Monty Python cast member John Cleese—have ultimately relegated the goose-step to the realm of the ridiculous. In his short-lived but still beloved mid-1970s British sitcom *Fawlty Towers*, Cleese played Basil Fawlty, proprietor of a hotel where, in one classic episode, a group of Germans has come to stay. "Don't mention the war!" becomes Fawlty's ruling mantra as he tries to accommodate his guests. But of course he can't do anything *but* mention it, and at one point even finds himself goose-stepping around the dining room, turning a method of propaganda into a punch line.

Daddy Gets His Brain Back

What spilled out when I cracked my head open.

BY MICHAEL LEWIS

April 3, 2003

WHEN I CAME TO, the first thing I noticed was that wherever I was I had never been there before. Flat on my back, an oxygen mask on my face, I looked up and saw a silver wall, some flashing lights, and a man in a dark blue jumpsuit, his back to me. The mask made it hard to call out. I tried to raise my arm but couldn't. My arms and my legs were strapped down. My head, too. My gaze was directed straight down at my bare chest and the several wires taped to it. My stomach, I could see, was caked with blood. My khakis, too, were a dull dry red. On the left side of my face I felt the warm pleasant drip-drip-drip of even more blood. Apparently, I'd been in some sort of accident: What sort? I had no idea. But I knew what I was meant to do, from TV shows. I wiggled my fingers, then my toes.

The man in the blue suit turned around and removed my oxygen mask. I now realized, again from TV shows, that I was in the back of an Emergency Rescue Unit.

"I can feel my toes and fingers," I reported, knowingly.

"What's your name?" he asked.

I told him. But my voice sounded strange and manufactured, not my natural own.

"That's good, Michael," he said, and smiled, with a terrifying condescension. This man knew something I didn't: What?

"Do you know what day it is?" he asked.

"I never know what day it is," I said.

"He says he never knows what day it is," he said. Out of the corner of my eye I now spotted a second man in a dark blue emergency rescue uniform. And I remembered something: Tallulah on an ice rink. I remembered skating over to her awkwardly, like a man pumping a Razor Scooter up a steep hill, and then skating back to my own beginner's ice-skating lesson. I also remembered that they had lumped the beginners together with the intermediates. I remembered a short, squat Irishman showing me how to spin. I recalled thinking: If I try to spin I'll kill myself. But what I couldn't remember is why I was ice skating in the first place.

"Do you know your address?"

I did, just.

"Michael, you've been a little funny for some time."

I now recalled why I was ice skating. I was ice skating because Tallulah's mother had conceived that the three of us should do something meaningful together. Just one thing, to remind Tallulah that she was still special. We cast about for one meaningful thing and landed upon ice skating. Tabitha knew how to ice skate, Tallulah and I did not. Tallulah and I would learn together, side by side. In that briefly harmonious spirit we had set off, presumably not long before, for the local ice rink. What I couldn't remember is why we needed to remind Tallulah she was special.

"Where are my wife and daughter?" I asked.

"They're outside in your car," he said. "Do you remember what kind of car you have?"

I did, a bit more clearly. "How long have I been unconscious?" I asked. He didn't answer.

"What year is it?" he asked. A wave of irritation crashed over me. My head pounded. I didn't care what year it was, or what car I owned, or what I had eaten for dinner. I had bigger problems.

Such as: Who was I? Or rather: Was I the same me as I had been before whatever had happened to me happened to me? I needed for the man to sit down and listen to my life story, from the beginning, to see if it all felt familiar. Then I remembered something else: the book! Before I fell on my head, I was writing a book.

"Can you remember what year it is?" asked the emergency rescue worker.

I told him what year it was. This time the answer came to me easily.

"Do you remember falling?"

"No."

"What do you remember?"

"I remember that if I don't hand in my book in six weeks, I'm fucked."

He looked at me a little strangely. "OK," he said. "That's a start."

And so I told him about my literary problems. How thrilling it had been to be handed material so rich that I was limited only by my ability to handle it. How for months I'd been haunted by the sense that something would interfere with my finishing it. How, a few months earlier, with about a third of the book done, the manuscript had been stolen, along with everything I had ever written and not published, including 15 years of private journals and biographies I had kept of my two daughters. How a fancy truck with darkened windows—it was spotted by a neighbor—had rolled up alongside my office in broad daylight. How its occupants had picked the lock to my office, stolen my computer, all my backup files (from a separate room) and . . . nothing else. How they'd left no fingerprints, only a mystery.

Then, by some miracle of brain chemistry, I realized I sounded like a lunatic. "I know this sounds nuts," I said.

"This all happened?"

"This all happened," I said.

I explained to the man—who continued to stare calmly at me; how I do not know—how my wife had understood, or pretended to, that to compensate for the loss of my manuscript I needed to abandon most of my responsibilities as a father. How I had spent several months redefining what is meant by "the bare minimum"—how little a husband and father can do and still not trigger screams of terror when he walks in the front door. How I had a genius for it—and an excuse. A deadline. How Dixie didn't seem to mind—a father doesn't add much to the life of a 6-month-old child—but that Tallulah was different. The moment I put some space between me and her, she set about trying to drive her mother insane. She'd eat nothing but sugar, do nothing but watch cartoons. Denied sugar and cartoons, she took to calling her mother "you stupid lady." Told not to talk to her mother that way she'd spit, absurdly, "Jack-n-Ass!" Somewhere in there she got her first bad report card: Her teacher said that the normally ebullient Tallulah was now, occasionally, "morose." On my brief visits home I saw more truculence than moroseness, but that was as alarming, in its way. On Christmas morning, the moment she realized that she'd ripped open her last present she looked up and said, "Oh, shit." Fucking hell, I thought, where did that come from?

When I spoke that last line the ambulance man laughed. "He's OK," he shouted out to his colleague. They changed their plan to drive me to the trauma center to determine if I'd suffered brain damage. Instead, they would drive me to the emergency room, to have my head sewn up. Before they did they invited Tabitha into the truck to tell me that she and Tallulah would be right behind me, in the aforementioned car. My wife is at her best in such moments; she's as good in a crisis as ice on a burn. After making it clear to me that I was a wimp to be concerned about the state of my brain, she said that I didn't need to worry about Tallulah: She had hustled her off the ice before she could see her father lying in a lake of blood. It's astonishing how much trouble we take to prevent our children from seeing the world as it is. It's even more astonishing how, even when we might think we have earned a right to forget about our children for a moment, we haven't.

The ambulance started, the siren wailed. I remembered another thing: Tallulah needed to feel special because I had spent too much time working on my book. I was learning how to ice skate because someone had broken into my office and stolen my book. The theft of my computer memory had led to this assault on my own.

The emergency rescue worker was back to fiddling with one of the machines hooked up to me. He seemed to think we were done talking. We weren't. My mind wasn't right, and I knew it wasn't right. I thought: When you hit your head and you are never again the same, how do you know? If you have that thought does that mean you are the same? I didn't know; and I was certain the only way I would know was to talk and talk and talk. "I've got to finish this book soon," I said, a little desperately.

"Uh-huh," he said.

"No," I said, "I still have a problem."

"Yeah?"

"I can't remember what the book's about."

"Give me a moment," he said. He didn't even try to hide it: I was boring him. I was boring the emergency rescue worker! I must have fallen asleep, as the next thing I knew I was looking up not at an emergency rescue worker but a lady doctor. "I hear you're a writer," she said, making conversation. "What do you write about?"

She was soon sorry she had asked. For it was then I remembered: baseball! I was writing a book about baseball. As she stitched me back together I offered her, free of charge, my literary autobiography. Every last detail, including the various articles I'd written for this magazine. I told her, for instance, I'd written about the birth of my child, which had occurred in this very hospital. I told her I'd lived in Paris, and written a letter from Paris. It was then that she perked up.

"I read those!" she said.

Inexplicably, I feel better.

"I loved those descriptions of you with your son in the Luxembourg Gardens."

"That was Adam Gopnik," I said. For the first time I felt something I knew I had always felt. The surge of irritation, the choking back of indignation—oh the horror, oh, the smallness of existence—was so breathtakingly familiar that I couldn't deny it: I was still me.

Hello, Moon

Has America's low-rise obsession gone too far?

BY AMANDA FORTINI

Oct. 10, 2003

AMERICA IS IN THE THROES of a crack epidemic. Sitting in a booth with a friend at an excruciatingly hip restaurant in downtown Manhattan a few weeks ago, I glanced up to see a fleshy forest of crevices and multiple folds of skin and G-strings that three women in their late 20s were displaying for the world. It was then that I knew: This low-rider style has gone too far.

On the street, on television, even in the office, women of all ages and sizes are wearing tight, low-slung, butt-hugging jeans and pants that hit at, or often far below, the hip. The trend isn't new— it began around 1995 or so—but what is new are the unlovely depths to which the pants have now, as it were, sunk. The crotch-to-waist measurement, or rise, on a standard pair of jeans (the sort we haven't seen much of since the early 1990s) is somewhere between 10 and 12 inches. Early low-riders had a rise of about 7 inches. Over the past couple of years, the rise has dipped as low as 3 or 4 inches. Low-rise, it seems, has become synonymous with no-rise. Gasoline, a Brazilian company, has even created Down2There jeans, which feature a bungee cord that allows the wearer to lower her pants as she sees fit, as though adjusting a set of Venetian blinds.

Usually paired with midriff-baring shirts—even tops that aren't cropped can't cover the exposed expanse of abdominal flesh—the jeans have redefined our collective understanding of cleavage. Then there's the oft-visible G-string that, like a bra strap, creates strange fleshy bulges as it strains against the body. But there are worse bulges yet. These are the love handles that materialize on even the thinnest women—models and anorexics excepted—because the jeans hit a woman's body at its fleshiest point, below the hips, just above the buttocks. Of course, the feminist in me wants to applaud the insouciance with which women of all shapes now flaunt their imperfections, but the aesthete in me objects. This is a style that suits only 12-year-olds and celebrities who have the luxury of devoting entire afternoons to sculpting their obliques. For the rest of us, wearing these jeans is like putting our hips and buttocks on some humiliating reality show.

Yet the real problem with extremely low-riding pants is that they're impractical. Sitting is difficult: If you can't find a chair with a closed back, you have to tie a shirt around your waist—always highly attractive—or risk scandalizing the room. If you drop something, or need to tie your shoe, abandon all hope; bending over with dignity is next to impossible. You must perfect the art of squatting, back straight, head up, as though preparing to curtsy. Low-riders also tend to slide down, requiring the wearer to hitch them up repeatedly. In their way, low-rider jeans bear a creepy

similarity to Chinese foot-binding—they constrict a woman's action, rendering her ornamental. And like foot-binding, the jeans can have deleterious medical consequences. In 2001, the *Canadian Medical Association Journal* published a doctor's report stating that low-rise jeans can cause a condition called *meralgia paresthetica*, characterized by numbness or tingling in the thighs, by pinching a nerve located at the hip. Left untreated, the numbness can become permanent. Forget the question of style: This is a human rights issue.

So, how did we go so low? In America, the first low-rise jeans, called hip-huggers, became popular during the late 1960s, with the ascendance of the hippie counterculture and rock-and-roll. Icons of rock like Jimi Hendrix and Jim Morrison helped to popularize the style. In the 1970s, the pants went mainstream and became a staple of disco culture—people danced "The Hustle" in their Wrangler hip-huggers. In the late 1970s and early 1980s, waistlines moved higher as the culture, and fashion, grew increasingly conservative. Throughout the 1980s and into the 1990s, as more women entered the corporate workforce, the high waist continued to reign. Even Madonna, who arguably is responsible for today's exposed abdomens, didn't wear low-rise. In pictures of her from that decade, her hip bones are always covered by the waistband of her pants.

Then, around 1992, Alexander McQueen sent models down the runway in his shockingly low-slung "Bumsters." In 1995, Tom Ford's first (and wildly popular) collection for Gucci included his now-famous velvet hip-hugger suit, worn by Madonna, among other celebrities. By the mid-1960s, hip-huggers had infiltrated popular culture: Juliette Lewis wore a red pair in *Natural Born Killers* and Mark Wahlberg memorably peeled his off in *Boogie Nights*. But it took Britney, Christina, and Jennifer Lopez to bring the style, riding lower than ever, back into the mainstream over the past five years.

By the time a trend hits malls across America, high fashion is already calling it déclassé. *Vogue* declared low-rise pants over in May 2002, and that spring Tom Ford himself showed a trouser with a higher waist, wider legs, and dropped crotch. In spring 2003, several other designers showed high-waisted pants for fall. And in August 2003, Sarah Jessica Parker, an arbiter of style, told *Vogue* that she doesn't consider low-rise pants to be age-appropriate for a woman like herself.

It usually takes only a couple of months for a trend to go from the fashion magazines to the streets, and yet somehow, like the G-strings it popularized, this trend clings tenaciously on. It could be that the pants are a feminist statement, demanding as they do an ecumenical embrace of body type by wearer and viewer alike, and as such, women are loath to abandon them. It could be that the dark fissures and peek-a-boo undies they reveal are physical emblems of our confessional culture, the sartorial equivalent of the tell-all memoir. It could simply be that letting your belly hang free is comfortable. Or that women, buying these pants for lack of choice, have unwittingly created a false sense of demand. But the strongest argument for the persistence of the trend might simply be that we want to dress like the 1970s because we feel like we're starring in a reprise of that decade: Our economy is bad; we're entrenched in an occupation abroad; we mistrust our government at home.

I'm not advocating that we abandon this style in favor of Katharine Hepburn-type trousers belted just below the rib cage. As a fashionable friend recently said, low-slung trousers, with their rock-and-roll connotations, simply look "groovier." But *moderately* low-rise pants can be worn with style and class. There's a famous photograph of Jackie Kennedy Onassis, taken by the celebrity photographer Ron Galella in the early 1970s. In it, Jackie walks along a Manhattan street, holding only her keys. The wind musses her hair, and she looks over her shoulder at the camera. Perhaps surprisingly, she is wearing hip-huggers with a slim-fitting ribbed knit sweater. Not surprisingly, she bares no midriff. And a G-string is nowhere in sight.

Mime Is Money

My dreadful career as a street performer.

BY EMILY YOFFE

Oct. 30, 2003

As I PUT THE FINAL TOUCHES on my makeup for my debut as a Washington, D.C., street performer, the loving words of my husband echoed in my head: "You look like Bette Davis in *What Ever Happened to Baby Jane?*" He had a point. The combination of pigtails, crow's-feet, and rouged cheeks was so disturbing that I wondered if I could actually go through with standing on a downtown corner and doing my act. I desperately wanted a combination of Xanax for my anxiety and Zantac for my stomach acid. Now, there was a drug I could use: Xanzan—the pill for the talentless street performer.

Becoming a street performer was a challenge posed by a particularly cruel reader of previous installments of Human Guinea Pig—the column in which I explore odd, intriguing, but mostly odd corners of life. The challenge was compounded by the fact that I possess none of the skills that normally persuade passers-by to put money in a hat. I play no instruments, and my singing has been compared to the death throes of a moose. So, I decided to go for a more conceptual approach. I would dress up like a mechanical doll and tinkle various toy instruments; enchanted Washingtonians would throw money at my feet.

Washington isn't a great city for street performers. Checking out the scene with my husband the week before I started, we saw only two entertainers: a man singing Joni Mitchell songs and strumming guitar and another playing "Someone To Watch Over Me" on the saxophone. "My people!" I remarked.

"They're not your people," my husband replied. "They're good."

Undeterred, I went to a costume store and bought a powder-blue princess outfit, made of polyester and lint, complete with puffy sleeves, petticoat, and peplum. When I previewed it for my family, the response was not encouraging.

"This is catastrophic," said my husband, who literally shielded his eyes from the sight. "I am going to get a call from the day room at St. Elizabeth's saying I have to come sign you out."

"It's OK, Dad," said my 7-year-old daughter as she inspected me. "You can see she shaves her underarms. That means people will know she's not crazy."

I suggested that I could vastly increase the lucrativeness of this venture if I attached a large cardboard key to my back, then brought my daughter along and had her pretend to wind me up.

"You are keeping our daughter out of this," said my husband slowly. Violating this decree, I could see, would result in his starting a file labeled "custody battle."

I decided to make my first appearance at the downtown corner where *Slate* has its offices. For moral support, and protection in case the crowds became unruly, my editor David Plotz acted as my manager, standing a discreet distance away. He also conducted interviews about my work with the lawyers, lobbyists, regulators, and clerical workers who make up a D.C. lunchtime crowd.

The hardest part was making my entrance from the *Slate* building onto the street. This must be how people who want gender reassignment must feel the first time they go out in public as a member of the opposite sex, I thought. Not making eye contact, I walked to the corner of 18th and M Streets and put down a straw hat—seeded with $1.35 borrowed from David. I laid my props next to me: tambourine, maracas, plastic pan flute, and a bag of beads with smiley faces embossed on them that I planned to give as gifts to anyone who dropped money in my hat. I put a frozen smile on my face, picked up the maracas, and stiffly started shaking them.

Washingtonians are not easily enchanted. These are people who are grimly important; the lanyards around their necks holding their IDs announce just how important they are. They were determined to ignore me. About a quarter walked by without acknowledgment. The other three-quarters lost a visible struggle with their facial muscles and smiled. But even the smilers refused to stop at the beckoning of my maracas and throw some coins into my hat.

David, meanwhile, was conducting his interviews. The reaction, I later heard on the tape, fell into two schools. My fans: "It's silly and fantastic." "D.C.'s not that wacky and this is nice and wacky." "This is very interesting. Is she a mechanical doll?" And my detractors: "Is she on something?" "She's stiff. She's got no dance, no performance." "I keep looking back at her to try to say something good, but sorry." "I thought she was possibly a little loony." Sure, everyone's a critic. These are the people who would have told the young Meryl Streep to forget that acting nonsense and go to law school.

Hoping to loosen people's wallets with a change of instruments, I switched from my maracas to a plastic pan flute. But playing it turned out to be exhausting and dangerous. After a few minutes of hard blowing, David came over to remark, "Do you know your nose is bleeding?" But I wasn't about to let something like a possible aneurysm stop me, although I realized the trickle of blood was probably depressing the crowd and my income. I made a sad clown face and mopped myself up.

Gratifyingly, at one point a high-school classmate of mine, whom I had seen two nights before at an event at the school both our children attend, walked right past me without recognition. I had David bring him over, but when he finally realized who I was, even after I explained what I was doing, he seemed deeply disturbed and scurried away. (The next day, when we were picking up our kids at school, his wife said, "I understand you're now working downtown as a mime.")

My biggest financial score came from a man who watched me from his parked car for a few minutes then beckoned me over. He asked me if I could speak, hear, and write, but I just smiled and shook my maracas. He took out a business card, wrote his home phone number on it, and handed it to me with $2. Either he thought I had promise or he was into demented chicks.

As I was about to pack up after 90 minutes of entertaining (total take: $4.15), a homeless man started to approach. I was worried he was going to steal my money. I watched as he moved in, then stepped away, then moved closer. I caught his eye, smiled, and shook my maracas. He smiled back at me and winked. *No lanyards for us*, our looks said.

Having not even made the equivalent of the minimum wage, I was determined to find a more congenial crowd. A couple of days later, I decided to take the Metro downtown and perform in front of the Smithsonian's National Museum of Natural History. Again my husband expressed deep misgivings.

"You can't ride the Metro in that outfit," he said. "You're going to be arrested." I assured him that though Washington was a town of stiffs, it was not yet run by Mullah Omar.

I set up in front of the museum next to one of the concrete barriers. Immediately two security guards walked by me. I suddenly wondered, is it legal to perform as a mechanical doll on federal property? I smiled, blew my flute, and saluted them frenetically. They returned the salute and walked on. Older tourists gave me a wide berth, obviously having been warned not to make contact with any of D.C.'s depraved citizens. But the kids loved me, dropping coins in my hat as they stared in disbelief. One toddler was so taken with me that he tried to steal my act by scooping up all my instruments and running off with them. A couple of young women deposited a dollar, then one put her arm around me while the other snapped our picture.

I felt looser and more in command of my act. To people talking on cell phones, I would make a yackety-yak motion with my hand. For a woman with magenta hair, I pointed at her head and gave her a thumbs-up. I ran after a girl with a smiley-face sweatshirt and handed her one of my smiley-face beads. In 45 minutes I made $6.50.

Then a huge bus slowly pulled up in front of the museum. I got so excited—I could harass each tourist into dropping money into my hat as they disembarked. I started jumping up and down and waving wildly at the bus. It stopped in front of me, the doors opened, and the bus driver gave me a long look. Then she leaned toward me and said, with a note of panic in her voice, "Are you our tour guide?"

I sadly shook my head. I realized at that moment that I was not a true performer. A true performer would have nodded yes and led the crowd into the museum. Now, that would have been art.

Bobos in Purgatory

Can you hate Bush but love his tax cuts?

BY DANIEL GROSS

Nov. 13, 2003

Driving around a leafy Fairfield County, Conn., town the other day, I came upon a not uncommon sight. A woman sat behind the wheel of a midnight blue BMW so brand new that the gummy residue of the dealer's sticker was still visible on the window; in the back seat, a pile of Howard Dean yard signs spilled onto the floor.

Intent on divining a trend, I mounted a search for other such juxtapositions of conspicuous consumer spending and conspicuous anti-Bush sentiment. At both the macro and micro levels, there's plenty of evidence that well-off liberals are using their increased disposable income—much of which can be attributed to the Bush tax cuts—to sate their desires for luxury goods *and* for political revenge. This odd condition of consumerist self-indulgence and political indignation—fueled by the same source—has reached epidemic proportions in areas where high-income Democrats tend to congregate. Many people I know are finding themselves simultaneously coping with a sense of greater well-being and a niggling sense of unease when they stop to consider to whom they owe their good fortune.

For lack of a better name, you could call it *Bushenfreude*.

We've all seen the symptoms. A table of four raging over Bush's Iraq policy while sampling the $58 tasting menu at Virot, an expensive new bistro on the Upper West Side. A middle-aged man clucking over the deficit while fondling home furnishings at Restoration Hardware. The thirtysomething lawyer seething over the neutering of the Environment Protection Agency with one side of her brain, while weighing that classic conundrum—Cape Cod or Tuscany next summer?—with the other side.

Bushenfreude began in the summer of 2001, when the first Bush tax-cut rebates were sent. Back then it was easy to deal with those one-time windfalls if you resented the source. You could send the check back, or sign it over to People for the American Way. Refusing to spend it—and hence refusing to stimulate the economy— was a gratifying protest against Bush's risky skewed-to-the-wealthy tax scheme. Yet in the aftermath of Sept. 11—particularly in New York—promptly spending any disposable cash seemed to be the right thing for the right-thinking to do.

This year's tax cuts—which brought a fresh round of rebates, speeded up the already enacted marginal rate reductions and cut taxes on capital gains and dividends—gave liberal beneficiaries yet more cause to squirm. Many higher-income families weren't eligible for the rebates, so it was harder for them to dispose of them symbolically.

Instead, over the past several months, the tax cuts have quietly wormed their way into our financial lives. Many people won't calculate the taxes they owe on dividends until next spring, for example. Psychologically, it's nice to regard today's larger paycheck as the consequence of a raise you so richly deserve but that your employer has been too cheap to actually give you.

As an economic strategy, the tax cuts have plainly worked. People—particularly high-income people—are feeling wealthier and are buying more goods and services. But it's a questionable political strategy. Bush's tax cuts don't seem to have converted many Democrats, particularly the high-income Democrats who fuel his opponents' campaigns. Wealthy Democrats generally would prefer to pay less taxes rather than more, but they don't wake up each morning raging at the government's confiscation of their income. Their dander is far more easily aroused by attempts to stock the bench with right-wing ideologues, or by Dick Cheney's insistence on linking Saddam Hussein to 9/11, or by the general hash the president has made of trade and fiscal policy.

In fact, many wealthy Democrats are just getting angrier. Groups like the Center for American Progress have tapped into the growing pool of Bush-hostile capital. Billionaire trader George Soros, perhaps one of the single largest beneficiaries of the Bush tax cuts, has made defeating President Bush "the central focus of my life." He has contributed at least $15 million to anti-Bush groups. The tax cuts have also made more money available for less-wealthy (but just as angry) liberals to buy best-selling anti-Bush screeds like *Big Lies*, *Lies and the Lying Liars Who Tell Them*, or *The Great Unraveling*. And those who have been so amply rewarded for Bush-bashing—that's you, Joe Conason and Al Franken and Paul Krugman—will get to keep a much bigger chunk of their royalty payments.

Bushenfreude is only likely to intensify if the economy continues to recover. So we had all better learn to cope and start dispelling the stigma surrounding the dread condition. In my darker moments, when I contemplate twin Excel files showing the ever-more imminent bankrupting of Social Security and my projected tax payments for 2003, I, too suffer from a mild case of the malady. But rather than buy David Corn's *Lies of George W. Bush* or make a political contribution, I calculate how much I'm saving in taxes. Then I put a fraction of that sum in a retirement plan. After all, the fiscal recklessness of the past few years means I'm highly unlikely to get the Social Security benefits to which I'm theoretically entitled. I also put a fraction of that sum in an account for my kids, who will have to foot the bill for this party when they grow up. And then—and only then—do I go to Dean & DeLuca and search for that perfect manchego.

2004

WE STARTED CONSIDERING an exit strategy from Microsoft. Though Microsoft had always supported *Slate* and respected its editorial independence, we were finding it hard to develop the business side of the magazine. Microsoft, which at one point in the late 1990s was publishing several dozen content sites, had shut them all down except *Slate* and its MSNBC joint venture, and we began to feel we would be better off at a media company. So, in the middle of the year, Editor Jacob Weisberg and Microsoft executives began exploring the possibility of selling *Slate*. The Washington Post Company emerged as the most suitable buyer, and in the fall, Microsoft struck a deal to sell *Slate* to the *Post*.

In the meantime, we were busy with the presidential election. Our "Swingers" series took *Slate* reporters to every tossup state in the campaign. The "Election Scorecard," William Saletan's tool to analyze state polls, proved one of our most popular features ever, as readers frantically crunched and recrunched the data to see whether Bush or Kerry had the edge. And Henry Blodget returned from his Internet-era notoriety to cover the Martha Stewart trial for us.

Full Disclosure

Dispatches from the Martha Stewart trial.

BY HENRY BLODGET

Jan. 7, 2004

Given the current state of my reputation, along with the other considerations laid out below, readers may want to take everything I say with a grain of salt. There are literally dozens of reasons why my observations about these proceedings might be biased.

First, although I don't want to insult Martha Stewart by drawing comparisons—my "story" is, at its most mythical, only a faint echo of hers—there are obviously parallels. Like Stewart, I was, for a while, bathed in the golden glow of prosperity, a symbol of American capitalism and the optimism of the Internet Age, and, now, like Stewart, in the harsh light of the bust, I am seen by some as a symbol of "excess," a "fallen star," a "disgrace." Like Stewart, I have been charged with securities fraud. Like Stewart, I have been the object of adulatory and venomous press coverage. Like Stewart, I have had the bizarre experience of watching legions of people I have never met come to trust me, look to me for guidance, regard me as a "guru," and then decide that I am, in fact, a scumbag.

About a year ago, in connection with a wide-ranging investigation into conflicts of interest between the research and investment banking divisions of Wall Street brokerage firms, I was accused of civil securities fraud. One of the agencies that charged me, the Securities and Exchange Commission, has also filed a civil insider-trading charge against Martha Stewart. In my case, the SEC alleged that, among other things, my research team and I made some statements in e-mails that were inconsistent with our published research reports. Along with other defendants, I settled the charge without admitting or denying the allegations, agreed to pay a fine and "disgorgement" totaling $4 million, and agreed to a permanent prohibition against working in the securities industry.

One of my former employers, Merrill Lynch, is also a former employer of Martha Stewart's stockbroker, co-defendant, and alleged co-conspirator, Peter Bacanovic. I don't know Bacanovic, but some of my former colleagues do. Furthermore, two of Martha Stewart's lawyers, Bob Morvillo and Jack Tigue, represented Merrill in connection with the research proceedings described above. I still have professional relationships with Merrill, Morvillo, and Tigue. I also still have professional relationships and/or agreements with parties on the regulator-prosecutor side of the aisle.

Next, I have pre-existing impressions of Martha Stewart that are, on balance, positive. For one thing, I admire her decision to fight the charges. Given how much she has lost already—her job, her reputation, her board seats, two years of her life (and counting), and some $400 million of her net worth—she must have been tempted to settle, especially given the massive amount of time, effort, money, stress, and luck that will be required for her to achieve even the Pyrrhic vindication of an acquittal. (In this country, we can indeed get "our day in court"—and this alone is cause to wave the flag around—but it is no mystery why people sometimes plead guilty to crimes they didn't commit.)

I don't know Martha Stewart personally, but I have met her on two occasions. The first was in a business meeting. I sat next to her, and halfway through the meeting, she turned to me and kindly offered to "marry me off." The second was a few years later, when I was already under investigation but before she was. My wife (I had managed to marry myself off, eventually) and I were carrying our 3-month-old daughter out of a New York restaurant just as Martha and her daughter were walking in. I would like to say that my daughter aced this first brush with celebrity by smiling sweetly or cooing a proto-hello, but she didn't. Instead, she barfed on Martha's shoes. Given that even a person of average temperament might have found this annoying, let alone someone with a reputation for being, well, impatient, I was grateful for the good humor that Martha displayed (she even helped clean up the mess). I should add that I find Martha Stewart not only charming but physically attractive. Studies have shown that human beings tend to be favorably disposed toward people they find charming and attractive.

Lastly, I admire Martha Stewart's business accomplishments, especially her having built a high-quality company that now employs more than 500 people. After watching thousands of smart, talented entrepreneurs try to do this and fail, I have a sense of how hard it is. I consider it so hard, in fact, that I find many of the common jabs at Martha ("arrogant," "control freak," "workaholic," "demanding," "bitch") so petty as to border on the absurd. Anyone who can manage the pressures, responsibilities, and hassles of running a major corporation without occasionally evoking such descriptions should be beatified. Lest this make it sound as though I admire all business success and anyone who achieves it, I don't. On the contrary, in my career, I have met plenty of conceited, incompetent (though well-compensated), rude, selfish, and unethical sleazebags, many of whom I would be thrilled to see get a legal and moral comeuppance. I am not sure that the density of such people is much greater in business than it is in other professions, though.

Martha Stewart sits at the same intersection of ethics, law, celebrity, politics, the stock market, and post-crash *schadenfreude* as I once did, and I am writing about her, in part, because I feel a sense of empathy, and, in part, because I believe (or at least hope) that my experiences give me insight into her situation. I believe that Stewart should be treated as innocent until proven guilty (and also that many observers are not treating her this way). But I also believe that lying to investigators and shareholders is and should be a crime, and that, if Stewart did this, she should have to take responsibility for it. In covering her case, I will try my best to evaluate the evidence in a fair-minded way.

This is the last of Henry Blodget's dispatches from the Martha Stewart trial. It was filed on March 5, 2004, a couple of hours after she was convicted:

I thought it would be close; it wasn't. I thought there was reasonable doubt; there wasn't. I thought if I were wrong, the aftermath would be sad; it was.

Just after lunch on Friday afternoon, a buzz developed outside the courtroom. First, the rumor was that there was another "note." Then that there was "news." Then, when we had all settled on our benches and observed that the head of the U.S. attorney's office and the husbands and/or wives of several of the players had begun to appear, the rumor was that there was a verdict.

As the jury filed in, not a single juror glanced in Stewart's direction. An experienced trial observer had just explained to me that if the jurors smiled at Stewart as they walked in, she would be acquitted, so this was the first clue. As Judge Cedarbaum read the verdict, Martha Stewart did not so much as flinch.

Conspiracy: guilty.

False statements: guilty.

False statements: guilty.

Obstruction of an agency proceeding: guilty.

These words hit the courtroom like punches; I can't imagine how hard they must have hit her. Seconds later, in the benches behind Stewart, her daughter, Alexis, was weeping, and two members of her media team were in tears. Stewart's own expression never changed.

Peter Bacanovic, too, remained calm as he learned that he had been convicted of conspiracy, making false statements, obstruction, and perjury (but not, interestingly, of forging the "@60" mark on the allegedly altered worksheet). As with Stewart, this news hit his family and counsel hard.

An hour later, one of the jurors, Chappelle Hartridge, explained that the jury had believed Douglas Faneuil and found Ann Armstrong's testimony about Stewart temporarily changing the Dec. 27 phone message particularly damning (one of the many ironies of the story, given that this act wasn't charged as a crime). Hartridge reportedly remarked that the verdict "was a victory for the little guy who loses money in the market because of this kind of transaction. It sends a message to bigwigs in corporations they have to abide by the law. No one is above the law." This was ironic because, although this case has always been trumpeted as a symbol of fat-cat insiders fleecing the "little guy," it didn't cost anyone but Martha Stewart, Peter Bacanovic, and the government a dime (anyone, that is, except the shareholders of Martha Stewart Living Omnimedia, who lost $250 million Friday afternoon).

Little guys get "secret tips," too, of course. And little guys also are rude to assistants and conspire, obstruct justice, and lie to the feds. But from the moment news of Stewart's ImClone sale was leaked, at the height of the post-crash, post-Enron, post-Tyco rage, the themes and morals of this case have remained the same: Martha Stewart, one of the most visible symbols of the golden 1990s, was now a symbol of something else: corporate excess and greed (which, in many other cases, did ream little guys). Argue what you will about the legality of Stewart's trade, it was a personal act, not a professional one, and no one was swindled by it. No "bigwigs in corporations" learned not to treat shareholders like dupes. No one learned anything other than that, in the current climate, if you happen to be a high-profile business executive, your personal and professional behavior had better be exemplary, because you have a gigantic bull's-eye on the back of your head. That—and this: When the phone rings and there is a government investigator on the other end, you've already made your mistake (even if, in your mind, you didn't do anything wrong). No matter how much of a bigwig you are, the phone call has just rendered you a little guy. So it's time to brush up on words like "deference" and "respect" and go in, be forthright, and kiss the ring.

After Stewart had descended the steps of the courthouse (to a cheer) and slipped into an SUV, she posted a statement on her Web site thanking her friends, family, and supporters, reiterating her faith in the system, and announcing her intention to appeal. For a brief period, her statement also said that she took comfort from knowing that she had done nothing wrong. Then, without fanfare, this assertion disappeared.

The New Vanity Press Moguls

Welcome, Philip Anschutz!
Bruce Wasserstein! Roger Hertog!

BY JACK SHAFER

Feb. 27, 2004

WE IN THE JOURNALISM RACKET would like to welcome Colorado billionaire **Philip Anschutz** to our inner sanctum of power and influence. Anschutz, the primary owner of Qwest Communications who owns entertainment properties, real estate, and chunks of the Los Angeles Lakers and Los Angeles Kings, just paid $20 million for the company that owns the *San Francisco Examiner*. It sounds like a lot of money to pay for the doomed No. 2 paper in a market dominated by the *San Francisco Chronicle*, but it's a smaller percentage of Anschutz's net worth ($5.2 billion) than $119 was of my net worth ($4,100) when I invested that sum in a Smith Corona manual typewriter to gain entry to the same business 30 years ago. Welcome, Philip!

And a friendly howdy to **Bruce Wasserstein**, mergers and acquisitions wizard and head of Lazard, who needs no introduction. Wasserstein joined the journalism cult while in college, working on the *Michigan Daily*, and even slummed at *Forbes* one summer while pursuing his MBA and law degree at Harvard. Bruce returned to his first love in the late 1990s after making Wall Street millions by purchasing the *American Lawyer*, other legal publications, and launching the M&A tip machine, *The Deal*. Wasserstein just won *New York* magazine at auction for $55 million, a magazine that made only $1 million last year on revenues of $43 million, beating old-school vanity press mogul **Mortimer Zuckerman** (real estate, *U.S. News & World Report*, the *Daily News*, and a couple of years ago the *Atlantic Monthly*). Even though Wasserstein has been a bit of a tightwad at the *American Lawyer*—compared to former owners—we priests at the temple of journalism give him our blessing: May all your deadlines be happy, Bruce!

Multimillionaire money managers **Roger Hertog** and **Michael Steinhardt** (**Herthardt** to you) bought their way into the *New Republic* in 2002 at the bottom of the market, partnering with vanity-mogul-by-way-of-his-wife's-inheritance **Martin Peretz**, who still holds an interest in the publication and the editor in chief title. Peretz, you may recall, flopped in his labors to mogul his way to media riches (*Washington Weekly*, the Electronic Newsstand, *Journal of NIH Research*, and TheStreet.com). Herthardt also owns a chunk of that vanity of vanity newspapers, the *New York Sun*, and Hertog serves as chairman emeritus of the Manhattan Institute, which publishes the wonk mag *City Journal*. "There's no fear they'll go broke doing this," Michael Tomasky wrote in 2002, in deliberate understatement. Long may Herthardt publish, or at least until a bigger spender comes along!

What's their Rosebud? What possesses such wealthy gentlemen as Anschutz, Wasserstein, Hertog, Steinhardt, and all the rest—**David Bradley** (*National Journal*, *Atlantic Monthly*), **Bill Gates** (*Slate*), convicted felon **Rev. Sun Myung Moon** (*Washington Times*, *Insight*, *World & I*, UPI), **Richard Mellon Scaife** (*Pittsburgh Tribune-Review*), **Paul Newman** (*The Nation*), **Leonard Stern** (former owner of the *Village Voice* chain of alt-weeklies), **Harvey Weinstein** (*Talk*), **John Warnock** (*Salon*), **Arthur L. Carter** (*New York Observer*, one-time owner of *The*

Nation), **Adam Hochschild** (*Mother Jones*), **John F. Kennedy Jr.** (*George*)—who've made their money in birdseed, software, consulting, Hollywood, Wall Street, real estate, inheritance, banking, religion, and other enterprises to stray from their ultra-profitable fields into ours?

Don't get me wrong. We journalists celebrate whenever non-publishers move their money from the security of blue chip stocks into the volatile world of publishing. Without the vanity posse, scores of vital newspapers and magazines might fold tomorrow, reducing the size of the inner sanctum, which would be a very bad thing for us.

Typical vanity moguls are confident beasts but most wear their publications as emblems of their insecurities. They usually join the game because they're already bulging at the seams with profitable investments and are bored with their yachts, airplanes, mansions, sports franchises, race horses, and priceless works of art, and they view publications (correctly) as exciting diversions from their conventional holdings. Some vanity moguls buy into journalism for ideological reasons (Scaife, Hochschild, convicted felon Moon), hoping their investment will move the public debate in their direction. For others, the attraction is political: They're frustrated politicians who don't have the time, patience, talent, or résumé to sell themselves to voters (Hertog, Peretz, Zuckerman). **Michael Bloomberg** of Bloomberg News is the rare publisher, vanity or straight, who practices politics rather than preaches them.

Other vanity moguls are frustrated reporters who want in the game (Bradley, Wasserstein, Zuckerman again). Bradley and Wasserstein may fancy themselves journalists, but both accept that pounding words into a keyboard is a financial waste of their time. This maxim is lost on Mort Zuckerman, who skanks up both *U.S. News* and the *Daily News* with his pitiable column. (Note to Mort: Spend more time on your pieces—or at the very least hire a better ghost than Harry Evans. With a net worth of $1.3 billion, you can afford it.)

Never underestimate the intellectual currency one can extract from owning a piece of the right publication (Peretz, Herthardt, Bradley, Carter at *The Nation*). With the exception of Gates, every moneybags who invests in a publication becomes a more fascinating person overnight, acquiring cachet beyond their millions. Press moguls get talked about and written up in gossip columns. Civilians hang on their every utterance, politicians seek their counsel, and party-givers stroke them. For the very rich, buying a publication is the cheapest form of ego enhancement.

Every now and then, a vanity press mogul makes a go of his venture. We salute publishing heir **Rea Hederman** (*New York Review of Books, Granta*, a book division), who purchased and developed his properties with few grandiose notions about acquiring power and prestige. Genuine press moguls occasionally play vanity mogul—newspaper barons **Rupert Murdoch** (*New York Post, Weekly Standard*) and **Conrad Black** (*Spectator, New York Sun*) come to mind. But whenever they purchase or launch low- or no-profit vanity titles, they seem more accepting of the fact that the only income they'll earn from these publications will be psychic.

But in most cases, the vanity mogul's life cycle is every bit as predictable as that of a butterfly.

Stage 1: The tyro vanity mogul comes in with grand plans about restoring the publication to its former glory. He makes few noises about the immediate need to make money but hints that profits won't be hard to find because he brings the Midas touch to all of his investments. Quality, the mogul proclaims, will attract readers and advertisers.

Stage 2: He fires the editor and replaces him with a star (Michael Kelly, Shelby Coffey, Adam Moss), orders a redesign, and drops an expensive direct-mail package to recruit new subscribers. He expands the editorial and art budgets and moves the publication to better quarters, upgrades the paper stock, and thinks about building a publication empire, not just a stand-alone title.

Stage 3: Whoops! As fresh red ink flows, the mogul makes a few course adjustments, steering slightly away from quality to hire "names" who will write talked-about columns and during their TV appearances get the magazine's name chironed at the bottom of the screen.

Stage 4: Still losing money, the mogul reverts to his original economic instincts. "I know how to make money!" he mumbles. "I'm not running a charity here!" He cuts costs, eliminates employee perks, loses dead wood, cheapens the paper stock, increases the price of the product, reduces frequency of publication, and tightens everybody's shorts. David Bradley's *Atlantic* is sailing into such a space.

Stage 5: The mogul begins to doubt whether he can make money in publishing but realizes that the social standing that came with the magazine will evaporate if he cuts the budget too deeply or overmeddles in the editing. Some moguls, such as Mort Zuckerman, don't care if they become the laughingstock of the industry and proceed apace. Mort usually overcomes his depression at not making any money by firing his editor and hiring a new one and firing him, too. Already he feels better! Fire and hire again!

Stage 6: As the mogul cracks the cocoon, he must decide whether to fly or crawl or hold. Zuckerman usually crawls. At *U.S. News* he's cut medical benefits, closed the cafeteria, reduced the staff to bare bones, sacked the older (more expensive) employees, taken away the Christmas ham, and closed bureaus. "What Would a Slumlord Do?" guides Zuckerman. Recently, Zuckerman did what a slumlord would do, shopping for a new estate, *New York*, while neglecting his condemnable property, *U.S. News*.

Stage 7: Sometimes, just sometimes, good things happen to struggling moguls. Convicted felon Rev. Sun Myung Moon maintains a direct line to God through which he receives a steady stream of $100 bills that keep his *Washington Times* alive. *Times* officials confided in 1997 that the paper had lost $1 billion since its 1982 launch.

Stage 8: Before his losses reach the $1 billion mark, the average vanity mogul who has tired of his toy looks to unload his property on an entry-level mogul (Zuckerman to Bradley in the case of the *Atlantic*).

As the wheel of life turns, the cycle begins anew.

How Will the Universe End?

A cosmic detective story about the demise of the world.

BY JIM HOLT

March 5, 2004

ONE OF MY FAVORITE MOMENTS in Woody Allen's film *Annie Hall* is when Alvy Singer (Allen's alter ego) is shown having an existential crisis as a little boy. His mother summons a psychiatrist, one Dr. Flicker, to find out what's wrong.

"Why are you depressed, Alvy?" Dr. Flicker asks.

"The universe is expanding," Alvy says. "The universe is everything, and if it's expanding, some day it will break apart and that will be the end of everything."

"Why is that your business?" interrupts his mother. Turning to the psychiatrist, she announces, "He's stopped doing his homework!"

"What's the point?" Alvy says.

"What has the universe got to do with it!" his mother shouts. "You're here in Brooklyn! Brooklyn is not expanding!"

Dr. Flicker jumps in: "It won't be expanding for billions of years, Alvy, and we've got to enjoy ourselves while we're here, eh? Ha ha ha." (Cut to a view of the Singer house, which happens to be under the Coney Island roller coaster.)

I used to take Dr. Flicker's side in this matter. How silly to despond about the end of everything! After all, the cosmos was born only around 13 billion years ago, when the Big Bang happened, and parts of it will remain hospitable to our descendants for a good hundred billion years, even as the whole thing continues to spread out.

A half-dozen years ago, however, astronomers peering through their telescopes began to notice something rather alarming. The expansion of the universe, their observations indicated, was not proceeding at the stately, ever-slowing pace that Einstein's equations had predicted. Instead, it was speeding up. Some "dark energy" was evidently pushing against gravity, sending galaxies hurtling away from one another at a runaway rate. New measurements earlier this year confirmed this strange finding. Last July 22, the *New York Times* ran an ominous headline: "ASTRONOMERS REPORT EVIDENCE OF 'DARK ENERGY' SPLITTING THE UNIVERSE." David Letterman found this so disturbing that he mentioned it several consecutive nights in his *Late Show* monologue, wondering why the Times buried the story on Page A–13.

Until recently, the ultimate destiny of the universe looked a little more hopeful—or remote. Back around the middle of the last century, cosmologists figured out that there were two possible fates for the universe. Either it would continue to expand forever, getting very cold and very dark as the stars winked out one by one, the black holes evaporated, and all material structures disintegrated into an increasingly dilute sea of elementary particles: the Big Chill. Or it would eventually stop expanding and collapse back upon itself in a fiery, all-annihilating implosion: the Big Crunch.

Which of these two scenarios would come to pass depended on one crucial thing: how much stuff there was in the universe. So, at least, said Einstein's theory of general relativity. Stuff— matter and energy—creates gravity. And, as every undergraduate physics major will tell you, gravity sucks. It tends to draw things together. With enough stuff, and hence enough gravity, the expansion of the universe would eventually be arrested and reversed. With too little stuff, the gravity would merely slow the expansion, which would go on forever. So, to determine how the universe would ultimately expire, cosmologists thought that all they had to do was to weigh it. And preliminary estimates—taking account of the visible galaxies, the so-called "dark matter," and even the possible mass of the little neutrinos that swarm though it all—suggested that the universe had only enough weight to slow the expansion, not to turn it around.

Now, as cosmic fates go, the Big Chill might not seem a whole lot better than the Big Crunch. In the first, the temperature goes to absolute zero; in the second, it goes to infinity. Extinction by fire or by ice—what's to choose? Yet a few imaginative scientists, haunted, like Woody Allen, by visions of the end of the universe, came up with formulations of how our distant descendants might manage to go on enjoying life forever, despite these unpleasant conditions. In the Big Chill scenario, they could have an infinity of slower and slower experiences, with lots of sleep in between. In the Big Crunch scenario, they could have an infinity of faster and faster experiences in the run-up to the final implosion. Either way, the progress of civilization would be unlimited. No cause for existential gloom.

So, Letterman had reason to be upset by the dark-energy news. It spells inescapable doom for intelligent life in the far, far future. No matter where you are located, the rest of the universe would eventually be receding from you at the speed of light, slipping forever beyond the horizon of knowability. Meanwhile, the shrinking region of space still accessible to you will fill up with a kind of insidious radiation that would eventually choke off information processing—and with it, the very possibility of thought. We seem to be headed not for a Big Crunch or a Big Chill but something far nastier: a Big Crackup. "All our knowledge, civilization and culture are destined to be forgotten," one prominent cosmologist has declared to the press. It looks as if little Alvy Singer was right after all. The universe is going to "break apart," and that will indeed mean the end of everything—even Brooklyn.

Hearing this news made me think of the inscription that some-one once said should be on all churches: *important if true*. Applied to cosmology—the study of the universe as a whole—that is a big "if." Cosmic speculations that make it into the newspapers should often be taken with a pinch of salt. A few years ago, some as-tronomers from Johns Hopkins made headlines by announcing that the cosmos was turquoise; two months later they made head-lines again by announcing that, no, it was actually beige. This may be a frivolous example, but even in graver matters—like the fate of the universe—cosmologists tend to reverse themselves every decade or so. As one of them once told me, cosmology is not really a science at all since you can't do experiments with the universe. It's more like a detective story. Even the term that is sometimes applied to theorizing about the end of the universe, "eschatology" (from the Greek word for "furthest"), is borrowed from theology.

Before I was going to start worrying about the extinction of ab-solutely everything in some inconceivably distant epoch, I thought it would be a good idea to talk to a few leading cosmolo-gists. Just how certain were they that the cosmos was undergoing a disastrous runaway expansion? Was intelligent life really doomed to perish as a result? How could they, as scientists, talk about the ultimate future of "civilization" and "consciousness" with a straight face?

It seemed natural to start with Freeman Dyson, an English-born physicist who has been at the Institute for Advanced Study in Princeton since the 1940s. Dyson is one of the founding fathers of cosmic eschatology, which he concedes is a "faintly disrep-utable" subject. He is also a fierce optimist about the far future, one who envisions "a universe growing without limit in richness and complexity, a universe of life surviving forever and making it-self known to its neighbors across unimaginable gulfs of space and time." In 1979, he wrote a paper called "Time Without End," in which he used the laws of physics to show how humanity could flourish eternally in a slowly expanding universe, even as the stars died and the chill became absolute. The trick is to match your metabolism to the falling temperature, thinking your thoughts ever more slowly and hibernating for longer and longer periods while extraneous information is dumped into the void as waste heat. In this way, Dyson calculated, a complex society could go on perpetually with a finite energy reserve, one equivalent to a mere eight hours of sunlight.

The day I went to see Dyson, it was raining in Princeton. It took me a half-hour to walk from the train station to the Institute for Advanced Study, which sits by a pond in 500 acres of woods. The institute is a serene, otherworldly place. There are no students to distract the eminent scientists and scholars in residence from pursuing their intellectual fancies. Dyson's office is in the same building where Einstein spent the last decades of his career fruitlessly searching for a unified theory of physics. An elfin, courtly man with deep-set eyes and a hawklike nose, Dyson frequently lapsed into silence or emitted snuffles of amusement. I started by asking him whether the evidence that the universe was caught up in an accelerated expansion had blighted his hopes for the future of civilization.

"Not necessarily," he said. "It's a completely open question whether this acceleration will continue forever or whether it will peter out after a while. There are several theories of what kind of cosmic field might be causing it and no observations to determine which of them is right. If it's caused by the so-called 'dark energy' of empty space, then the expansion will keep speeding up forever, which is bad news as far as life is concerned. But if it's caused by some other kind of force field—which, out of ignorance, we label 'quintessence'—then the expansion might well slow down as we go into the future. Some quintessence theories even say that the universe will eventually stop expanding altogether and collapse. Of course, that, too, would be unfortunate for civilization since nothing would survive the Big Crunch."

Well, then, I said, let's stick with the optimistic scenario. Suppose the acceleration does turn out to be temporary and the future universe settles into a nice cruise-control expansion. What could our descendants possibly look like a trillion trillion trillion years from now, when the stars have disappeared and the universe is dark and freezing and so diffuse that it's practically empty? What will they be made of?

"The most plausible answer," Dyson said, "is that conscious life will take the form of interstellar dust clouds." He was alluding to the kind of inorganic life forms imagined by the late astronomer Sir Fred Hoyle in his 1957 science fiction novel, *The Black Cloud.* "An ever-expanding network of charged dust particles, communicating by electromagnetic forces, has all the complexity necessary for thinking an infinite number of novel thoughts."

How, I objected, can we really imagine such a wispy thing, spread out over billions of light-years of space, being conscious?

"Well," he said, "how do you imagine a couple of kilograms of protoplasm in someone's skull being conscious? We have no idea how that works either."

Practically next door to Dyson at the institute is the office of Ed Witten, a gangly, 50-ish fellow who is widely regarded as the smartest physicist of his generation, if not the living incarnation of Einstein. Witten is one of the prime movers behind superstring theory, which, if its hairy math is ever sorted out, may well furnish the Theory of Everything that physicists have long been after. He has an unnerving ability to shuffle complicated equations in his head without ever writing anything down, and he speaks in a hushed, soft voice. Earlier this year, Witten was quoted in the press calling the discovery of the runaway expansion of the universe "an extremely uncomfortable result." Why, I wondered, did he see it that way? Was it simply inconvenient for theoretical reasons? Or did he worry about its implications for the destiny of the cosmos? When I asked him, he agonized for a moment before responding, "Both."

Yet Witten, too, thought there was a good chance that the runaway expansion would be only temporary, as some of the quintessence theories predicted, rather than permanent, as the dark-energy hypothesis implied. "The quintessence theories are nicer, and I hope they're right," he told me. If the acceleration does indeed relax to zero, and the Big Crackup is averted, could civilization go on forever? Witten was unsure. One cause for concern was the possibility that protons will eventually decay, resulting in the dissolution of all matter within another, oh, 10^{33} years or so. Freeman Dyson had scoffed at this when I talked with him, pointing out that no one had ever observed a proton decaying, but he insisted that intelligent beings could persist even if atoms fell to pieces, by re-embodying themselves in "plasma clouds"—swarms of electrons and positrons. I mentioned this to Witten. "Did Dyson really say that?" he exclaimed. "Good. Because I think protons probably do decay."

Back at the Princeton railroad station after visiting Witten and Dyson, waiting for the train to New York, and munching on a vile "veggie" sandwich that I had picked up at the convenience store across the parking lot, I pondered proton decay and Dyson's scenario for eternal life. How would his sentient Black Clouds, be they made up of cosmic dust or of electron-positron plasma, while away the eons in an utterly freezing and dark universe? What passions would engross their infinite number of ever-slowing thoughts? After all (as Alvy Singer's alter ego once observed), eternity is a long time, especially toward the end. Maybe they would play games of cosmic chess, in which each move took trillions of years. But even at that rate they would run through every possible game of chess in a mere $10^{10^{70}}$ years—long before the final decay of the burnt-out cinders of the stars. What then? Would they come around to George Bernard Shaw's conclusion (reached by him at the age of 92) that the prospect of personal immortality was an "unimaginable horror"? Or would they feel that, subjectively at least, time was passing quickly enough? After all, as Fran Lebowitz pointed out, once you've reached the age of 50, Christmas seems to come every three months.

It was almost with a sense of relief that I spoke to Lawrence Krauss a few days later. Krauss, a boyish fellow in his late 40s who teaches at Case Western Reserve in Cleveland, is one of the physicists who guessed on purely theoretical grounds, even before the astronomical data came in, that the cosmos might be undergoing a runaway expansion. "We appear to be living in the worst of all possible universes," Krauss told me, clearly relishing the note of anti-Leibnizian pessimism he struck. "If the runaway expansion keeps going, our knowledge will actually decrease as time passes. The rest of the universe will be literally disappearing before our very eyes surprisingly soon—in the next 10 or 20 billion years. And life is doomed—even Freeman Dyson accepts that. But the good news is that we can't prove we're living in the worst of all possible universes. No finite set of data will ever enable us to predict the fate of the cosmos with certainty. And, in fact, that doesn't really matter. Because, unlike Freeman, I think that we're doomed even if the runaway phase turns out to be only temporary."

What about Dyson's vision of a civilization of sentient dust clouds living forever in an expanding universe, entertaining an infinite number of thoughts on a finite store of energy? "It turns out, basically for mathematical reasons, that there's no way you can have an infinite number of thoughts unless you do a lot of hibernating," Krauss said. "You sleep for longer and longer periods, waking up for short intervals to think—sort of like an old physicist. But what's going to wake you up? I have a teenage daughter, and I know that if I didn't wake her up, she'd sleep forever. The

Black Cloud would need an alarm clock that would wake it up an infinite number of times on a finite amount of energy. When a colleague and I pointed this out, Dyson came up with a cute alarm clock that could actually do this, but then we argued that this alarm clock would eventually fall apart because of quantum mechanics."

The Misunderestimated Man

How Bush chose stupidity.

BY JACOB WEISBERG

May 7, 2004

THE "BUSHISMS" COLLECTED over the years in *Slate* may leave the impression that President George W. Bush is a dimwit. Let's face it: A man who cannot talk about education without making a humiliating grammatical mistake ("The illiteracy level of our children are appalling"); who cannot keep straight the three branches of government ("It's the executive branch's job to interpret law"); who coins ridiculous words ("Hispanos," "arbolist," "subliminable," "resignate," "transformationed"); who habitually says the opposite of what he intends ("the death tax is good for people from all walks of life!") sounds like a grade-A imbecile.

And if you don't care to pursue the matter any further, that view will suffice. George W. Bush has governed, for the most part, the way any airhead might, undermining the fiscal condition of the nation, squandering the goodwill of the world after Sept. 11, and allowing huge problems (global warming, entitlement spending, AIDS) to metastasize toward catastrophe through a combination of ideology, incomprehension, and indifference. If Bush isn't exactly the moron he sounds, his synaptic misfirings offer a plausible proxy for the idiocy of his presidency.

In reality, however, there's more to it. Bush's assorted mala-propisms, solecisms, gaffes, spoonerisms, and truisms tend to imply that his lack of fluency in English is tantamount to an absence of intelligence. But as we all know, the inarticulate can be shrewd, the fluent fatuous. In Bush's case, the symptoms point to a specific malady—some kind of linguistic deficit akin to dyslexia—that does not indicate a lack of mental capacity per se.

Bush also compensates with his nonverbal acumen. As he notes, "Smart comes in all kinds of different ways." The president's way is an aptitude for connecting to people through banter and physicality. He has a powerful memory for names, details, and figures that truly matter to him, such as batting averages from the 1950s. Bush also has a keen political sense, sharpened under the tutelage of Karl Rove.

What's more, calling the president a cretin absolves him of responsibility. Like Reagan, Bush avoids blame for all manner of contradictions, implausible assertions, and outright lies by appearing an amiable dunce. If he knows not what he does, blame goes to the three puppeteers: Cheney, Rove, and Rumsfeld. It also breeds sympathy. We wouldn't laugh at FDR because he couldn't walk. Is it less cruel to laugh at GWB because he can't talk? The soft bigotry of low expectations means Bush is seen to outperform by merely getting by. Finally, elitist condescension, however merited, helps cement Bush's bond to the masses.

But if "numskull" is an imprecise description of the president, it is not altogether inaccurate. Bush may not have been born stupid, but he has achieved stupidity, and now he wears it as a badge of honor. What makes mocking this president fair as well as funny is that Bush is, or at least once was, capable of learning, reading, and thinking. We know he has discipline and can work hard (at least when the goal is reducing his time for a 3-mile run). Instead he chose to coast, for most of his life, on name, charm, good looks, and the easy access to capital afforded by family connections.

The most obvious expression of Bush's choice of ignorance is that, at the age of 57, he knows nothing about policy or history. After years of working as his dad's spear-chucker in Washington, he didn't understand the difference between Medicare and Medicaid, the second- and third-largest federal programs. Well into his plans for invading Iraq, Bush still couldn't get down the distinction between Sunni and Shiite Muslims, the key religious divide in a country he was about to occupy. Though he sometimes carries books for show, he either does not read them or doesn't absorb anything from them. Bush's ignorance is so transparent that many of his intimates do not bother to dispute it even in public. Consider the testimony of several who know him well:

Richard Perle, foreign policy adviser: "The first time I met Bush 43 . . . two things became clear. One, he didn't know very much. The other was that he had the confidence to ask questions that revealed he didn't know very much."

David Frum, former speechwriter: "Bush had a poor memory for facts and figures. . . . Fire a question at him about the specifics of his administration's policies, and he often appeared uncertain. Nobody would ever enroll him in a quiz show."

Laura Bush, spouse: "George is not an overly introspective person. He has good instincts, and he goes with them. He doesn't need to evaluate and reevaluate a decision. He doesn't try to overthink. He likes action."

Paul O'Neill, former treasury secretary: "The only way I can describe it is that, well, the President is like a blind man in a roomful of deaf people. There is no discernible connection."

A second, more damning aspect of Bush's mind-set is that he *doesn't want* to know anything in detail, however important. Since college, he has spilled with contempt for knowledge, equating learning with snobbery and making a joke of his own anti-intellectualism. ("[William F. Buckley] wrote a book at Yale; I read one," he quipped at a black-tie event.) By O'Neill's account, Bush could sit through an hourlong presentation about the state of the economy without asking a single question. ("I was bored as hell," the president shot back, ostensibly in jest.)

Closely related to this aggressive ignorance is a third feature of Bush's mentality: laziness. Again, this is a lifelong trait. Bush's college grades were mostly Cs (including a 73 in Introduction to the American Political System). At the start of one term, the star of the Yale football team spotted him in the back row during the shopping period for courses. "Hey! George Bush is in this class!" Calvin Hill shouted to his teammates. "This is the one for us!" As governor of Texas, Bush would take a long break in the middle of his short workday for a run followed by a stretch of video golf or computer solitaire.

A fourth and final quality of Bush's mind is that it does not think. The president can't tolerate debate about issues. Offered an option, he makes up his mind quickly and never reconsiders. At an elementary school, a child once asked him whether it was hard to make decisions as president. "Most of the decisions come pretty easily for me, to be frank with you." By leaping to conclusions based on what he "believes," Bush avoids contemplating even the most obvious basic contradictions: between his policy of tax cuts and reducing the deficit; between his call for a humble foreign policy based on alliances and his unilateral assertion of American power; between his support for in-vitro fertilization (which destroys embryos) and his opposition to fetal stem-cell research (because it destroys embryos).

Why would someone capable of being smart choose to be stupid? To understand, you have to look at W.'s relationship with father. This filial bond involves more tension than meets the eye. Dad was away for much of his oldest son's childhood. Little George grew up closer to his acid-tongued mother and acted out against the absent parent—through adolescent misbehavior, academic failure, dissipation, and basically not accomplishing anything at all until well into his 40s.

Dubya's youthful screw-ups and smart-aleck attitude reflect some combination of protest, plea for attention, and flailing attempt to compete. Until a decade ago, his résumé read like a sendup of his dad's. Bush senior was a star student at Andover and Phi Beta Kappa at Yale, where he was also captain of the baseball team; Junior struggled through with gentleman's C's and, though he loved baseball, couldn't make the college lineup. *Père* was a bomber pilot in the Pacific; *fils* sat out 'Nam in the Texas Air National Guard, where he lost flying privileges by not showing up. Dad drove to Texas in 1947 to get rich in the oil business and actually did; Son tried the same in 1975 and drilled dry holes for a decade. Bush the elder got elected to Congress in 1966; Shrub ran in 1978, didn't know what he was talking about, and got clobbered.

Through all this incompetent emulation runs an undercurrent of hostility. In an oft-told anecdote circa 1973, GWB—after getting wasted at a party and driving over a neighbor's trash can in Houston—challenged his dad. "I hear you're lookin' for me," W. told the chairman of the Republican National Committee. "You want to go *mano a mano* right here?" Some years later at a state dinner, he told the Queen of England he was being seated far away because he was the black sheep of the family.

After half a lifetime of this kind of frustration, Bush decided to straighten up. Nursing a hangover at a 40th-birthday weekend, he gave up Wild Turkey, cold turkey. With the help of Billy Graham, he put himself in the hands of a higher power and began going to church. He became obsessed with punctuality and developed a rigid routine. Thus did Prince Hal molt into an evangelical King Henry. And it worked! Putting together a deal to buy the Texas Rangers, the ne'er-do-well finally tasted success. With success, he grew closer to his father, taking on the role of family avenger. This culminated in his 1994 challenge to Texas Gov. Ann Richards, who had twitted dad at the 1988 Democratic convention.

Curiously, this late arrival at adulthood did not involve Bush becoming in any way thoughtful. Having chosen stupidity as rebellion, he stuck with it out of conformity. The promise-keeper, reformed-alkie path he chose not only drastically curtailed personal choices he no longer wanted, it also supplied an all-encompassing order, offered guidance on policy, and prevented the need for much actual information. Bush's old answer to hard questions was, "I don't know and, who cares." His new answer was, "Wait a second while I check with Jesus."

A remaining bit of poignancy was his unresolved struggle with his father. "All I ask," he implored a reporter while running for governor in 1994, "is that for once you guys stop seeing me as the son of George Bush." In his campaigns, W. has kept his dad off-stage. (In an exceptional appearance on the eve of the 2000 New Hampshire primary, 41 came onstage and called his son "this boy.") While some describe the second Bush presidency as a restoration, it is in at least equal measure a repudiation. The son's harder-edged conservatism explicitly rejects the old man's approach to such issues as abortion, taxes, and relations with Israel.

This Oedipally induced ignorance expresses itself most dangerously in Bush's handling of the war in Iraq. Dubya polished off his old man's greatest enemy, Saddam, but only by lampooning 41's accomplishment of coalition-building in the first Gulf War. Bush led the country to war on false pretenses and neglected to plan the occupation that would inevitably follow. A more knowledgeable and engaged president might have questioned the quality of the evidence about Iraq's supposed weapons programs. One who preferred to be intelligent might have asked about the possibility of an unfriendly reception. Instead, Bush rolled the dice. His budget-busting tax cuts exemplify a similar phenomenon, driven by an alternate set of ideologues.

As the president says, we misunderestimate him. He was not born stupid. He chose stupidity. Bush may look like a well-meaning dolt. On consideration, he's something far more dangerous: a dedicated fool.

A Medical Quest

BY MASHA GESSEN

June, 2004

Subject: In Which I Find Out That I Am Genetically Mutant. Posted June 13, 2004

"IF YOU ARE ANYTHING LIKE ME," my doctor says, "you are looking at your kids and thinking you just want to be around for their college graduation." My doctor and I both are Ashkenazi Jewish women in midlife, each with two young children, so there is the basis for comparison. But I've always figured on a long life with an extended middle part. I thought I might choose to have a third child some years down the road, when these two are in school. There didn't seem to be any reason I shouldn't; I come from good stock: My grandmothers are still going strong in their 80s, my great-grandparents lived into their 90s, and generations of women in my family have had babies well into their 40s. But somewhere in this terrific soup is a single genetic mutation that caused my mother and her aunt to die of cancer in middle age. As it turns out, I have it too—literally a fatal flaw that means I just might end up on the wrong side of the law of averages. That is, I may not make it to midlife at all.

In fact, the law of averages is not about mathematical middles but about probability, which, it holds, will determine everything in the long run. That's the bad news for me. My flaw is located in the 39th amino acid position of a protein called BRCA1, which stands for "Breast Cancer 1." There is also another known mutation that causes breast and ovarian cancer that is sometimes found in this gene, and one found in BRCA2, another gene. All three of these are relatively common among Ashkenazi Jews; about 5 percent may have one. In numerical terms, "my" mutation means, roughly, that every decade of my life, starting at age 30, increases my risk of breast cancer by 20 percentage points. So, one in five women with the BRCA1 mutation develops breast cancer by the age of 40; two in five by the age of 50; three in five by 60; and so on. But the estimates aren't as precise as they sound: The literature states that somewhere between 55 percent and 87 percent of women with a BRCA1 mutation will develop breast cancer. Which raises two questions: Are the missing 13 percent those who would have developed breast cancer if something else hadn't killed them first? Or is the lower estimate correct, which would mean the odds are more like 50/50, odds I could maybe live with?

Not that I have much of a choice about living with it. But I can hold some sway over the probabilities. The standard recommendation for a woman in my situation in the United States is to have a preventive oophorectomy—which means having her ovaries removed—"when she has completed child bearing," but preferably no later than at age 35. The Canadians, generally less scalpel-happy, recommend the surgery at the age of 40. There are two reasons for the recommendation. One is that early surgical menopause, induced when the ovaries are removed, reduces the risk of breast cancer by about half (which means it's still a lot higher than in the general population). Two, both BRCA1 and BRCA2, mutations also mean a vastly increased risk of ovarian cancer—and ovarian cancer, unlike breast cancer, is virtually never caught early. There are ultrasounds and there is a blood test, but the basic truth is that when one of these comes back positive, the cancer has probably already spread beyond the ovaries. My great-aunt died of ovarian cancer three days before her 53rd birthday. My mother died of breast cancer a week before her 50th birthday. I'm 37.

Another way to prevent breast cancer—an obvious one—is to have a preventive mastectomy. There is a maddening disconnect between the cutting-edge science of oncogenetics and the barbaric state-of-the-art response to the discovery of a mutation: Hack everything off before it goes bad. The counselors at the Cancer Risk & Prevention Department of Adult Oncology at the Dana-Farber Cancer Institute (the name goes on, actually, but you get the basic coordinates) drive a hard bargain. When I raise objections to opting for early surgical menopause—the unpleasant effects of which include increased risk of heart disease, high blood pressure, osteoporosis, not to mention cognitive problems and depression (as well as inelastic skin and weight gain, which seem downright frivolous to mention)—Judy Garber, the director, who personally counsels women like me, says, "The payoff is keeping you here." I can accept that kind of singular vision as a characteristic of a true scientist, but, at that moment, it also occurred to me that the best way to prevent cancer of the breasts and the ovaries would be to shoot myself tomorrow: That way, I could make sure I died of something other than cancer.

I like my doctor a lot, partly for her alarmism. She also explicitly allows me to ask the question that was at the tip of my tongue: "What would you do?" She says she might have another child right away. Then she'd probably have an oophorectomy. She'd consider a mastectomy, but the thought weirds her out—not because she is worried about finding a mate (she has one) but because she has used her breasts to nurse her two children and can't imagine not breast-feeding the third.

I'd actually thought that if I tested positive I might want to get pregnant again right away. As it turns out, I don't: I feel that if I have only a couple of premenopausal years left, I don't want to go missing, as one does in pregnancy. Which just leaves the question of what I will do, and when. I decided to look for the answer right here, in Cambridge, Mass., the geographic location of the genetic frontier: the home of the Human Genome Project is less than 2 miles from my house, as are a slew of biotech companies working on things like fixing tragic genetic misfires like mine. Perhaps more important, I feel like there are people right here at Harvard, where I am spending a year as a journalism fellow, who know things about people—the sorts of things I could use to guide me to a decision. So, I have set out, over the next week, to systematically pick their brains. I plan to come to a decision by the end of the week—and this series of dispatches.

Subject: In Which It Is Mathematically Proven That the Doctors Were Right After All
Posted June 15, 2004

When I enter David Laibson's office in Harvard's economics department, he is on the phone saying things like, "This one is a .4 chance" and "She is no more than a .5 chance." He is going down a list of prospective graduate students, each of whom has a rating based on the chances of his or her accepting an offer from Harvard. This is why I came to see David: He really thinks this way. One of the little-known facts about economics is that it's actually a study of how people make decisions—the problem is, for most of the history of the dismal science, economists have based their suppositions on the blatantly absurd assumption that people will always act rationally and in their own best interest. David is a behavioral economist, which means that he tries to figure out how people really act. In his popular Harvard course "Psychology and Economics," he and his co-teacher, Andrei Shleifer, discuss things like lotteries, the Milgram obedience experiment, and how the media cooks the news (although they happen to be all wrong about journalism) and try to talk about the way people make decisions—and why their decisions are often wrong. I hope that because David has studied decision-making mistakes, he can help me avoid them.

Instead, David first does what anyone would do: He tries to find a way to avoid making a decision. He tells me about two NYU economists who have done a study showing that people don't really want to know what will happen to them, especially when it's not clear what to do with the knowledge. I tell him there are in fact two other studies, specifically concerning the BRCA mutations, which show that women do want to know whether they have the mutation. "They just *say* they want to know," David responds. So, I finally tell him I have a BRCA mutation, which elicits the predictable sympathetic look from David. (I am not making light; it was obvious to me his sadness and sympathy were sincere—it's just that I still haven't figured out what I, a healthy woman with more knowledge and options than most women in a similar situation, should do with that kind of sympathy.) Then he suggests we make a spreadsheet.

In the left column of the spreadsheet David puts ages, year by year, starting at 37 (which happens to be his age as well as mine). Across the top, he places the options: "Oophorectomy," "Mastectomy," "Oophorectomy and Mastectomy," and "Do Nothing." Now we devise the formulas for figuring out the value of life under each possible decision for each possible year. "Let's normalize not being alive as having a utility of 0," suggests David. "Further, let's normalize a year of healthy life to have a utility of 100. Should we assume that life without breasts is equally good?" Sure, I say, provided the surgery goes well—as we know, people adjust very quickly to radical change. What would be the value of life with cancer? That's harder to calculate, since the value gets higher as probability gets lower: The longer a woman lives after the initial diagnosis, the more likely it is that her life will once again approach normalcy. We consider equating a diagnosis of cancer with death, which has a value of 0, but then David decides to calculate the values more precisely—or as precisely as algebra will allow what he calls the "pseudoscience" of behavioral economics, to become.

He switches from his computer screen to the huge dry-erase board opposite his desk and gives up on the spreadsheet. Here is roughly what we come up with (where *we* is the sum of David's genius and my clumsily conveyed supply of information). If you cannot stomach equations, now is a good time to skip to the conclusion of this piece.

$$V(G) = 100 + B\,[(.98)V(G) + (.02)V(\text{illness})]$$

Translated, that says:

The value of a year of life in what we consider a "good state"—apparent health with none of the possible disadvantages of surgery—is equal to 100 (this is the utility we have assigned to a year of normal healthy life). The value of an entire life that begins in the good state is 100 plus "the discount factor" B multiplied by the value of the state that starts next year, if I survive. B reflects the normal mortality risk for young people, which is about $1/4$ of 1 percent. The value of life in the next period is in brackets. The first term is the 98 percent likelihood of staying in the "good state," and the second term is the 2 percent likelihood of a diagnosis of cancer.

Now we have to decide what the value of life with cancer would be. To prevent, eh, reader attrition, I'll skip the calculation that leads us to the utility of 70 for life with cancer (compared to 100 for health and 0 for death). Then

$$V(\text{illness}) = 70 + B[(.8)V(\text{illness})+(.2)X_0] =$$
$$(\text{skipping the algebra here}) = 347$$

What that means is that while life—actual life—with cancer might have a utility flow of 70 utils per year, which is not all that far from normal healthy life, the likelihood of death makes the *value* of life with cancer just 347. Plugging this value into the first equation, we find out that life in the "good state" has a value of 4,752, even allowing for the 2 percent annual risk of breast cancer.

I already know that if I got a mastectomy, the utility of one year of life would be essentially the same because I would adjust. The *value* of life, however, would actually increase because the risk of breast cancer would be cut by 90 percent. Still, after the age of 40 the risk of ovarian cancer would kick in, also to the tune of about

2 percent a year, bringing the value of my now breastless life right back down to 1,500. What if I got an oophorectomy? Sure, that would cut my ovarian cancer risk by 95 percent. But it might make me instantly old, susceptible to heart disease, high blood pressure, osteoporosis, and so forth. I suggest David look at my collection of all the age-specific risk statistics of all these diseases. David's solution is far more elegant: He just changes our "discount factor" (B') to reflect the mortality risk of an older person—someone over 65. The assumption here is that the mortality risk is a good enough expression of all the disadvantages of life after menopause. That mortality risk is about 1.5 percent a year, rather than a quarter of a percent, as it is for young people. The utility of life in a state we termed "Good/old" turned out to be 95 (as compared to 100 for good/young). And the value?

$$V(G/old) = 95+B'[V(G/old)] = 9,500$$

Huh? Does that mean it is better to be old and cancer-risk-free than young and at risk?

"Hey," says David. "Being old isn't so bad. I can't do many of the things I could do when I was 20, and I don't miss them."

I think about this. The truth is, physically, I don't feel that different than when I was 20. True, to achieve this state of well-being I have to drink a lot less, smoke not at all, and work out a lot, but these don't count as costs. (On the other hand, when I was 20, I could actually follow this kind of math with pleasure.)

"You know what?" continues David. "Having a 1 percent chance of dying from being old just doesn't compare to having a 2 percent chance of getting cancer." Sure it does. It's only half as bad.

"It seems the doctors are right," concludes David: Surgery is the solution. We stare at each other for a minute; this is an outcome neither of us expected. I, for one, had been almost sure we'd prove that the absurd-sounding recommendation of a preventive oophorectomy was wrong.

Unfairenheit 9/11

The lies of Michael Moore.

BY CHRISTOPHER HITCHENS

June 21, 2004

ONE OF THE MANY PROBLEMS with the American left, and indeed *of* the American left, has been its image and self-image as something rather too solemn, mirthless, herbivorous, dull, monochrome, righteous, and boring. How many times, in my old days at *The Nation* magazine, did I hear wistful and semi-envious ruminations? Where was the radical *Firing Line* show? Who will be our Rush Limbaugh? I used privately to hope that the emphasis, if the comrades ever got around to it, would be on the first of those and not the second. But the meetings themselves were so mind-numbing and lugubrious that I thought the danger of success on either front was infinitely slight.

Nonetheless, it seems that an answer to this long-felt need is finally beginning to emerge. I exempt Al Franken's unintentionally funny Air America network, to which I gave a couple of interviews in its early days. There, one could hear the reassuring noise of collapsing scenery and tripped-over wires and be reminded once again that correct politics and smooth media presentation are not even distant cousins. With Michael Moore's *Fahrenheit 9/11*, however, an entirely new note has been struck. Here we glimpse a possible fusion between the turgid routines of MoveOn.org and the filmic standards, if not exactly the filmic skills, of Sergei Eisenstein or Leni Riefenstahl.

To describe this film as dishonest and demagogic would almost be to promote those terms to the level of respectability. To describe this film as a piece of crap would be to run the risk of a discourse that would never again rise above the excremental. To describe it as an exercise in facile crowd-pleasing would be too obvious. *Fahrenheit 9/11* is a sinister exercise in moral frivolity, crudely disguised as an exercise in seriousness. It is also a spectacle of abject political cowardice masking itself as a demonstration of "dissenting" bravery.

In late 2002, almost a year after the al-Qaida assault on American society, I had an onstage debate with Michael Moore at the Telluride Film Festival. In the course of this exchange, he stated his view that Osama Bin Laden should be considered innocent until proven guilty. This was, he said, the American way. The intervention in Afghanistan, he maintained, had been at least to that extent unjustified. Something—I cannot guess what, since we knew as much then as we do now—has since apparently persuaded Moore that Osama Bin Laden is as guilty as hell. Indeed, Osama is suddenly so guilty and so all-powerful that any other discussion of any other topic is a dangerous "distraction" from the fight against him. I believe that I understand the convenience of this late conversion.

Fahrenheit 9/11 makes the following points about Bin Laden and about Afghanistan, and makes them in this order:

1. The Bin Laden family (if not *exactly* Osama himself) had a close if convoluted business relationship with the Bush family, through the Carlyle Group.

2. Saudi capital in general is a very large element of foreign investment in the United States.

3. The Unocal company in Texas had been willing to discuss a gas pipeline across Afghanistan with the Taliban, as had other vested interests.

4. The Bush administration sent far too *few* ground troops to Afghanistan and thus allowed far too many Taliban and al-Qaida members to escape.

5. The Afghan government, in supporting the coalition in Iraq, was purely risible in that its non-army was purely American.

6. The American lives lost in Afghanistan have been wasted. (This I divine from the fact that this supposedly "anti-war" film is dedicated ruefully to all those killed there, as well as in Iraq.)

It must be evident to anyone, despite the rapid-fire way in which Moore's direction eases the audience hastily past the contradictions, that these discrepant scatter shots do not cohere at any point. Either the Saudis run U.S. policy (through family ties or overwhelming economic interest), or they do not. As allies and patrons of the Taliban regime, they either opposed Bush's removal of it, or they did not. (They opposed the removal, all right: They wouldn't even let Tony Blair land his own plane on their soil at the time of the operation.) Either we sent too many troops or were wrong to send any at all—the latter was Moore's view as late as 2002—or we sent too few. If we were going to make sure no Taliban or al-Qaida forces survived or escaped, we would have had to be more ruthless than I suspect that Mr. Moore is really recommending. And these are simply observations on what is "in" the film. If we turn to the facts that are deliberately left out, we discover that there is an emerging Afghan army, that the country is now a joint NATO responsibility and thus under the protection of the broadest military alliance in history, that it has a new constitution and is preparing against hellish odds to hold a general election, and that at least a million and a half of its former refugees have opted to return. I don't think a pipeline is being constructed yet, not that Afghanistan couldn't do with a pipeline. But a highway from Kabul to Kandahar—an insurance against warlordism and a condition of nation-building—is nearing completion with infinite labor and risk. We also discover that the parties of the Afghan secular left—like the parties of the Iraqi secular left—are strongly in favor of the regime change. But this is not the sort of irony in which Moore chooses to deal.

He prefers leaden sarcasm to irony and, indeed, may not appreciate the distinction. In a long and paranoid (and tedious) section at the opening of the film, he makes heavy innuendoes about the flights that took members of the Bin Laden family out of the country after Sept. 11. I banged on about this myself at the time and wrote a *Nation* column drawing attention to the groveling Larry King interview with the insufferable Prince Bandar, which Moore excerpts. However, recent developments have not been kind to our Mike. In the interval between Moore's triumph at Cannes and the release of the film in the United States, the 9/11 Commission has found nothing to complain of in the timing or arrangement of the flights. And Richard Clarke, Bush's former chief of counterterrorism, has come forward to say that he, and he alone, took the responsibility for authorizing those Saudi departures. This might not matter so much to the ethos of *Fahrenheit 9/11*, except that—as you might expect—Clarke is presented throughout as the brow-furrowed ethical hero of the entire post-9/11 moment. And it does not seem very likely that, in his open admission about the Bin Laden family evacuation, Clarke is taking a fall, or a spear in the chest, for the Bush administration. So, that's another bust for this windy and bloated cinematic "key to all mythologies."

A film that bases itself on a big lie and a big misrepresentation can only sustain itself by a dizzying succession of smaller falsehoods, beefed up by wilder and (if possible) yet-more-contradictory claims. President Bush is accused of taking too many lazy vacations. (What is that about, by the way? Isn't he supposed to be an unceasing planner for future aggressive wars?) But the shot of him "relaxing at Camp David" shows him side by side with Tony Blair. I say "shows" even though this photograph is on-screen so briefly that if you sneeze or blink, you won't recognize the other figure. A meeting with the prime minister of the United Kingdom, or at least with this prime minister, is not a goof-off.

The president is also captured in a well-worn TV news clip, on a golf course, making a boilerplate response to a question on terrorism and then asking the reporters to watch his drive. Well, that's what you get if you catch the president on a golf course. If Eisenhower had done this, as he often did, it would have been presented as calm statesmanship. If Clinton had done it, as he often did, it would have shown his charm. More interesting is the moment where Bush is shown frozen on his chair at the infant school in Florida, looking stunned and useless for seven whole minutes after the news of the second plane on 9/11. Many are those who say that he should have leaped from his stool, adopted a Russell Crowe stance, and gone to work. I could even wish that myself. But if he had done any such thing then (as he did with his "Let's roll" and "dead or alive" remarks a month later), half the Michael Moore community would now be calling him a man who went to war on a hectic, crazed impulse. The other half would be saying what they already say—that he knew the attack was coming, was using it to cement himself in power, and couldn't wait to get on with his coup. This is the line taken by Gore Vidal and by a scandalous recent book that also revives the charge of FDR's collusion over Pearl Harbor. At least Moore's film should put the shameful purveyors of that last theory back in their paranoid box.

But it won't because it encourages their half-baked fantasies in so many other ways. We are introduced to Iraq, "a sovereign nation." (In fact, Iraq's "sovereignty" was heavily qualified by international sanctions, however questionable, which reflected its noncompliance with important U.N. resolutions.) In this peaceable kingdom, according to Moore's flabbergasting choice of film shots, children are flying little kites, shoppers are smiling in the sunshine, and the gentle rhythms of life are undisturbed. Then—wham! From the night sky come the terror weapons of American imperialism. Watching the clips Moore uses, and recalling them well, I can recognize various Saddam palaces and military and police centers getting the treatment. But these sites are not identified as such. In fact, I don't think Al Jazeera would, on a bad day, have transmitted anything so utterly propagandistic. You would also be led to think that the term "civilian casualty" had not even been in the Iraqi vocabulary until March 2003. I remember asking Moore at Telluride if he was or was not a pacifist. He would not give a straight answer then, and he doesn't now, either. I'll just say that the "insurgent" side is presented in this film as justifiably outraged, whereas the 30-year record of Baathist war crimes and repression and aggression is not mentioned once. (Actually, that's not quite right. It is briefly mentioned but only, and smarmily, because of the bad period when Washington preferred Saddam to the likewise unmentioned Ayatollah Khomeini.)

That this—his pro-American moment—was the worst Moore could possibly say of Saddam's depravity is further suggested by some astonishing falsifications. Moore asserts that Iraq under Saddam had never attacked or killed or even threatened (his words) any American. I never quite know whether Moore is as ignorant as he looks, or even if that would be humanly possible. Baghdad was for years the official, undisguised home address of Abu Nidal, then the most-wanted gangster in the world, who had been sentenced to death even by the PLO and had blown up airports in Vienna and Rome. Baghdad was the safe house for the man whose "operation" murdered Leon Klinghoffer. Saddam boasted publicly of his financial sponsorship of suicide bombers in Israel. (Quite a few Americans of all denominations walk the streets of Jerusalem.) In 1991, a large number of Western hostages were taken by the hideous Iraqi invasion of Kuwait and held in terrible conditions for a long time. After that same invasion was repelled—Saddam having killed quite a few Americans and Egyptians and Syrians and Brits in the meantime and having threatened to kill many more—the Iraqi secret police were caught trying to murder former President Bush during his visit to Kuwait. Never mind whether his son should take that personally. (Though why should he not?) Should you and I not resent any foreign dictatorship that attempts to kill one of our retired chief executives? (President Clinton certainly took it that way: He ordered the destruction by cruise missiles of the Baathist "security" headquarters.) Iraqi forces fired, *every day, for 10 years,* on the aircraft that patrolled the no-fly zones and staved off further genocide in the north and south of the country. In 1993, a certain Mr. Yasin helped mix the chemicals for the bomb at the World Trade Center and then skipped to Iraq, where he remained a guest of the state until the overthrow of Saddam. In 2001, Saddam's regime was the only one in the region that openly celebrated the attacks on New York and Washington and described them as just the beginning of a larger revenge. Its official media regularly spewed out a stream of anti-Semitic incitement. I think one might describe that as "threatening," even if one was narrow enough to think that anti-Semitism only menaces Jews. And it was after, and not before, the 9/11 attacks that Abu Mussab al-Zarqawi moved from Afghanistan to Baghdad and began to plan his now very open and lethal design for a holy and ethnic civil war. On Dec. 1, 2003, the *New York Times* reported—and the David Kay report had established—that Saddam had been secretly negotiating with the "Dear Leader" Kim

Jong-il in a series of secret meetings in Syria, as late as the spring of 2003, to buy a North Korean missile system, and missile-production system, right off the shelf. (This attempt was not uncovered until after the fall of Baghdad, the coalition's presence having meanwhile put an end to the negotiations.)

Thus, in spite of the film's loaded bias against the work of the mind, you can grasp even while watching it that Michael Moore has just said, in so many words, the one thing that no reflective or informed person can possibly believe: that Saddam Hussein was no problem. No problem at all. Now look again at the facts I have cited above. If these things had been allowed to happen under any other administration, you can be sure that Moore and others would now glibly be accusing the president of ignoring, or of having ignored, some fairly unmistakable "warnings."

The same "let's have it both ways" opportunism infects his treatment of another very serious subject, namely domestic counterterrorist policy. From being accused of overlooking too many warnings—not exactly an original point—the administration is now lavishly taunted for issuing too many. (Would there not have been "fear" if the harbingers of 9/11 had been taken seriously?) We are shown some American civilians who have had absurd encounters with idiotic "security" staff. (Have you ever met anyone who can't tell such a story?) Then we are immediately shown underfunded police departments that don't have the means or the manpower to do any stop-and-search: a power suddenly demanded by Moore on their behalf that we know by definition would at least lead to some ridiculous interrogations. Finally, Moore complains that there isn't enough intrusion and confiscation at airports and says that it is appalling that every air traveler is not forcibly relieved of all matches and lighters. (Cue mood music for sinister influence of Big Tobacco.) So—he wants even more pocket-rummaging by airport officials? Uh, no, not exactly. But by this stage, who's counting? Moore is having it three ways and asserting everything and nothing. Again—simply not serious.

Circling back to where we began, why did Moore's evil Saudis not join "the Coalition of the Willing"? Why instead did they force the United States to switch its regional military headquarters to Qatar? If the Bush family and the al-Saud dynasty live in each other's pockets, as is alleged in a sort of vulgar sub-Brechtian scene with Arab headdresses replacing top hats, then how come the most reactionary regime in the region has been powerless to stop Bush from demolishing its clone in Kabul and its buffer regime in Baghdad? The Saudis hate, as they did in 1991, the idea that Iraq's recuperated oil industry might challenge their near-monopoly. They fear the liberation of the Shiite Muslims they so despise. To make these elementary points is to collapse the whole pathetic edifice of the film's "theory." Perhaps Moore prefers the pro-Saudi Kissinger/Scowcroft plan for the Middle East, where stability trumps every other consideration and where one dare not upset the local house of cards, or killing-field of Kurds? This would be a strange position for a purported radical. Then again, perhaps he does not take this conservative line because his real pitch is not to any audience member with a serious interest in foreign policy. It is to the provincial isolationist.

I have already said that Moore's film has the staunch courage to mock Bush for his verbal infelicity. Yet it's much, much braver than that. From *Fahrenheit 9/11* you can glean even more astounding and hidden disclosures, such as the capitalist nature of American society, the existence of Eisenhower's "military-industrial complex," and the use of "spin" in the presentation of our politicians. It's high time someone had the nerve to point this out. There's more. Poor people often volunteer to join the army, and some of them are duskier than others. Betcha didn't know that. Back in Flint, Mich., Moore feels on safe ground. There are no martyred rabbits this time. Instead, it's the poor and black who shoulder the packs and rifles and march away. I won't dwell on the fact that black Americans have fought for almost a century and a half, from insisting on their right to join the U.S. Army and fight in the Civil War to the right to have a desegregated Army that set the pace for post-1945 civil rights. I'll merely ask this: In the film, Moore says loudly and repeatedly *that not enough* troops were sent to garrison Afghanistan and Iraq. (This is now a favorite cleverness of those who were, in the first place, against sending any soldiers at all.) Well, where does he think those needful heroes and heroines would have come from? Does he favor a draft—the most statist and oppressive solution? Does he think that only hapless and gullible proles sign up for the Marines? Does he think—as he seems to suggest—that parents can "send" their children, as he stupidly asks elected members of Congress to do? Would he have abandoned Gettysburg because the Union allowed civilians to pay proxies to serve in their place? Would he have supported the anti-draft (and very anti-black) riots against Lincoln in New York? After a point, one realizes that it's a waste of time asking him questions of this sort. It would be too much like taking him seriously. He'll just try anything once and see if it floats or flies or gets a cheer.

Indeed, Moore's affected and ostentatious concern for black America is one of the most suspect ingredients of his pitch package. In a recent interview, he yelled that if the hijacked civilians of 9/11 had been black, they would have fought back, unlike the stupid and presumably cowardly white men and women (and children). Never mind for now how many black passengers were on those planes—we happen to know what Moore does not care to mention: that Todd Beamer and a few of his co-passengers, shouting "Let's roll," rammed the hijackers with a trolley, fought them tooth and nail, and helped bring down a United Airlines plane, in Pennsylvania, that was speeding toward either the White House or the Capitol. There are no words for real, impromptu bravery like that, which helped save our republic from worse than actually befell. The Pennsylvania drama also reminds one of the self-evident fact that this war is not fought only "overseas" or in uniform but is being brought to our cities. Yet Moore is a silly and shady man who does not recognize courage of any sort even when he sees it because he cannot summon it in himself. To him, easy applause, in front of credulous audiences, is everything.

Moore has announced that he won't even appear on TV shows where he might face hostile questioning. I notice from the *New York Times* of June 20 that he has pompously established a rapid-response team, and a fact-checking staff, and some tough lawyers, to bulwark himself against attack. He'll sue, Moore says, if anyone insults him or his pet. Some right-wing hack groups, I gather, are planning to bring pressure on their local movie theaters to drop the film. How dumb or thuggish do you have to be in order to counter one form of stupidity and cowardice with another? By all means go and see this terrible film, and take your friends, and if the fools in the audience strike up one cry, in favor of surrender or defeat, feel free to join in the conversation.

However, I think we can agree that the film is so flat-out phony that "fact-checking" is beside the point. And as for the scary lawyers—get a life, or maybe see me in court. But I offer this, to Moore and to his rapid-response rabble. Any time, Michael my boy. Let's redo Telluride. Any show. Any place. Any platform. Let's see what you're made of.

Some people soothingly say that one should relax about all this. It's only a movie. No biggie. It's no worse than the tomfoolery of Oliver Stone. It's kick-ass entertainment. It might even help get out "the youth vote." Yeah, well, I have myself written and presented about a dozen low-budget made-for-TV documentaries, on subjects as various as Mother Teresa and Bill Clinton and the Cyprus crisis, and I also helped produce a slightly more polished one on Henry Kissinger that was shown in movie theaters. So I know, thanks, before you tell me, that a documentary must have a "POV," or point of view, and that it must also impose a narrative line. But if you leave out absolutely everything that might give your "narrative" a problem and throw in any old rubbish that might support it, and you don't even care that one bit of that rubbish flatly contradicts the next bit, and you give no chance to those who might differ, then *you have betrayed your craft*. If you flatter and fawn upon your potential audience, I might add, you are patronizing them and insulting them. By the same token, if I write an article and I quote somebody and for space reasons put in an ellipsis like this (. . .), I swear on my children that I am not leaving out anything that, if quoted in full, would alter the original meaning or its significance. Those who violate this pact with readers or viewers are to be despised. At no point does Michael Moore make the smallest effort to be objective. At no moment does he pass up the chance of a cheap sneer or a jeer. He pitilessly focuses his camera, for minutes after he should have turned it off, on a distraught and bereaved mother whose grief we have already shared. (But then, this is the guy who thought it so clever and amusing to catch Charlton Heston, in *Bowling for Columbine*, at the onset of his senile dementia.) Such courage.

Perhaps vaguely aware that his movie so completely lacks gravitas, Moore concludes with a sonorous reading of some words from George Orwell. The words are taken from *1984* and consist of a third-person analysis of a hypothetical, endless, and contrived war between three superpowers. The clear intention, as clumsily excerpted like this (. . .) is to suggest that there is no moral distinction between the United States, the Taliban, and the Baath Party and that the war against *jihad* is about nothing. If Moore had studied a bit more, or at all, he could have read Orwell really saying, and in his own voice, the following:

> The majority of pacifists either belong to obscure religious sects or are simply humanitarians who object to taking life and prefer not to follow their thoughts beyond that point. But there is a minority of intellectual pacifists, whose real though unacknowledged motive appears to be hatred of western democracy and admiration for totalitarianism. Pacifist propaganda usually boils down to saying that one side is as bad as the other, but if one looks closely at the writing of the younger intellectual pacifists,

one finds that they do not by any means express impartial disapproval but are directed almost entirely against Britain and the
United States . . .

And that's just from Orwell's *Notes on Nationalism* in May 1945.
A short word of advice: In general, it's highly unwise to quote Orwell if you are already way out of your depth on the question of
moral equivalence. It's also incautious to remind people of Orwell
if you are engaged in a sophomoric celluloid rewriting of recent
history.

If Michael Moore had had his way, Slobodan Milosevic would
still be the big man in a starved and tyrannical Serbia. Bosnia and
Kosovo would have been cleansed and annexed. If Michael
Moore had been listened to, Afghanistan would still be under Taliban rule, and Kuwait would have remained part of Iraq. And Iraq
itself would still be the personal property of a psychopathic crime
family, bargaining covertly with the slave state of North Korea for
WMD. You might hope that a retrospective awareness of this kind
would induce a little modesty. To the contrary, it is employed to
pump air into one of the great sagging blimps of our sorry,
mediocre, celeb-rotten culture. Rock the vote, indeed.

What Did Bush Know?

And what did he think his intelligence agencies knew about Iraqi WMD?

BY FRED KAPLAN

July 14, 2004

SEVERAL INTRIGUING QUESTIONS are raised by a story in today's *New York Times*, which reports that the White House is refusing to give Senate investigators the one-page "President's Summary" of the CIA's 2002 National Intelligence Estimate dealing with Iraqi weapons of mass destruction.

The first question: The "President's Summary" was *one page?* This CIA estimate was a 93-page document, filled with caveats, qualifiers, and footnotes of interagency dissent on several key points. It would take a dedicated master of pith to whittle the NIE's findings and equivocations to a single page. (By the *Times*' account, the summarizer didn't bother with the equivocations.)

Which leads to the second question: Who wrote this summary? And what position had he or she taken on the estimate's controversies?

In graduate school, I had a professor who had served on several top-secret national security panels over the years. The way he bolstered his own influence on these panels, he told me, was always to volunteer for the subpanel that wrote the report. That way, he could shape which points were emphasized and which points were not.

Both of these questions are ancillary to the main question here: What did the president know about Iraqi WMD—or, more to the point, what did he think (or what was he led to think) his intelligence agencies knew?

This is why the Senate Intelligence Committee wants the summary released. It's the same reason the 9/11 commission wanted the White House to release the president's daily intelligence briefing of August 6, 2001 (the one headlined, "Bin Laden Determined To Strike in U.S."). They want to know what the president knew. Did he have reason to see Osama Bin Laden's attack coming—and, if so, should he have done something about it? Did he know about internal disputes over the evidence of Iraqi weapons programs—and, if so, should he have thought twice about going to war?

If all George W. Bush knew about the Iraqi threat was gleaned from a one-page summary that stated the case for WMD—and that did not even acknowledge the existence of a case for skepticism—that's important to know. It's important for citizens who want some insight on why we went to war. And it's important for the president, who may decide to read a longer document the next time there's trouble.

Perhaps no president can be expected to read a 93-page document. (Some presidents would have, though. Bill Clinton was an inveterate reader of intelligence reports. Jimmy Carter once asked to see the engineering blueprints for the KH–11 photoreconnaissance satellite. The latter is a case of a control freak gone too far.) Still, the president's summary should stretch beyond the margins of a single page—at least when the fate of nations is at stake.

A National Intelligence Estimate is not an ordinary report. It marks the one occasion when the Central Intelligence Agency warrants its name, acting as a *central* entity that pulls together the assessments of all the myriad intelligence departments, noting where they agree and where they differ. Most NIEs are produced on an annual basis. Occasionally, the CIA is asked to produce what used to be called a "special" NIE. The 2002 estimate in question, titled "Iraq's Continuing Program for Weapons of Mass Destruction," was such a document. It was ordered so that the president could decide, in an informed manner, whether to go to war. The president is the main consumer of the NIE; it is written entirely for his benefit. To shrink the thing into a single page—to remove all distinctions between certainty and guesswork—is to evade the whole point.

Would Bush have acted any differently if he'd known that the State Department's intelligence branch thought Iraq had imported aluminum tubes for purposes other than building centrifuges? Or that Air Force Intelligence thought Iraq's drones were unsuitable for spraying chemical or biological weapons? Or that several agencies were far less sure than others that Iraq was reconstituting its nuclear weapons program? Maybe not. But a president at least should be told of such things. And citizens should know whether he was told—or wanted to be told—of such things.

This is not an academic exercise. The controversy over the "missile gap," during Dwight Eisenhower's administration, is a dramatic case in point. In 1958, when everybody thought that the Soviet Union far outgunned the United States in intercontinental ballistic missiles (hawks of the day called it "the missile gap"), the CIA's science and technology division started to notice something odd. The Soviets had stopped testing their ICBMs; the whole program was slowing down. The previous year's NIE had predicted the Soviets would have 1,000 ICBMs by 1959 or 1960. But where were they? The CIA's top managers were loath to revise the estimate. A U.S. Air Force panel had concluded a few years earlier that the Soviets intended, in the near future, to launch a nuclear first strike against the United States with such power that we couldn't retaliate. The entire intelligence community agreed. The 1957 NIE seemed consistent with this view. Even the analysts in the CIA's science and technology shop were puzzled by their findings; they agreed with the consensus on the Soviet threat, too.

Months passed, then years. The Soviets still hadn't ginned up an ICBM program. Finally, the CIA broke ranks. The 1960 NIE was crammed with footnotes. Air Force Intelligence stuck to its initial predictions, merely setting the target dates back a couple of years. But the Army and Navy Intelligence branches, which had their own parochial reasons to oppose the Air Force, issued dissenting footnotes. The CIA joined the dissent, saying the Soviets would have only 50 ICBMs. (As it turned out, at the start of 1961, the Soviets had a mere four ICBMs.)

The dispute was jolting. It wasn't a matter of mere numbers. With 1,000 missiles, the Soviets could launch a disarming first strike; with 50 missiles, they couldn't. The dispute about Soviet arsenals translated—inevitably—into a dispute about Soviet intentions. All this was kept secret, even from Congress. President Eisenhower knew about the split, however, and he also knew about the new, super-secret satellite photographs that supported the CIA's position. When leading hawks, who in those days were Democrats, protested that the CIA was grossly underestimating the Soviet threat—just as Bush's hawks protested that the CIA was grossly underestimating the Iraqi threat—Eisenhower politely disagreed but said nothing more. While running for president in 1960, John F. Kennedy had been among those most loudly criticizing the "missile gap." When he took office in 1961, he realized that there was no gap—or that the gap favored the United States.

A similar story could be told about Iraqi's WMD—except for the ending. "Everybody" assumed Iraq possessed stockpiles of chemical and biological weapons; some also believed Saddam Hussein was trying to rebuild his nuclear program. The CIA, which shared this assumption, kept coming up short on supporting evidence and even found some evidence to dispute it. Footnotes of dissent and ambiguity crept into the NIE. But this time, the president did not side with the dissenters. The question is: Did he know there *were* dissenters? And: Did he care?

Racist Like Me

Why am I the only honest bigot?

BY DEBRA DICKERSON

Aug. 11, 2004

IN A NATION RIVEN to its very core by race, I appear to be the only remaining racist. Off and on, I'm homophobic and anti-Semitic, too, but mostly, I'm racist. Yet unlike the rest of you, I'm honest about it.

I'm the only person I know who routinely admits to being a racist. When I redeemed my Mother's Day spa package, I was assigned a lovely young black woman as my aesthetician. As we chatted, I found myself searching for words. Eventually, I realized I was trying to find a way to ask about her credentials. In 20 years of spa trips, I have never had a black aesthetician, and I have never thought, let alone asked, about one's competence, even when they disappoint me. It appears that I, too, think black people are stupid, uninformed, and graceless. Criminal, too—day before yesterday, after finalizing the details of working in a public housing complex, I dreamt that night of herds of rapacious, animalistic blacks robbing, assaulting, and generally terrorizing me there. (*Birth of a Nation* was more subtle.) So, counting yesterday's incident, which I will recount shortly, that makes twice just this week that I was a racist.

It was yesterday's incident that got me thinking about how racism is lived. The *New York Times* recently won a Pulitzer for a series on how *race* is lived, but that's not quite the same thing, is it? Most of us agree that racism is far from dead and that we're all responsible for helping to end it. And yet, so charged is the issue of race that it is virtually impossible for those who do not already agree about it to discuss it. Without a free exchange of ideas, progress is not very likely; conservatives will continue to preach to their choir and liberals will do the same.

Here's an example: A gay friend was being cavalier and dismissive, I thought, about the least divergence from the gay agenda, even by a pro-gay person like me. He wouldn't even entertain the notion that, say, lesbians in a women's locker room could legitimately give one pause. It shouldn't be a long pause (given that they've always been there), but give me a break. From the look on his face, you'd have thought that I had said he was going to sodomite hell. "Oh Debra. From you?" I argued that a man would never be allowed into a women's locker room—even if he were physically incapable of either sex or violence (I also made him blind for good measure). My friend sighed deeply, looked to the heavens as if praying for patience, and then grandly "forgave" me by abruptly changing the subject. Clearly, he considered any such discussion homophobic, a designation I escaped solely on the strength of our friendship. But why couldn't we discuss it? The notion that "victim" status exempts him from the need to examine, explain, or defend his beliefs is a dangerous one indeed. That was the perfect moment both to prove to himself that he'd thought things through, and to educate someone who could go forth and spread knowledge. Instead, we just showed each other that you can love and respect someone and yet know that they can sometimes be self-righteous, intolerant, and anti-intellectual.

One reason for bigotry's maddening intractability is that a determination—however knee-jerk, superficial, or unthinkingly made—that something or someone is racist ends the discussion, as happened with my friend. The verdict is "guilty" and the only punishment is forfeiture of the right to consider yourself a decent human being. Better to be a necrophiliac than an admitted bigot. Yet if we are to evolve on the issue of race, the notion that you, or someone else, is racist ought to function as the *beginning* of the attainment of full humanity, not the proof that you've relinquished it. Realizing with each incident that I was operating from a no-longer-quite-subconscious script about race allowed me to recognize, and then confront, the hateful notions I have internalized about blacks. Worse, it allowed me to see that having experienced racism had helped turn me into one: It turns out that I have a problem with whites, too.

Yesterday, I watched a white man park his truck in my driveway and walk off down the road without even a glance to see if the owners were about so he could ask permission. The sense of entitlement and ownership he exuded pushed every race-, gender- and class-based button a black girl from the inner city has to push. Guys like that have been pushing the world (read: me) around forever. Still, I tried to shrug it off. Then, when I went out for the mail two hours later, I was furious to see his truck still on my property. In full Gloria Steinem meets Fannie Lou Hamer mode, I marched down the road to the construction site where I figured he'd gone.

At the site, a gaggle of "Joe College"-type shirtless white boys were goofing off, and a grandfatherly black man halfheartedly directed nonexistent traffic. As I approached, the black man perked up, glad to see me in this extremely white part of an extremely white city in an extremely white region. Or perhaps he was glad because now he wasn't the only adult. The white guys, suddenly busy with their rakes, feigned blindness.

"Whose truck—"

The black man strode over and pointed gleefully at the man who was clearly in charge. "The green hat! That's *his* truck." How had he known what I was going to say?

With happy spite, the black man watched as I exchanged a few words with my squatter and saluted me as the man who must be his boss followed me shamefacedly to move his truck. As I passed the brother, I said evilly, "If I'd parked on *his* property, the police would be here."

"You got that right," he agreed grimly, as if I'd narrowly escaped the noose. It's a wonder we didn't flash each other black power salutes. But the moment the words were out of my mouth, I was ashamed. Worse: I felt stupid.

Who am I kidding? I'm an attorney. The lots are so big in my deer-filled suburb that I had to drive from neighbor to neighbor to collect petition signatures for a local election. In fact, we rarely even use that usurped driveway because we have two. My architect husband is white as are our two children. (So far. Biracial kids often darken over time.) The local police are just as respectful of me as they are of my neighbors, whatever they might be thinking. Whether or not I *should* fear them, I don't.

It is a testament to the enduring legacy of racism that a black grandfather still doing manual labor bothered to side with either me or my squatter. He should have said to hell with the both of you and played dumb, leaving the two of us to fight over our possessions. I'm guessing he'd also witnessed his feudal lord take arrogant possession of a stranger's property and that this had pushed all his buttons, too. The fact that I turned out to be black was the icing on the cake.

In a way, I'm arguing for class warfare to replace racial warfare. Class conflict makes sense; it keeps the powerful from riding roughshod over senior citizens who can't retire from manual labor in the hot sun. The truth is, I have far more in common with the rich white man than I do with that poor black grandfather (who would never dare to park on private property in this neighborhood). A world of perfect harmony would be lovely, but until the rapture comes I'd rather blue-collar types of all races faced off against us "suits" than one race against the other. There is nothing logical, natural, or beneficial about a world organized by race—the very concept is irrational. Any system divided along racial lines, implicitly or overtly, will be immoral, inefficient, and unstable. (Take, for example, poor whites' hatred of slaves, rather than of slavery, for depressing wages.)

Class conflict, on the other hand, is natural and rational. It brought us the minimum wage, OSHA, Social Security, the weekend, overtime, pensions, and the like. While none of those are unmitigated successes, a system organized along class lines acknowledges that capitalism doesn't police itself and that labor must have a voice—it wasn't the capitalists who pushed for child labor laws and the eight-hour workday. Everybody loses when societal goods are distributed on the basis of race, even those in the front of the bus. Bigotry is just plain stupid, but as long as the price of examining one's prejudices is expulsion from the human race, we're never going to be able to quash it.

When I realized that I had internalized the world's loathing of blacks, my first response was, counterintuitively, relief. Finally, I have proof that blacks' obsession with racism isn't crazy. If I secretly think that many poor blacks are animalistic and stupid, you'll never make me believe that lots of other people don't, too. My lasting response has been chagrined amusement to realize that I hold such ridiculous, illogical notions. Most of all, acknowledging my own racism has given me a measure of compassion for how difficult it is to retain one's humanity in such a politicized and inhumane world. I'm black and I make my living thinking about race, but I still wasn't immune to the insidious bigotry in our world. How much harder it must be for those with far less time to contemplate and come to terms with these vexing social issues.

It's not bigotry per se that hamstrings us in the struggle to achieve a just society. It's our inability to talk about and think our way through our preconceptions. We have to learn how to forgive each other, and more importantly, ourselves, when we're stupid.

Trying Really Hard to Like India

BY SETH STEVENSON

September, 2004

Sept. 28, 2004

I HAVE A PROBLEM with backpackers. The problem is that wherever they are, I don't want to be.

Partly, it's that I don't go somewhere like India so I can hang out with a bunch of 19-year-old German dudes (though I'm sure they're lovely people). Also, it's that I look at all these backpackers . . . and I see myself. And frankly, I don't like what I see.

For one, I'm not properly bathed. And for another, I've got this massive, geeky pack on my back, which dwarfs my torso and bends me near double under its weight. (Because of this, I have, I'll admit somewhat irrationally, refused to use a backpack on this trip. Instead I've brought a wheeled carry-on suitcase, which has worked quite nicely. Just try to call me a backpacker now! No backpack here, Heinrich!)

But above all, I hate the ambience that forms around a back-packer enclave. The ticky-tacky souvenir shops. The sketchy tour guides. The rabbit warren hostels. And the way the locals start to eye me like I'm nothing but an ambulatory wallet.

There are two ways to escape the backpackers. The first is to get off the beaten path, wander around, and discover a private Eden not yet ruined by backpacking hordes. This takes more time than my vacation will allow. So I've opted for the second (much quicker) method: money.

Yes, the simplest way to find solitude is to buy it. Thus we've arrived here at the Casino Group Marari Beach Resort.

This idyllic spot is on the west coast of India in the state of Kerala (the setting for *The God of Small Things*). The resort's lovely bungalows are tucked between groves of palm trees. The beach is wide, empty, silent. Each evening the sun melts down into the Arabian Sea. By day we lounge around a heated pool eating big plates of samosas. Nearby, in the recreation area, an older Italian woman is playing badminton in a bikini.

Wait, you say, why bother to go to India for this? If a beach resort's all you want, there are plenty back home, right? I assure you this is different for several reasons, such as . . .

The food: Each night, we enjoy delicious Indian specialties, prepared by actual Indian chefs, in India. (Pause to lick tandoori chicken from fingers.) You just can't get that at home.

The cost: We're paying about $70 a night for our bungalow. Pretty much anywhere in the States—for a luxury resort with a private beach—you'd pay at least quadruple that. Consider the fact that Sir Paul McCartney once stayed here. When I can afford a hotel Paul McCartney stays at, you can be certain it's a bargain.

The sheer solitude: You'll rarely find a beach this nice that's also this utterly empty. There's nothing here (as my pictures attest). Several hundred yards away are a few wooden fishing boats, which haul up their catch on the beach each afternoon. Also— and I swear this is somehow charming (remember, it's hundreds of yards away)—you'll see a few village folk squatting amid the tides. This is because they don't have indoor plumbing.

The world beyond the hotel gates: Walk outside your beach resort in Florida . . . and you're still in Florida. Walk outside your beach resort in India and . . . oh, man, you are unmistakably in India. Lots of heartbreaking rural poverty. Lots of sad-yet-edifying tableaux (which is no doubt what you came here for, correct?). It's sort of the best of both worlds for the tourist who fancies himself culturally aware: Live right next to the picturesque misery—but not in it.

Before you condemn me to hell, remember: Unless you're Gandhi—and you're not—you can't come here without diving headfirst into a salty sea of unpleasant contradictions.

For yet another lesson on this theme, take our last night at Marari Beach. We somehow end up drinking in the bar with a thirtysomething American woman—let's call her "Debbie"—who is six stiff drinks ahead of us. Between sips of some tropical concoction, she delivers a slurry monologue explaining that she has come to India on business. Her business: designing doormats. No joke.

One of Kerala's big industries is coir—a textile made from coconut husks. On a bike ride we took around the village (yes, "the world beyond the hotel gates"), we could see into huts that had looms and people weaving coir into simple mats. These mats get trimmed and finished (by some big export factory) to Debbie's design specs. Then they get shipped to North America and end up in some middlebrow home-furnishings catalog where you can buy them for $26.99.

Debbie is drinking heavily because her job here is wicked depressing. She buys in bulk from the big exporter, who pays a shady middleman, who (barely) pays the villagers here. The villagers can make about three mats per week—all of excellent quality—and for this they get paid a few cents per mat. The middleman of course takes all the profit.

Debbie, good-hearted human that she is, is on the verge of drunken tears as she describes all this. She knows the whole thing is grossly unfair. And that she perpetuates it. But if she wants to keep her job with the American firm she works for, and still make deals with Indian exporters, there's not a damn thing she can do about it.

And unless you have carefully avoided buying any products made by Third World labor—and chances are you have not—you're really no better than Debbie. Let's drink to that. Believe me, Debbie already has.

Sept. 30, 2004

Our first day out in Mumbai (formerly Bombay), we were approached by a man who—I'm fairly certain of this—planned to kidnap us. He gave us this carefully polished spiel about needing to cast a few extras for a Bollywood movie and how we'd be perfect for this scene he was shooting, so if we would just hop into his car with him . . . Tempting, but no dice. (It sort of cooled our jets when, in the middle of the pitch, this other Indian guy ran over and shouted, "Be careful with this man! This is a dangerous man!")

I'll admit, this Bollywood scam was brilliant. It played on my vanity and my long-held desire to appear in a Bollywood movie (preferably in a dance scene). I salute you, my would-be abductor.

But other pitches were not as well-crafted. For instance, there was this guy who smiled weakly and asked us, with a halfhearted shrug, "Monkey dance?" Our eyes followed the leash in his hand, which led to the neck of a monkey. The most jaded, world-weary monkey I've ever seen. The Lou Reed of monkeys. He looked like he was about to sit down, pull out his works, and shoot a big syringe full of heroin into his paw. Needless to say, we declined the monkey dance—which I'm guessing would have been some sort of sad, simian death-jig.

The upshot of all this: Mumbai is not the place to go for a care-free, relaxing vacation. Just stepping out on the streets can be a difficult ordeal. The air smells like twice-baked urine, marinated in more urine. The sidewalks are a slalom of legless beggars and feral dogs. Hundreds of times each day you walk right past something so unfathomably sad, so incomprehensibly surreal, so horribly unfair . . .

The only way to cope is to stop resisting. Embrace the chaos. If you see a woman rolling around in the gutter clutching at the massive, bulbous wart on the side of her face and moaning loudly . . . well, that's part of the scenery. No one else here (certainly no native Mumbaian) will pay her any attention. So why should you? Just say to yourself: Wow, that's crazy stuff and marvelously edifying. Doo-dee-doo, keep on walking.

That's harsh and simplistic. The truth is, the chaos can be wonderful sometimes, too. There's a goofy sense of freedom that comes with it. A sense of unknowing.

Back home in the States, it can feel like we've got life figured out, regulated, under control, under wraps. But here in India, nothing seems even close to figured out. Nothing seems remotely under control. You're never quite sure what will happen next, and you're working without a net.

Terrifying? Yes. But also invigorating. On the train ride up from Goa, I perused a women's magazine (sort of an Indian *Cosmo*) that we'd bought at a newsstand. The cover story was about women who'd lived abroad—mostly in the United States and Britain—but moved back because they liked India better. All these former NRIs (Non-Resident Indians) had gotten homesick . . . *for the chaos!* Yes, the West was clean and orderly. But that was sort of boring. They missed the hubbub, the craziness, the randomness of India.

I see what they're saying. But in honesty, I prefer to see it from several stories up, in the air-conditioned cocktail lounge of the Oberoi Hotel. Ahhhh. Soft music. Lovely view. No legless beggars.

From up here, sure, all that chaos is beautiful. It's amazing to ponder (while calmly sipping a stiff rum and Coke) how one billion people manage to coexist in a single, sprawling democracy. It truly is impressive that this country keeps chugging along—massive, bulbous face warts and all.

In fact, I've come not just to like, but to love India—in a way—from afar. It's the underdog. It's dirty, and hectic, and insane . . . and I find myself rooting for it.

Trading Family Values

How the old conservative/liberal stereotypes break down when it comes to parenting.

BY ANN HULBERT

Oct. 22, 2004

DADS SAY THE DARNEDEST THINGS about their kids during presidential debates. "I'm trying to put a leash on them," President Bush joked in a rare light moment during the first debate. "Well, I don't know. I've learned not to do that, Mr. President," Kerry responded with a smile, basking in the compliment the president had bestowed a few moments earlier. ("I admire the fact that he is a great dad," Bush had told Jim Lehrer.) The final debate ended with another round of mutual flattery about the candidates' good-guy parenting (on display in their *Dr. Phil* appearances, too). No old-style fathers here: That was the unmistakable message. With the exception of the Mary Cheney flap, we have been treated to the unusual spectacle of red-blue convergence on the classically divisive issue of family values.

But look again at the dads and listen to the kids who are everywhere on the campaign trail, and an even odder development stands out. The parties show signs of having flip-flopped on a parenting debate that dates back to 1968, when Nixon deplored the "fog of permissiveness" that he felt had engulfed the country. Then it was conservatives who complained that unruly youths had been "Spocked when they should have been spanked"; in the 1980s and 1990s, dare-to-discipline crusaders like Focus on the Family's James Dobson pursued the anti-permissive theme as the culture war heated up. These days, though, it's Democrats who come across as no-nonsense parental taskmasters, certainly compared to their Republican opponents.

By now, the Bush dynasty is famous for its failure to impose a tight-leash parenting policy. However you judge the particular youthful exploits of either W. or his twins, they don't add up to an advertisement for the character education and abstinence-training that conservative child-rearing experts like Dobson have trumpeted in "the battle for the hearts and minds of our kids" (the subtitle of his and Gary Bauer's 1990 manifesto, *Children at Risk*). By contrast, the Kerry-Edwards entourage is positively strait-laced. Their family tableau telegraphs hardworking, public-spirited wholesomeness—even wonkiness.

The super-conscientious tradition, in fact, can be traced back to their Democratic antecedents, from the high-achieving Chelsea Clinton on through the golden Gore girls, to homely Amy Carter (who worried about nuclear proliferation, remember?). The parents have been no slouches, either. Who would have thought pop-culture policewoman Tipper could be topped? When Theresa Heinz claims she "was a *witch* with my children"—requiring written reports on the snippets of television she let them watch, for example—you can readily believe she ran a strict, Old World household. She's the woman who yanked Jack Edwards' thumb out of his mouth, after all. Dr. Spock would have spanked *her*.

It's obvious why the Democrats are eager to play up the tough-love aura. They hope it will appeal to the family-values crowd and help counter the party's "soft" image. But the hard-driving display isn't simply spin at work. These liberal parents—even the libidinal Bill Clinton—are all too credible as goody-goody exemplars of the get-ahead grind's approach, beginning early in life: They're moms and dads who can plausibly preach do-as-I-did to their kids and who aren't about to let them slack off. Watch clips of Kerry as a pompous young striver—famously unpopular with his peers—on the recent *Frontline* program "The Choice 2004," and you'll be convinced that Vanessa Kerry isn't faking when she describes a dad on her case, monitoring homework and keeping close tabs on the partying. If he ever really learned a no-leash approach, it was late in the game.

What's somewhat more mysterious is the absence of Republican chagrin at their side's failure to live up to the industrious competition. It's clear, of course, that Bush is eager to humanize his "hard" profile. He evidently figures it doesn't hurt to be the laid-back dad, especially since that lets him avoid the awkward don't-do-as-I-did stance that nearly tripped him up in the last election. (When a hidden drunken-driving arrest surfaced from his dissolute past, his excuse was that he'd wanted to shield his daughters.) It's also little wonder that he lets his girls loose in their designer clothes to gab about MTV and *The O.C.* They're plainly being deployed to promote the notion that being a young Republican isn't dorky.

Still, you might expect a hint of defensiveness, given the Christian fundamentalist followers whom Bush is said to care so much about pleasing. But there's a reason the campaign goes ahead and flaunts the "when we were young and irresponsible, we were young and irresponsible" ethos that the twins displayed at the convention: It has the anti-elitist appeal the party assumes its Red state base thrives on. Filtered through a populist prism, such an attitude needn't suggest decadence; it can convey a spirit of down-home, defiant independence. After all, studiousness and parental pushiness, however virtuous, are also part of the pointy-headed approach to life. To snub TV is snobby, and adult hypervigilance can look a lot like elitist cosseting. You can see the cultural contradictions of populism at work: "Hit the books" is not presumed to be what Joe Six-Pack wants to hear.

You know the winds have changed when the obstreperous Bill O'Reilly gets up on a conservative parenting soapbox that once emphasized a mind-your-manners-and-act-mature message. In his brand-new *O'Reilly Factor for Kids*, aimed at middle-schoolers and teens, the conservative icon adopts an I'm-your-pal style, and a don't-do-the-dumb-stuff-I-did tack—only to find himself in just the mess his own savvy advice is supposed to prevent. ("Guys, if you exploit a girl, it will come back to get you. That's called 'karma.'") He's not a preacherly Dr. Dobson type, that's for sure. If O'Reilly has a model, it's John Rosemond, the upstart right-wing author of *Because I Said So* and other popular parenting books, who likes to bill himself as a "loose cannon."

Rosemond comes right out and says that "conservatives believe that where government is concerned, the less, the better. The same applies to the governing of children." By this, he means parents should do less micromanaging and let kids learn from their mistakes—as he presumes they will, pulling themselves up by their own bootstraps. (He boasts of overcoming the "pot-addled excesses" of his youth.) But Bush's own record on that score is less than inspiring, and his daughters can probably count on getting bailed out, just as he was. Their special no-consequences dispensation is not part of the official populist parenting message, of course. It should, though, get wider airing in Red states where incomes and education levels lag. Hard-driving parents and kids in the well-educated, blue-state elite are easy to mock, but they're onto an important secret: The luxury of screwing up and still coming out on top isn't something regular Americans can count on.

What I Like About Scrooge

In praise of misers.

BY STEVEN E. LANDSBURG
Dec. 9, 2004

HERE'S WHAT I LIKE about Ebenezer Scrooge: His meager lodgings were dark because darkness is cheap, and barely heated because coal is not free. His dinner was gruel, which he prepared himself. Scrooge paid no man to wait on him.

Scrooge has been called ungenerous. I say that's a bum rap. What could be more generous than keeping your lamps unlit and your plate unfilled, leaving more fuel for others to burn and more food for others to eat? Who is a more benevolent neighbor than the man who employs no servants, freeing them to wait on someone else?

Oh, it might be slightly more complicated than that. Maybe when Scrooge demands less coal for his fire, less coal ends up being mined. But that's fine, too. Instead of digging coal for Scrooge, some would-be miner is now free to perform some other service for himself or someone else.

Dickens tells us that the Lord Mayor, in the stronghold of the mighty Mansion House, gave orders to his 50 cooks and butlers to keep Christmas as a Lord Mayor's household should—presumably for a houseful of guests who lavishly praised his generosity. The bricks, mortar, and labor that built the Mansion House might otherwise have built housing for hundreds; Scrooge, by living in three sparse rooms, deprived no man of a home. By employing no cooks or butlers, he ensured that cooks and butlers were available to some other household where guests reveled in ignorance of their debt to Ebenezer Scrooge.

In this whole world, there is nobody more generous than the miser—the man who *could* deplete the world's resources but chooses not to. The only difference between miserliness and philanthropy is that the philanthropist serves a favored few while the miser spreads his largesse far and wide.

If you build a house and refuse to buy a house, the rest of the world is one house richer. If you earn a dollar and refuse to spend a dollar, the rest of the world is one dollar richer—because you produced a dollar's worth of goods and didn't consume them.

Who exactly gets those goods? That depends on how you save. Put a dollar in the bank and you'll bid down the interest rate by just enough so someone somewhere can afford an extra dollar's worth of vacation or home improvement. Put a dollar in your mattress and (by effectively reducing the money supply) you'll drive down prices by just enough so someone somewhere can have an extra dollar's worth of coffee with his dinner. Scrooge, no doubt a canny investor, lent his money at interest. His less conventional namesake Scrooge McDuck filled a vault with dollar bills to roll around in. No matter. Ebenezer Scrooge lowered interest rates. Scrooge McDuck lowered prices. Each Scrooge enriched his neighbors as much as any Lord Mayor who invited the town in for a Christmas meal.

Saving *is* philanthropy, and—because this is both the Christmas season and the season of tax reform—it's worth mentioning that the tax system should recognize as much. If there's a tax deduction for charitable giving, there should be a tax deduction for saving. What you earn and don't spend is your contribution to the world, and it's equally a contribution whether you give it away or squirrel it away.

Of course, there's always the threat that some meddling ghosts will come along and convince you to deplete your savings, at which point it makes sense (insofar as the taxation of income ever makes sense) to start taxing you. Which is exactly what individual retirement accounts are all about: They shield your earnings from taxation for as long as you save (that is, for as long as you let others enjoy the fruits of your labor), but no longer.

Great artists are sometimes unaware of the deepest meanings in their own creations. Though Dickens might not have recognized it, the primary moral of *A Christmas Carol* is that there should be no limit on IRA contributions. This is quite independent of all the other reasons why the tax system should encourage saving (e.g., the salutary effects on economic growth).

If Christmas is the season of selflessness, then surely one of the great symbols of Christmas should be Ebenezer Scrooge—the old Scrooge, not the reformed one. It's taxes, not misers, that need reforming.

2005

THE SALE TO THE Washington Post Company went through in January, making us a sister publication to the *Washington Post* newspaper and *Newsweek* magazine. *Slate* closed its Seattle office and settled almost the entire staff in New York and Washington. Michael Kinsley, who had left briefly to run the *Los Angeles Times* opinion section, returned as a columnist. Our multimedia efforts grew. We started publishing the best newspaper political cartoons—a portfolio that now features 14 Pulitzer Prize–winning cartoonists. In December, *Slate* and Magnum Photos began collaborating on Today's Pictures, a daily slide show of photographs from Magnum's extraordinary archives. Witold Rybczynski signed on as our first architecture critic.

Technological innovation, once a weakness, was becoming a strong point. *Slate* was one of the first major media outlets to begin podcasting, and our podcast is consistently one of iTunes' most popular. We launched our first regular video feature, Robert Wright's "Meaning of Life TV."

What happened in a decade? When we began in 1996, we published once a week. By the beginning of 2006, we were publishing 10 times a day and putting up as many stories in 24 hours as we used to post in a week. In 1996, *Slate* was lucky to get 10,000 readers a day. In 2006, we often have 1 million readers a day. *Slate's* childhood is over. We're looking forward to an unruly adolescence.

Doctor, Please Reattach My . . .

How long can you wait before sewing a severed body part back on?

BY DANIEL ENGBER

Feb. 22, 2005

LATE SATURDAY NIGHT in Anchorage, Alaska, a man's girlfriend cut off his penis and flushed it down the toilet. A municipal worker recovered the penis; surgeons had sewed it back on by morning. How long can you wait before reattaching a severed body part?

A day or two, at least. The man in Alaska was lucky to have his penis sawed off in a frigid climate (though the incident did occur indoors). A severed finger can survive for at least 12 hours in a warm environment and up to a couple of days if refrigerated. Some reports indicate that body parts can survive for as many as four days before being reattached.

Doctors suggest that a severed penis or other body part should be sealed in a plastic bag and placed on ice. Direct contact with the ice can cause frostbite and damage the tissue, and suspending severed body parts in water has been shown to make reattachment more difficult.

Not every part of the body is as resilient as the finger. Muscle tends to have a faster metabolism than other kinds of tissue, so a severed arm or leg will deteriorate more quickly than your pinkie (a full limb must be reattached within 6 to 12 hours). Cartilage has a particularly slow metabolism, so a severed ear or nose can be quite durable. The types of tissues in the penis actually make it an excellent candidate for longer stretches in the ice bucket.

The first step in reattaching a body part is to restore blood flow by reconnecting the arteries. For the procedure to work, the severed tissue must be alive, and the severed arteries must be large enough to manipulate using microsurgical techniques. The blood vessels in the finger are about 1 or 1.5 millimeters wide (depending on where you cut); vessels in the penis tend to be somewhat bigger and easier to work with.

You also need to reattach the veins, or blood won't be able to flow out of the severed part. Without a conduit for outflow, the body part will swell, which can cause tissue damage. When veins can't be sewn up right away, surgeons apply live leeches. A single leech can suck up 10 cubic centimeters of blood from a severed penis; a chemical in its saliva, hirudin, keeps blood from clotting and allows continued drainage.

Tendons, bone, and nerves must also be reattached. In general, the cleaner the cut, the more simple the operation. Ears, which have small arteries and which, when severed, are often ripped off or bitten off, tend to be tricky.

Even in the case of a clean cut, surgeons often remove some tissue to shorten the appendage. When the veins and arteries are stretched, tension on the stitches can jeopardize the procedure; shortening the severed part allows a bit of slack. In situations where significant shortening is undesirable, vein grafts from other parts of the body can provide some leeway.

Rappers and Bloggers

Separated at birth!

BY JOSH LEVIN

Feb. 23, 2005

P. DIDDY GARGLES CRISTAL as his yacht sails from San Tropez to Ibiza. Atrios stares at his computer screen and ponders the effect of "increased central bank diversification out of dollar holdings." Nelly takes in the NBA All-Star Game from the first row while gabbing on a cell phone made out of a giant shoe. InstaPundit digests the latest developments in the Dartmouth board of trustees race and takes note of an update to C-SPAN's early morning schedule. What, do I need to draw you a Venn diagram? Rappers and bloggers—they're the same!

Those of you obsessed with external appearances may think I'm kidding. What, you ask, could those champagne-swilling, "bitch"-shouting rappers have in common with those Jolt-pounding, "read the whole thing"-writing bloggers?

For starters, both groups share a love of loose-fitting, pajama-style apparel. Still not satisfied? Bloggers and rappers are equally obsessed with social networking. Every rapper rolls with his entourage; every blogger rolls with his blog roll. Women can't win an audience in either profession without raunching it up like Lil' Kim or Wonkette.

And don't forget those silly, silly names. Even if he didn't flaunt his devotion to pimping and pit bulls, you'd probably guess Snoop Dogg is a rapper. And Fedlawyerguy—yeah, probably a blogger. But the "blogger or rapper?" parlor game can stump even the nerdiest gangsta. Does uggabugga hate on wack emcees or wack Charles Krauthammer? What about Mad Kane? Big Noyd, Justus League, Uppity Negro, Little Brother, Cold Fury, and South Knox Bubba? (Answers: blogger, blogger, rapper, rap group, blogger, rap group, blogger, blogger.)

Essentially, blogging is sampling plus a new riff. Political bloggers take a story in the news, rip out a few chunks, and type out a few comments. Rap songs use the same recipe: Dig through a crate of records, slice out a high hat and a bass line, and lay a new vocal track on top. Of course, the molecular structure of dead-tree journalism and classic rock is filthy with other people's research and other people's chord progressions. But in newspaper writing and rock music, the end goal is the appearance of originality—to make the product look seamless by hiding your many small thefts. For rappers and bloggers, each theft is worth celebrating, another loose item to slap onto the collage.

Rap music and blogging are populist, low-cost-of-entry communication forms that reward self-obsessed types who love writing in first person. Maybe that's why both won so many converts so quickly. If you want to become MC I'm Good at Rapping, all you have to do is rustle up a microphone and a sampler. If you want to blog as AngryVeganCatholicGOPMom, bring a computer, an Internet connection, a working knowledge of Ctrl-C and Ctrl-V, and a whole lot of spare time.

Although bloggers and rappers are free to write about whatever they damn well please, they mostly talk to each other and about each other. That's partly because it's so easy to communicate with your fellow working professionals. If Nas disses you for not having a mustache, it's easy enough to come right back and tell him you slept with the mother of his child. When Markos from Daily Kos offhandedly admits that he doesn't read many books, Little Green Footballs steps up to hammer the softball.

But rappers' and bloggers' self-importance also has something to do with the supremely annoying righteousness that rides along with those who believe they're overturned the archaic forms of expression favored by The Man—that is, whitey and/or the mainstream media. Ninety percent of rap lyrics are self-congratulatory rhymes about how great the rapper is at rapping, the towering difficulties of succeeding in the rap game, or the lameness of wanksta rivals. Blogging is a circle jerk that never stops circling: links to posts by other bloggers, following links to newspaper stories about bloggers, following wonderment at the corruptions and complacency of old-fashioned, credentialed journalism.

Sure, there are a few differences between the blogosphere and the blingosphere. Although bloggers have a certain buzz about them these days, they'll never be cool the way rappers are cool. The blogger lifestyle is dangerous—staying up all night and eating Cheetos will eventually kill you—but not *sexy* dangerous. Rappers can afford to be more conspicuous with their triumphalism because selling millions of records is more financially rewarding than getting millions of hits. But if that blog ad gravy train ever comes in, I guarantee you that Josh Marshall will pick up his mail in a gold-plated tank and Nick Denton will put a hit on any linkmonger who looks at him cross-eyed.

But don't get caught up in those piddling distinctions. Public Enemy's Chuck D once said that rap music was the black CNN. After busting a cap in Eason Jordan's ass, what are bloggers now if not the white CNN? If only the two schools recognized they could inflict more damage with a little teamwork. Today, Mickey Kaus sits alone in Los Angeles, valiantly spewing bile at hidebound East Coast elites. Just think how much more pungent that bile would be with a hot backing track by Dr. Dre. Hey, maybe that podcasting thing won't be totally useless after all.

Not Dead at All

Why Congress was right to stick up for Terri Schiavo.

BY HARRIET McBRYDE JOHNSON

March 23, 2005

THE TERRI SCHIAVO CASE is hard to write about, hard to think about. Those films are hard to look at. I see that face, maybe smiling, maybe not, and I am reminded of a young woman I knew as a child, lying on a couch, brain-damaged, apparently unresponsive, and deeply beloved—freakishly perhaps but genuinely so—living proof of one family's no-matter-what commitment. I watch nourishment flowing into a slim tube that runs through a neat, round, surgically created orifice in Ms. Schiavo's abdomen, and I'm almost envious. What effortless intake! Due to a congenital neuromuscular disease, I am having trouble swallowing, and it's a constant struggle to get by mouth the calories my skinny body needs. For whatever reason, I'm still trying, but I know a tube is in my future. So, possibly, is speechlessness. That's a scary thought. If I couldn't speak for myself, would I want to die? If I become uncommunicative, a passive object of other people's care, should I hope my brain goes soft and leaves me in peace?

My emotional response is powerful, but at bottom it's not important. It's no more important than anyone else's, not what matters.

The things that ought to matter have become obscured in our communal clash of gut reactions. Here are 10 of them:

1. Ms. Schiavo is not terminally ill. She has lived in her current condition for 15 years. This is not about end-of-life decision-making. The question is whether she should be killed by starvation and dehydration.

2. Ms. Schiavo is not dependent on life support. Her lungs, kidneys, heart, and digestive systems work fine. Just as she uses a wheelchair for mobility, she uses a tube for eating and drinking. Feeding Ms. Schiavo is not difficult, painful, or in any way heroic. Feeding tubes are a very simple piece of adaptive equipment, and the fact that Ms. Schiavo eats through a tube should have nothing to do with whether she should live or die.

3. This is not a case about a patient's right to refuse treatment. I don't see eating and drinking as "treatment," but even if they are, everyone agrees that Ms. Schiavo is presently incapable of articulating a decision to refuse treatment. The question is who should make the decision for her, and whether that substitute decision-maker should be authorized to kill her by starvation and dehydration.

4. There is a genuine dispute as to Ms. Schiavo's awareness and consciousness. But if we assume that those who would authorize her death are correct, Ms. Schiavo is completely unaware of her situation and therefore incapable of suffering physically or emotionally. Her death thus can't be justified for relieving her suffering.

5. There is a genuine dispute as to what Ms. Schiavo believed and expressed about life with severe disability before she

herself became incapacitated; certainly, she never stated her preferences in an advance directive like a living will. If we assume that Ms. Schiavo is aware and conscious, it is possible that, like most people who live with severe disability for as long as she has, she has abandoned her preconceived fears of the life she is now living. We have no idea whether she wishes to be bound by things she might have said when she was living a very different life. If we assume she is unaware and unconscious, we can't justify her death as her preference. She has no preference.

6. Ms. Schiavo, like all people, incapacitated or not, has a federal constitutional right not to be deprived of her life without due process of law.

7. In addition to the rights all people enjoy, Ms. Schiavo has a statutory right under the Americans With Disabilities Act not to be treated differently because of her disability. Obviously, Florida law would not allow a husband to kill a nondisabled wife by starvation and dehydration; killing is not ordinarily considered a private family concern or a matter of choice. It is Ms. Schiavo's disability that makes her killing different in the eyes of the Florida courts. Because the state is overtly drawing lines based on disability, it has the burden under the ADA of justifying those lines.

8. In other contexts, federal courts are available to make sure state courts respect federally protected rights. This review is critical not only to the parties directly involved, but to the integrity of our legal system. Although review will very often be a futile last-ditch effort—as with most death-penalty habeas petitions—federalism requires that the federal government, not the states, have the last word. When the issue is the scope of a guardian's authority, it is

necessary to allow other people, in this case other family members, standing to file a legal challenge.

9. The whole society has a stake in making sure state courts are not tainted by prejudices, myths, and unfounded fears— like the unthinking horror in mainstream society that transforms feeding tubes into fetish objects, emblematic of broader, deeper fears of disability that sometimes slide from fear to disgust and from disgust to hatred. While we should not assume that disability prejudice tainted the Florida courts, we cannot reasonably assume that it did not.

10. Despite the unseemly Palm Sunday pontificating in Congress, the legislation enabling Ms. Schiavo's parents to sue did not take sides in the so-called culture wars. It did not dictate that Ms. Schiavo be fed. It simply created a procedure whereby the federal courts could decide whether Ms. Schiavo's federally protected rights have been violated.

In the Senate, a key supporter of a federal remedy was Iowa Sen. Tom Harkin, a progressive Democrat and longtime friend of labor and civil rights, including disability rights. Harkin told reporters, "There are a lot of people in the shadows, all over this country, who are incapacitated because of a disability, and many times there is no one to speak for them, and it is hard to determine what their wishes really are or were. So I think there ought to be a broader type of a proceeding that would apply to people in similar circumstances who are incapacitated."

I hope against hope that I will never be one of those people in the shadows, that I will always, one way or another, be able to make my wishes known. I hope that I will not outlive my usefulness or my capacity (at least occasionally) to amuse the people around me. But if it happens otherwise, I hope whoever is appointed to speak for me will be subject to legal constraints. Even if my guardian thinks I'd be better off dead—even if I think so my-self—I hope to live and die in a world that recognizes that killing, even of people with the most severe disabilities, is a matter of more than private concern.

Clearly, Congress' Palm Sunday legislation was not the "broader type of proceeding" Harkin and I want. It does not define when and how federal court review will be available to all of those in the shadows, but rather provides a procedure for one case only. To create a general system of review, applicable whenever life-and-death decisions intersect with disability rights, will require a reasoned, informed debate unlike what we've had until now. It will take time. But in the Schiavo case, time is running out.

Pity the Poor Prince

Charles is atoning for the sins of rich, middle-aged men everywhere.

BY JUNE THOMAS

April 7, 2005

POOR PRINCE CHARLES can't catch a break. He had to postpone his wedding day to accommodate a funeral 900 miles away; devotees of his deceased ex-wife are threatening to picket the nuptials; and wedding memorabilia is selling poorly—apparently, his future subjects don't want to dry their dishes on a towel bearing the likeness of his bride-to-be, Camilla Parker Bowles. His family and fellow royals won't even do him the honor of inventing decent excuses to skip the ceremony—his father refused to cancel a trip to Germany (*Germany!*); Sweden's crown princess is otherwise engaged opening an IKEA store in Japan—and his mother dashed his dreams of serving an organic feast at the reception.

Charles is an easy and usually deserving target. He's the squarest man in the world, a rich, underemployed old fogy who has dressed and acted like the 56-year-old he is for the last 40 years. But after a lifetime of feckless world travel, dilettantism, and endless chukkas of polo, he's finally coming good. Despite enduring years of unforgivably cruel jokes at the expense of the woman he loves, Charles is about to do something a Frenchman would never consider: He's going to marry his mistress.

If the groom in Saturday's ceremony were Charlie Windsor instead of "His Royal Highness Prince Charles Philip Arthur George, Prince of Wales, KG, KT, GCB, OM, AK, QSO, PC, ADC, Earl of Chester, Duke of Cornwall, Duke of Rothesay, Earl of Carrick, Baron of Renfrew, Lord of the Isles and Prince and Great Steward of Scotland," he would be a hero—a mensch of modern maturity. But somehow the British press doesn't see it that way. Instead of praising the prince for his devotion, the media have simply intensified the torture, gleefully reporting the many missteps on the way to the wedding.

Apart from doctrinal considerations—and since the British sovereign is the head of the Church of England, the royals are expected to be more *frum* than the person in the next pew—what's wrong with two divorcees correcting the mistakes of their youth and finally getting wed? Just take a look at them: Charles and Camilla are living proof that love is blind. Yes, they committed adultery, but according to veteran royal-watcher Ingrid Seward, the prince didn't resume his connection with Camilla until 1986, when his marriage had suffered an "irretrievable breakdown" and after Diana had cuckolded him at least twice—with Sgt. Barry Mannakee, one of her protection officers, and Maj. James Hewitt, a man she described as "her riding instructor."

Camilla is the anti-Di. Whereas Diana was forever getting her chakras balanced and her colon irrigated, Camilla is self-confident and well adjusted. Diana was obsessed with the trappings of celebrity, while Camilla, like the royals, prefers to hide her wealth behind a thick veneer of ordinariness. Her main interests are said to be horses, dogs, and farm prices—standard Buckingham Palace talking points, in other words.

Diana was the family student of self-help literature, but it's Charles who has jettisoned his self-defeating behaviors. In his

20s, when he set out on the long road to the royal rose ceremony, he foolishly listened to the advice of his great-uncle and mentor Lord Mountbatten, who judged Camilla an unsuitable princess because she was older than Charles—by 16 months—and because she was "experienced." Diana may have been a godsend for the House of Windsor's gene pool and for the tabloid press, but she was a terrible match for Charles. Pledging his troth to a Sloane Ranger 12 years his junior with experience of absolutely nothing beyond a little light child-minding worked out *annus-horribilis*ly for the prince of Wales. If Samuel Johnson was right, and second marriages represent the triumph of hope over experience, Charles and Camilla are an exception; in their case it is the long-deferred victory of experience over hope.

In an age when preposterously coiffed tycoons engage in serial matrimony with ever younger and more beautiful partners, Charles is doing his bit to atone for the sins of rich, middle-aged men everywhere. He's making an honest woman of his age-appropriate partner, a woman with whom he is well-matched in looks, habits, and hobbies, whom he has known and loved for more than 30 years. Charles' mistake was to get his weddings out of order: He married his first wife second and his trophy wife first.

The Way the Cookie Crumbles

How much did Proust know about madeleines?

BY EDMUND LEVIN

May 11, 2005

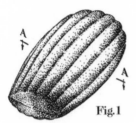

Fig.1

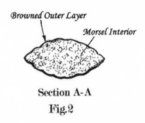

Browned Outer Layer

Morsel Interior

Section A-A

Fig.2

MARCEL PROUST'S MADELEINE is the cliché cookie—a highbrow reference that's penetrated pop culture. (Take the *Sopranos* episode in which Tony's Proustian madeleine is a slice of cappicola.) The great French author put madeleines on the map, and probably in our mouths, too. We surely have him to thank for those little packages at every Starbucks checkout.

But Proust left out one important detail: the recipe. And no one ever asked him for it.

Many cookbooks claim that you can reproduce Marcel Proust's magical madeleine in your own kitchen. But do any of the recipes yield the genuine article? I decided to reverse-engineer Proust's madeleine, using hints the author gives in *Remembrance of Things Past*, in an effort to find out.

In the renowned passage, the fleeting taste of this cake/cookie calls to life the world of the narrator's childhood in Belle Epoque France. For the attentive reader, the clues to The Recipe for The Madeleine are in the text:

> She (Marcel's mother) sent for one of those squat plump little cakes called *"petites madeleines,"* which look as though they had been molded in the fluted valve of a scallop shell . . . I raised to my lips a spoonful of the tea in which I had soaked a morsel of the cake. No sooner had the warm liquid mixed with the crumbs touched my palate than a shudder ran through me and I stopped, intent upon the extraordinary thing that was happening to me. An exquisite pleasure invaded my senses . . .
>
> And suddenly the memory revealed itself. The taste was that of the little piece of madeleine which on Sunday mornings at Combray . . . when I went to say good morning to her in her bedroom, my aunt Leonie used to give me, dipping it first in her own cup of tea or tisane . . . and the whole of Combray and its surroundings, taking shape and solidity, sprang into being, town and garden alike, from my cup of tea.

What can we glean from this passage? Proust's madeleine was quite dry. It demanded not just a quick dunk, but immersion to "soften" it (according to the new translation by Lydia Davis, said to be the most accurate). And, you'll note, Marcel never *bites* the cookie. The memory surge is triggered by *crumbs*.

The Crumb Factor is the key to this culinary mystery. A close analysis of the text yields the following sequence: Marcel 1) breaks off and drops the morsel into the tea. 2) The madeleine piece then wholly or partially disintegrates during its immersion. 3) Marcel then fishes about with his spoon, yielding a spoonful of tea mixed with crumbs.

The question, then: What recipe would deliver this dry, extraordinary crumb-producer?

Modern food science gives clear guidelines. To make a cake less moist, you put in less moisture and less fat. That means less butter and fewer eggs. And less sugar, too. Sugar is "hygroscopic"—meaning it helps baked goods retain moisture—so you want to keep it to a minimum. Also high on the list of no-nos: resting the batter. Resting allows the flour to absorb the batter's liquid and results in a moister product.

Running through this list of Proustian baking "tips"—which reads more like a catalogue of baking "don'ts"—the great man's signature dish was beginning to sound less than appealing: a pathetic, parched product, not a buttery treat.

My criteria knocked many supposedly "authentic" recipes out of contention. In *The Way To Cook*, Julia Child touts hers as "presumably the true Madeleine from Commercy, the one Marcel Proust dipped in his tea." But she turns out to be an incorrigible batter rester. Not only that, she *beats* the flour into the egg and sugar mixture, a sure way to develop the flour's gluten and produce a denser, uncrumby madeleine.

Dining With Proust, a cookbook that re-creates dozens of dishes from *Remembrance*, is co-authored by Anne Borrel, founder of the Proust Museum in Illiers-Combray. But the book's recipe calls for resting the batter a full hour-and-a-half and, worst of all, includes honey, notorious for its hygroscopic properties.

I found two recipes that looked promising. In the *Food Lover's Guide to Paris*, French food expert Patricia Wells champions dry madeleines. "The best, freshest madeleine has a dry, almost dusty taste when eaten on its own," she tells us. Being soaked in tea is what brings it to life. The relatively low butter, sugar, and egg content in Wells' recipe gave me hope.

In *The Making of a Cook*, Madeleine Kamman traces her recipe's lineage back to the 18th century and maybe even to "Madeleine Paumier . . . the young girl who . . . presented the first known madeleines to King Louis XV of France." She is adamant that the flour be *folded* into the batter, not beaten, to avoid the dreaded gluten development. Neither a batter beater, nor a batter rester, she was my strongest candidate.

I pulled out my mother's old early-Julia Child-era imported madeleine molds and set to work.

My first batch of the Kamman madeleines came out of the oven smelling great but looking terrible. I picked up one of the misshapen blobs. Not much resemblance to Proust's "little scallop shell pastry, so richly sensual under its severe, religious fold." But was it a crumb-producer?

I broke off a piece, dropped it into a glass of tea, and waited a minute. I prodded the cookie with my spoon. Looking very closely I saw only two small bits at the bottom of the glass. I stirred again, and a couple more appeared. The crumb production was underwhelming.

A madeleine morsel, it turns out, is a hardy little customer. Protected by a lightly browned layer, it does not disintegrate. Close examination revealed that it doesn't truly "soften" but absorbs liquid like a sponge, retaining its structural integrity. The locus of crumb production is confined to the narrow, exposed lens-shaped surface at the break-off line.

Would another recipe yield more Proustian results? Patricia Wells' fared no better. (Except, perhaps, in terms of taste. Her madeleines, supposedly "dry, dusty" tea-soaker-uppers, were delicious on their own. Half the batch disappeared while the tea was brewing.) Wells' madeleines produced no more crumbs than Kamman's. Julia Child's, as I expected, were equally crumb-free.

Things were looking bad for M. Proust. The sickly author, who hardly left his cork-lined bedroom in Paris for a dozen years, from 1910 until his death in 1922, supposedly channeled an entire world in all its precise sensations, setting it down on paper for us to re-experience. But my mind was afflicted with a blasphemous thought: Could Proust's madeleine ever have existed? Could it be he . . . *made it all up?*

I had one theory in reserve. Maybe Proust's Madeleine was *stale*. Unthinkable? Not necessarily. Proust was not finicky about his sensory stimuli—the fictional Marcel is even propelled into a reverie at one point by the dank smell of a lavatory.

I left my remaining madeleines outside, uncovered, defying instructions to keep them "stored in a tightly closed tin." After three days I brewed a glass of tea. I broke off a piece of madeleine and plopped it in. The result: about the same as before. I stirred, took a spoonful. A few brown bits swam in the spoon. I tasted. And here came the shocker: *I could not taste the crumbs.* Madeleine crumbs, once detached from the mother morsel, are quite delicate. They almost dissolve. It turns out they are *insensible to the tongue*.

I called my wife into the kitchen (her initial comment: "Does Proust explain who cleaned up?") for an objective opinion. She has a fine palate, but couldn't taste the crumbs either.

Confounded, I decided to confer with leading Proust authorities. I discovered a major obstacle: the eminent professor William Carter, author of *Marcel Proust: A Life*, who had supervised a re-creation of the famous scene for a PBS documentary. The professor was skeptical. He was turned off by my notion that Marcel had "dissolved pieces of madeleine floating around in his teacup," calling it "not likely." And, to my surprise, he asserted that Marcel does *dunk* and *bite* the madeleine—which would mean there's no crumb production mystery to be explained. The professor insisted that the crumbs are simply created *in the narrator's mouth* after he bites off a morsel and shmooshes it around.

I objected that no biting, or shmooshing, is mentioned in the text. The professor insisted it is "implied." But, in my view, Proust was simply too obsessed with detail to let something as significant as biting, let alone shmooshing, go unnoted if that's what he had in mind.

Much to my relief, I found firm support from MacArthur "genius" grant-winner Lydia Davis, the translator of the widely praised new edition of Proust's *Swann's Way*, in which the famed passage appears. She finds no "implied" biting in the text, and calls mere dunking "out of the question." She concurs that the crumby madeleine material is *already in the spoon* as it approaches Marcel's mouth. The tie-breaker was Stanford professor Joshua Landy, a Proust scholar who declares himself firmly in my "crumbs in the spoon" camp.

I'd given Proust a more-than-fair shot. His failure to account for extraordinary crumb production was manifest. Case closed, then: Proust's madeleine did not, does not, and never could have existed. To put it bluntly: Proust didn't know from madeleines.

This may be less than surprising. As it turns out, Proust's original model may have been a piece of soggy toast. In an early version of the scene, the narrator is offered a piece of "dry toast," which he dips in his tea. The "bit of sopped toast" triggers the familiar surge of memory.

This fact is not advertised to tourists making the pilgrimage to Illiers-Combray, where madeleines are sold by the bushel, and one patisserie does good business claiming Proust's family as patrons.

But Proust must have understood the madeleine's power. Otherwise he would have just left us the soggy toast. A well-made madeleine (and, please, rest the batter) is that rare thing: perfection itself. The shape, so pleasing to the eye, the double surface texture (ridged on one side, smooth on the other)—and, yes, the buttery, lemony taste. Make a batch. Take a bite. An "exquisite pleasure" will invade your senses. And you will have your own madeleine memories.

It's a Jerk!

Should men want to watch their wives give birth?

BY MEGHAN O'ROURKE

Aug. 29, 2005

A MAN WHO DOESN'T WANT TO WATCH his wife give birth is a jerk. This was the overwhelming consensus reached by a host of respected blogs after the publication last Tuesday in the *New York Times* of a piece by a therapist noting an unhappy trend: A number of his male patients have reported that after witnessing their wives have babies they no longer feel attracted to them. "I mean, how are you supposed to go from seeing that to wanting to be with . . . ?" one husband asked, unable to finish his sentence. It made no difference that these men were patients in search of help, not Neanderthals who'd ditched their wives; the bloggers—many of whom are usually temperate—were outraged. "Would it hurt if I call you a big pussy?" one woman queried, adding, "Luckily for me, I didn't marry a total asshole, so I didn't have this problem." According to one post, a husband who finds his libido gone in the wake of the delivery room merits the same scorn we'd direct at a man who leaves a woman after finding out that she has a black grandparent.

Dr. Keith Ablow, the author of the article, certainly can be faulted for blithely suggesting that the solution lies mostly in mothers' hands. But what was nonetheless striking about the debate was the vehemence of the hostility directed at these men.

The bloggers clearly felt that the men's desire (or lack of it) was objectively wrong, like that of a pedophile or a rapist, and ought somehow to be controllable. The animus against these men illuminates how powerful even relatively new cultural norms can be—and how dramatic the conflict is between what we think people should want and what they actually do want.

For most of human history, of course, men didn't go anywhere near women in labor, and any expectation that they would is relatively new: In Betty Smith's *A Tree Grows in Brooklyn*, set at the turn of the century, a father is sent off to the bar by the household women so he doesn't have to hear his wife's cries of pain. This changed in the 1960s, when a doctor named Robert Bradley put power in patients' hands, reducing the number of cesarean sections and episiotomies he performed and playing up natural ways of making childbirth less painful. One method, he discovered, was to invite the husband in to have him talk to his wife—a practice popularized in the 1970s. Putting husbands in the delivery room not only coincided with feminism but was intimately wrapped up with the natural childbirth movement and its effort to see the modern body in a more holistic fashion. (Bradley himself was no feminist; he told husbands to enforce a natural-foods diet he designed so that their "statuesque" wives wouldn't pack on pounds.)

The idea that childbirth was natural and therefore beautiful wasn't actually embraced by all feminists. Shulamith Firestone insisted that modern feminism shouldn't celebrate childbirth but should hope that science could soon render women's role in it obsolete. She writes, "Pregnancy is barbaric. . . . The husband's guilty waning of sexual desire, the woman's tears in front of the mirror at eight months are all gut reactions, not to be dismissed as cultural habits. . . . Three thousand years ago women giving birth 'naturally' had no need to pretend that pregnancy was a real trip, some mystical orgasm."

Today's women aren't celebrating pregnancy as a mystical orgasm, but they do see having the father in the delivery room as a necessary component of a healthy marriage, one in which both partners contribute equally to collective partnership. This is an absolutely reasonable request: Childbirth is scary and painful, and it makes sense to have reassurance and help from the person you're closest to (and your child's father). But the belief that men should be on duty no matter what assumes on some level that sex is just like all the other functions that the body performs. What the experience of the men in the therapist's article suggests is that, for at least some, this isn't true; for some, the erotic depends on maintaining a distinction between the sexual and the reproductive.

This doesn't mean, as bloggers seemed to believe, that the man who finds childbirth sexually traumatizing is nursing a retrograde desire for a Stepford wife and exposing his inability to confront his partner at less than her loveliest. In fact, these men were getting at a more distinct and elusive problem that Firestone alluded to: their psychological discomfort with the violent erosion of that sexual/reproductive boundary. Sexual attraction is highly variable and individualistic: Some relationships are grounded in hippie-ish holistic celebration of bodily plumbing (the kind of couples who don't close the bathroom door), and others thrive on a sharper separation between sex and the everyday framed in more ritualistic terms. The squeamishness of the men described in the *Times* article may be immature and even selfish. But I'm not sure it makes them sexist.

At the crux of the debate is one of the most important and vexed questions of modern feminism: How far into our imaginations should it reach? For one strain of feminism, epitomized by thinkers like Catharine MacKinnon, there's no room for a compartmentalization of sex from the rest of life, and the idea that sex requires a certain measure of artifice is utterly unacceptable. To have a "healthy" and "mature" relationship demands not only mutual respect in and out of the bedroom but an acceptance of womanhood in all its guises along a fluid (so to speak) spectrum. This approach—which effectively politicizes the bedroom—is a theo-retically valid way of conceptualizing equality between the sexes. And according to its terms, the men in the *Times* article truly are morally unlucky—stranded at an unfortunate crossroads of biol-ogy and culture.

But somehow this perspective seems ultimately impoverished. It's not just that it assumes individual male arousal is controllable, or that it assumes that even if it isn't we should despise these finicky men. It's that it aims to define which sexual feelings are and are not appropriate. Feminists (both female and male vari-eties) want to have it all ways: loving, unfaltering sexual devotion between husband and wife, and absolute domestic intimacy, too. But there's no room in this view for the notion that sexual devo-tion (and sexual obsession) might depend, in some cases, on the survival of an erotic vocabulary that's distinct from a biological one. What these men's concerns should make us wonder, for at least a moment, is just how far we can socialize sexual desire— and whether we want to even if we can.

How do we deal with the messy, intractable fact that our de-sires don't conform to our ideals for an egalitarian society? I'm to-tally sympathetic to the hostility women feel toward these men; ironically enough, a few days before the article appeared, a good male friend of mine told me he was uneasy about witnessing his future wife give birth, and I basically tore his head off. On a gut level most women, and plenty of men, feel anxious about the im-balance of power that stems from the fact that only women can give birth (among other things). And it seems absurdly unfair to do all the physical work of bringing a child into the world only to find that its squeamish father is too grossed out to make his way back to the marital bed.

But it doesn't help to pillory these men as blackguards and short-circuit a conversation that clearly needs to be had. (One blog even shut down its discussion thread about the article, claim-ing that the few posters defending the men were being unacceptably "narcissistic.") Until thirty or so years ago few men were in the delivery room, and now nearly all are: That's a huge cultural shift. Beginning a conversation about it doesn't mean we want to go back to the days when the father was sent down to the bar so he didn't have to hear what was taking place. It means acknowledging that perhaps a one-size-fits-all solution is foolish when it comes to complicated questions like sexual desire. The last few years have seen a rising movement among women to go ahead and have epidurals or say they want C-sections—to make individual choices about childbirth, in other words, rather than follow a doctrinaire routine imposed by dogmatic ideologists. It seems all the more odd, then, not to acknowledge that men, like women, aren't all wired the same way, even if we wish they were.

Miracle at Gainesville

How a poet and a resurrected dead man saved a Katrina evacuee.

BY BLAKE BAILEY

Nov. 22, 2005

RECENTLY I BEGAN TO FEEL neglected as a Hurricane Katrina evacuee. The CARE packages had become more sporadic, and my friends seemed less engaged by the odd allusion to our predicament. Also, as far as I can tell, there are very few evacuees in Gainesville, Fla.—where my wife and baby and I have been living these past few weeks—much less in this particular apartment complex, Windmeadows, where the residents don't strike me as the commiserating type. The media, too, has moved on, what with the distractive buffoonery of the present administration, which likewise has its mind (so to speak) on other matters. FEMA has entered a dormant phase. For the past two months—ever since receiving those first promising checks for Emergency Lodging and Rental Assistance—our online application status has remained unchanged, though the FEMA booklet promises an inspection within 10 days of a given disaster.

Finally I decided to give FEMA a call, and at length a human voice came on the line. During our conversation this woman seemed to be playing a vexing game of solitaire, or perhaps painting her nails a color she didn't much like.

"Can I help you?" she asked, after the dead air that followed my greeting.

I told her I was an evacuee from New Orleans and gave her my ZIP code and FEMA number. An interval passed.

"Can I help you?" she asked, not unfamiliarly.

"Yes, you may." I tried to sound friendly—not one of those whiny refugees, don't you know, but rather a chap who was weathering his little bad patch with a smile. "I was wondering if you could tell me when FEMA will be inspecting my house? See, I don't have flood insurance, so it's sort of import—"

"No."

"I'm sorry?"

"No . . . *sir*. I don't know when your inspection will be scheduled."

Silence. Perhaps she'd returned to her card game or nails.

"Well," I said, "have *any* inspections taken place?"

"Yes."

"But not in my ZIP code."

"I wouldn't know that, sir."

So what exactly would *you know, you idling oaf?* That's what I wanted to say, but I worried she might note any rude remarks in my FEMA file and hence I'd be inspected dead last or not at all. So instead I thanked her brightly and said goodbye.

Around this time we started looking at rental houses, since we're expected to vacate our borrowed apartment at Windmeadows by the end of the month. Given that we're still paying off a mortgage on our moldy ruined house back in New Orleans, we figured we could afford to spend maybe $1,000 a month, tops. This would have gotten us a pretty sweet crib in certain parts of New Orleans, but not in Gainesville.

Most of the houses in this price range look, on the outside, like a Walker Evans photo. Those we ruled out. When a place wasn't positively ghastly, though, we'd call the real-estate agent and schedule a visit. The first place I visited was very ugly indeed (orange concrete block), but in a fairly nice neighborhood with lots of trees. Once I got inside, though, I had to breathe through my mouth. The filthy gray wall-to-wall carpet not only reeked of mildew but was scored with cigarette burns, as if the place were a clubhouse for chain-smoking junkies. I thought of what Cheever had said about certain houses "where everything we see, touch, smell and hear urges us to commit murder or suicide or get drunk and perform some contemptible sexual obscenity."

"You'll never rent that place," I told the real-estate agent when I returned the key. "It's squalid."

He nodded as though I'd wished him a nice day. He was an old, old man who seemed tired of this line of work. "It belongs to that Presbyterian church across the way," he explained.

"They should replace the carpet."

"They'll mow the lawn for you," he said, and we parted in a mood of mutual dejection.

In a slightly higher price range we found places that were nice enough on the outside, but never, never on the inside. We began to accept that, for another few months at least, we'd have to live in drastically reduced circumstances—if we passed muster, that is. There was a lengthy application process.

"We'll be contacting your previous landlord," they all promise, after showing us their crepuscular, paneled dwellings. "And if he says you're OK, we'll take it from there."

"Sounds good," I say, rather than, "Actually, we *owned* a house, a *nice* house—though before that, I'm *very* sorry to say, we did rent a place from a guy who d****d us out of our security deposit, and who I therefore called a big d***, in effect, so I doubt he'll give us much of a reference."

No, I didn't say that, nor did I mention my Guggenheim or the fact that my wife is the first person in the history of her prestigious doctoral program to win the Florence Shafer Memorial Award for Therapeutic Excellence two years in a row. Instead I stood there clammily shaking hands and composing a sh**-eating epistle in my head to our former landlord.

Roughly two weeks before this dark juncture, I'd gotten a very curious e-mail. It was about seven weeks old when I read it, having been sent to my old Excite account—the one I check every other month, sifting through herbal Viagra flyers, urgent messages from exiled cousins of Sani Abacha, and the like. My correspondent, one James Kennedy in California, had read my first *Slate* column and professed to enjoy it. He wanted to *give* me ("no strings attached") a new house in a subdivision he was building in Mandeville, across the lake from New Orleans: "This is not a gimmick, not a scam," he wrote. He explained that he'd been killed recently, then revived, and thus "forever changed": "I vowed to myself after that, that I would do as much as humanly possible to help my fellow man, and make myself a better person."

It sounded way too good to be true, and never mind its super-hero-origin-story overtones. I replied, thanking him for his "exceptional generosity" but added that we had no plans to move back to New Orleans or its environs—and besides, he'd probably changed his mind by now and moved on (*like the rest of the world*, I sighed subtextually) and for that we could scarcely blame him, etc.

"I still want you to have the house," he replied. "Keep it, sell it, trade it—it's yours." Attached to this e-mail were professional sketches of the houses he proposed to build in Mandeville, circa spring 2006. They were very nice. There was no orange concrete. "If you do decide to pass for whatever reason (i.e., 'Kennedy's a weirdo [so he knew],' 'I don't believe it,' 'It's a scam,' etc.), at least you'll have the pleasure of knowing that at one time during your life, someone did something to restore your faith in humanity, and God."

Throughout this whole ordeal, the kindness of family, friends, and total strangers has done a lot to restore my faith in humanity— hitherto a shaky business to be sure. (God, alas, is a goner.) And I began to suspect that Kennedy was at least sincere in his desire to help. Besides, I enjoyed corresponding with him: He had a lot of advice about what to expect from Chase Home Finance once we let them know that we didn't intend to spend 30 years paying off a mortgage on an abandoned house. When I mentioned our rental woes, Kennedy researched the local market and recommended a number of places out of our price range. He was happy to pay a year's worth of rent in advance, he said, which would enable us to keep paying our mortgage while we waited to see how, if at all, FEMA could help us.

We were still swooning over the prospect when I was e-mailed by another *Slate* reader. This one was a notable poet and critic who teaches at the University of Florida (and prefers not to be identified). He mentioned my Cheever biography and said he had a funny story to tell me about Cheever's time at the Iowa Writers' Workshop 30 years ago.

"By the way," he added, "I assume you're well set up with housing while you're forced to stay in Gainesville; but I'll mention that we are off to England for eight months in mid-December and our large Victorian house will be available at a reasonable rent. Nice yard, quiet neighborhood (the Duck Pond), lots of room. . . . I'm terribly sorry for your losses."

As I write this down, I'm astonished all over again—but it's true. The poet's house is wonderful, the neighborhood is Arcadian, and the rent is comparable to what we would have paid for the stinky-rug place. And yes, James Kennedy in California—a heroic personage I may never meet—has paid our entire rent in advance. The check arrived by FedEx and has already cleared.

At this rate, my faith in God may soon be resurrected. The other day, following hard on these miraculous events, my wife got a call on her cell phone: FEMA! She shakily handed me the Samsung.

"Mr. Bailey, are you homeless?" a nice woman asked. "Because if so, we'd like to offer you a trailer."

A trailer seemed a good augury. Had there been no James Kennedy, no kindly poet living in the Duck Pond, still we'd be provided for, after a fashion, like the lilies of the field and the fowl of the air.

About the Contributors

Anne Applebaum is a columnist for, and member of the editorial board of, the *Washington Post*. Her book *Gulag: A History* won the 2004 Pulitzer Prize for General Nonfiction.

Blake Bailey is the author of *A Tragic Honesty: The Life and Work of Richard Yates*. He's working on a biography of John Cheever.

Emily Bazelon is a *Slate* senior editor.

Paul Berman was a regular book critic at *Slate* and is an occasional contributor. He is a writer-in-residence at New York University and the author of *Terror and Liberalism* and *Power and the Idealists*.

Henry Blodget, a former securities analyst, lives in New York City.

Frank Cammuso is co-author (with Hart Seely) of *2007-Eleven and Other American Comedies*. Cammuso is a political cartoonist for the *Syracuse Post-Standard* in Syracuse, N.Y.

Toby Cecchini is a co-owner of Passerby, a bar in New York City.

Bryan Curtis is a *Slate* staff writer.

Debra Dickerson is the author of *The End of Blackness* and *An American Story*.

David Edelstein, the longtime film critic for *Slate*, is a film critic at *New York* magazine.

Daniel Engber is a regular contributor to *Slate*, where he writes "The Explainer" column.

Amanda Fortini is a *Slate* contributor.

Atul Gawande, M.D., is a staff writer for *The New Yorker* and the author of *Complications: A Surgeon's Notes on an Imperfect Science.* He used to write the "Medical Examiner" column for *Slate.*

Masha Gessen is working on a book on medical genetics for Harcourt. Its working title is *Blood Matters: Travels Along the Genetic Frontier.* She is the author of *Ester and Ruzya: How My Grandmothers Survived Hitler's War and Stalin's Peace.*

Jeffrey Goldberg is a staff writer for *The New Yorker*. He covered organized crime for *New York* magazine and the *New York Times Magazine.* He is at work on a book about the Middle East.

David Greenberg writes *Slate*'s History Lesson column and teaches history and media studies at Rutgers University. He is the author of *Nixon's Shadow: The History of an Image* and has written for the *Atlantic Monthly,* the *New Republic, The New Yorker,* and other scholarly and popular publications.

Daniel Gross writes *Slate*'s "Moneybox" column.

Christopher Hitchens writes the "Fighting Words" column for *Slate.* He is a columnist for *Vanity Fair.* His most recent book is *Thomas Jefferson: Author of America,* and his most recent collection of essays is titled *Love, Poverty, and War.*

Jim Holt writes the "Egghead" column for *Slate.* He also writes for *The New Yorker* and the *New York Times Magazine.*

Ann Hulbert writes *Slate*'s "Sandbox" column. She is the author most recently of *Raising America: Experts, Parents, and a Century of Advice About Children.* She was a senior editor at the *New Republic* for many years and is currently a contributing writer for the *New York Times Magazine.*

Harriet McBryde Johnson is a disability-rights lawyer in Charleston, S.C., and author of a memoir, *Too Late to Die Young: Nearly True Tales From a Life*, and a novel, *Accidents of Nature*.

Fred Kaplan writes the "War Stories" column for *Slate*. He is also the author of *The Wizards of Armageddon* and a former Pentagon reporter and Moscow bureau chief for the *Boston Globe*.

Mickey Kaus, who writes *Slate*'s "Kausfiles" column, is author of *The End of Equality*.

Michael Kinsley is *Slate*'s founding editor.

Paul Krugman is an op-ed columnist for the *New York Times*. He is a professor of economics and international affairs at Princeton. He used to write about economics for *Slate*.

Steven E. Landsburg writes the "Everyday Economics" column for *Slate*. He is the author, most recently, of *Fair Play: What Your Child Can Teach You About Economics, Values, and the Meaning of Life*.

Edmund Levin is a writer/producer at ABC News. His work has also appeared in the *New Republic*, the *Atlantic Monthly*, the *Washington Post*, and the *New York Times*.

Josh Levin is a *Slate* assistant editor.

Michael Lewis is the author of *Moneyball, Liar's Poker, Coach*, and *The New New Thing*, among other books. He lives in Berkeley, Calif., with his wife, Tabitha Soren, and their two daughters.

Rebecca Liss is an associate producer at CBS's *60 Minutes*.

Dahlia Lithwick, a *Slate* senior editor, writes the magazine's "Supreme Court Dispatches."

Cullen Murphy was for 20 years the managing editor of the *Atlantic Monthly*. He is at work on a book about America and ancient Rome.

Deborah Needleman is the founding editor in chief of *Domino* magazine. She has written on gardening for the *New York Times* and *House & Garden* and penned "The Cranky Gardener" column for *Slate*.

Timothy Noah is a senior writer at *Slate*. Previously he was an assistant managing editor at *U.S. News & World Report*, a reporter in the Washington bureaus of the *Wall Street Journal* and *Newsweek*, a staff writer at the *New Republic*, and an editor at the *Washington Monthly*. Noah is editor of *The Woman at the Washington Zoo*, an anthology of writings by his late wife, Marjorie Williams, published in 2005.

Meghan O'Rourke is *Slate*'s culture editor and a poetry editor of the *Paris Review*. Her essays and poems have appeared in *Slate*, *The New Yorker*, the *New Republic*, the *New York Review of Books*, and elsewhere.

David Plotz is deputy editor of *Slate*. He is the author of *The Genius Factory: The Curious History of the Nobel Prize Sperm Bank*.

William Saletan is *Slate*'s national correspondent and author of *Bearing Right: How Conservatives Won the Abortion War*.

Mark Scheffler is a staff reporter at *Crain's Chicago Business* and produces multimedia content at Theglobalscene.com.

Hart Seely is co-author (with Frank Cammuso) of *2007-Eleven and Other American Comedies*. Seely is a reporter for the *Syracuse Post-Standard* in Syracuse, N.Y.

Jack Shafer, *Slate*'s editor at large, writes the "Press Box" column.

Herbert Stein was a contributor to *Slate* and creator of the "Dear Prudence" advice column. He was chairman of the Council of Economic Advisers under Presidents Nixon and Ford and a member of the board of contributors at the *Wall Street Journal*. He died in 1999.

Mike Steinberger is *Slate*'s wine columnist.

Jeffrey Steingarten, *Slate's* original food critic, is the food critic of *Vogue* and has won several James Beard Awards and a decoration from the French Republic.

Seth Stevenson is a frequent contributor to *Slate*, where he writes the "Ad Report Card" column.

June Thomas is *Slate's* foreign editor.

Jacob Weisberg is editor of *Slate* and co-author, with Robert E. Rubin, of *In An Uncertain World*.

Marjorie Williams was an op-ed columnist for the *Washington Post*, a contributing writer to *Vanity Fair*, and a member of *Slate's* "Book Club." She died in 2005. *The Woman at the Washington Zoo*, a collection of her writing edited by her husband, *Slate* writer Timothy Noah, was published in fall 2005.

Robert Wright, a Schwartz Senior Fellow at the New America Foundation and a contributor to *Slate*, is the author of *The Moral Animal* and *Nonzero*. He founded and runs the Web sites Meaningoflife.tv and Bloggingheads.tv.

Emily Yoffe, who writes *Slate's* "Human Guinea Pig" and "Dear Prudence" columns and is the author of *What the Dog Did: Tales From a Formerly Reluctant Dog Owner*.

Illustration Credits

Nina Frenkel: "Extroverted Like Me: How a month and a half on Paxil taught me to love being shy," p. 90; "Cold Shower: How to spit with the wine pros," p. 131; "Hello, Moon: Has America's low-rise obsession gone too far?" p. 151

Lilia Levin: "The Way the Cookie Crumbles: How much did Proust know about madeleines?" p. 255

Robert Neubecker: "Baby-Sitting the Economy: The baby-sitting co-op that went bust teaches us something that could save the world," p. 50; "Choking at the Bowl: Why do men have trouble urinating at ballparks?" p. 108; "Flag on the Field: Soccer, the last acceptable form of nationalism," p. 111; "An Unlikely Hero: The Marine who found two WTC survivors," p. 125; "Fifty-Fifty Forever: Why we shouldn't expect America's political 'tie' to be broken anytime soon," p. 136

Charlie Powell: "Lewis and Clark: Stop celebrating. They don't matter." p. 120

Mark Stamaty: "Trading Family Values: How the old conservative/liberal stereotypes break down when it comes to parenting," p. 233